SHIN YOSHIDA

We're powering up with Miyoshi's excellent art and Hikokubo on Duel design! This version of *ARC-V* is a bit different from the anime. The fun starts now!

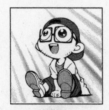

NAOHITO MIYOSHI

First *ZEXAL* and now this! I'm a lucky guy to work on *Yu-Gi-Oh!*, and I've faced a lot of new challenges in the process. I'm seriously excited about this. Here goes! I'll give it all I got!!

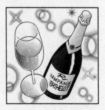

MASAHIRO HIKOKUBO

It's the start of a new Duel! Run among monsters through a world of Solid Vision and get yourself through tight spots with Action Cards! Smarts, strength and luck!! The curtain rises on entertainment duels!!

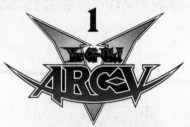

1

SHONEN JUMP MANGA EDITION

ORIGINAL CONCEPT BY
Kazuki Takahashi

PRODUCTION SUPPORT: **STUDIO DICE**

STORY BY
Shin Yoshida

ART BY
Naohito Miyoshi

DUEL COORDINATOR
Masahiro Hikokubo

TRANSLATION + ENGLISH ADAPTATION
Taylor Engel and John Werry, HC Language Solutions, Inc.
TOUCH-UP ART + LETTERING **John Hunt**
DESIGNER **Shawn Carrico**
EDITOR **Mike Montesa**

Printed in the U.S.A.

Published by VIZ Media, LLC
P.O. Box 77010
San Francisco, CA 94107

10 9 8 7 6 5 4 3 2 1
First printing, April 2017

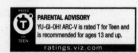

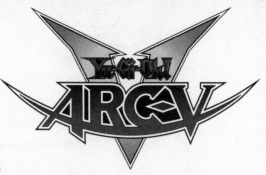

1

The Name Is Phantom!

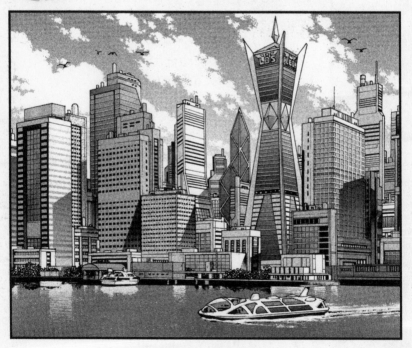

ORIGINAL CONCEPT BY **Kazuki Takahashi**

PRODUCTION SUPPORT: **STUDIO DICE**

STORY BY **Shin Yoshida**

ART BY **Naohito Miyoshi**

DUEL COORDINATOR **Masahiro Hikokubo**

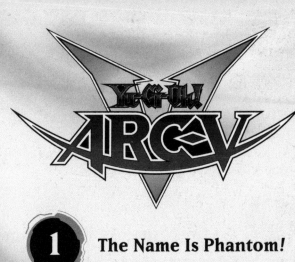

1 The Name Is Phantom!

SCALE **1** The Name Is Phantom!! 5

SCALE **2** Yuto vs. Sawatari!! 21

SCALE **3** Pendulum Summons!! 53

SCALE **4** The Hungry Assassin!! 85

SCALE **5** Assault! Raidraptors!! 117

SCALE **6** Feeling Alive!! 149

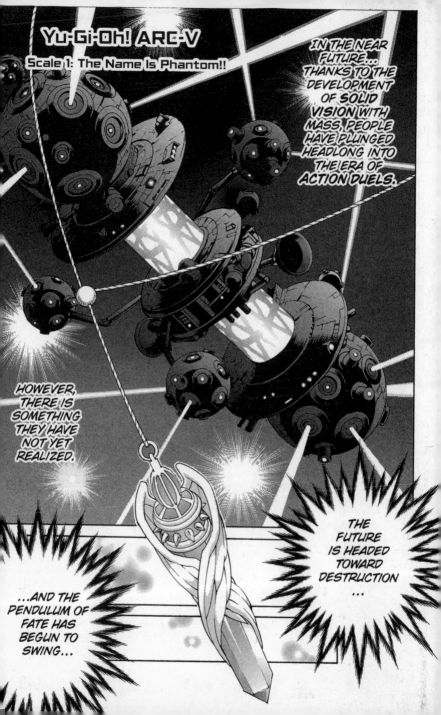

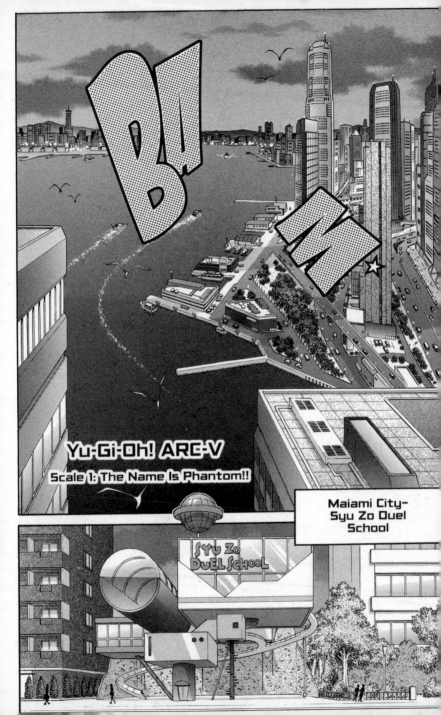

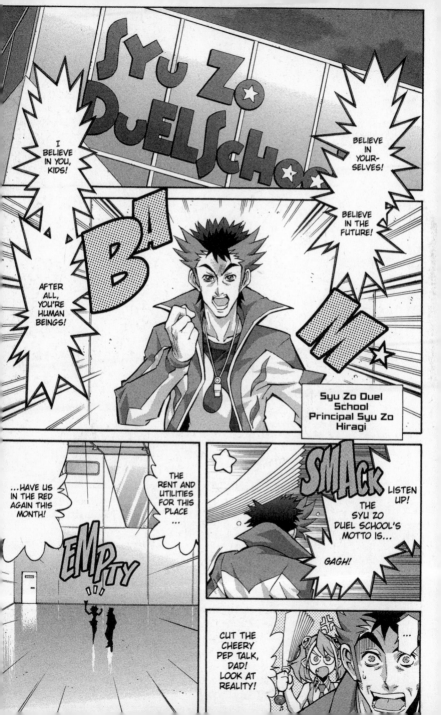

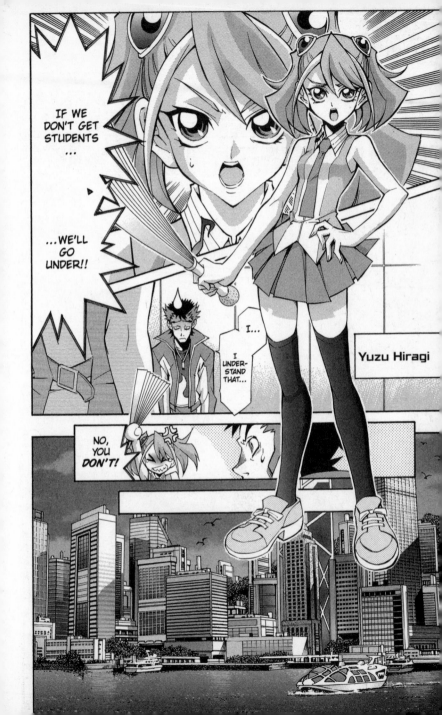

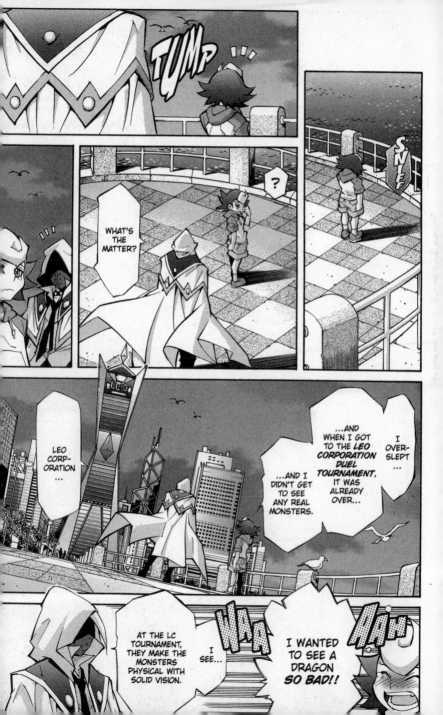

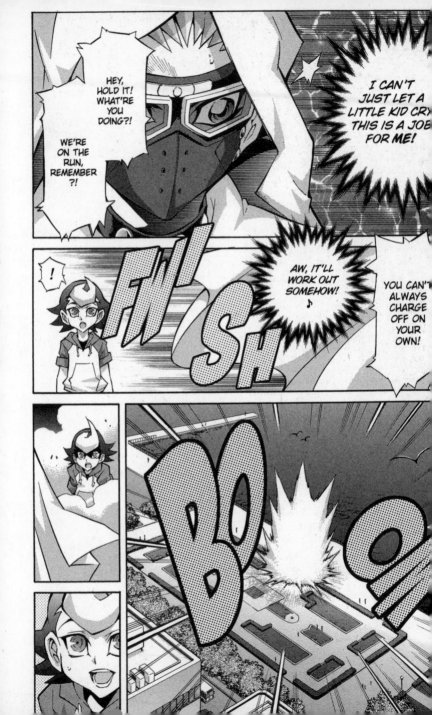

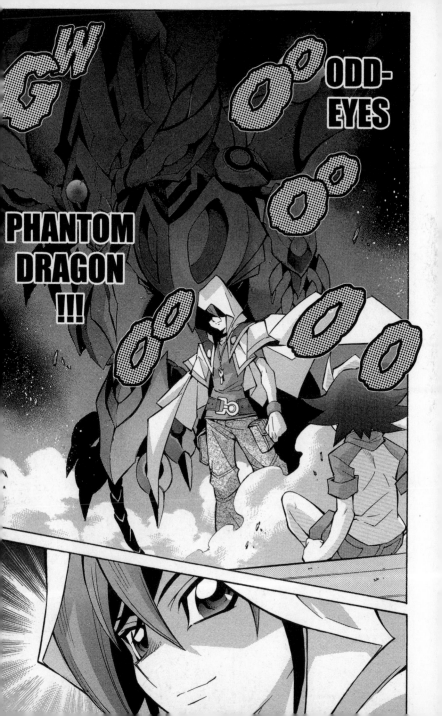

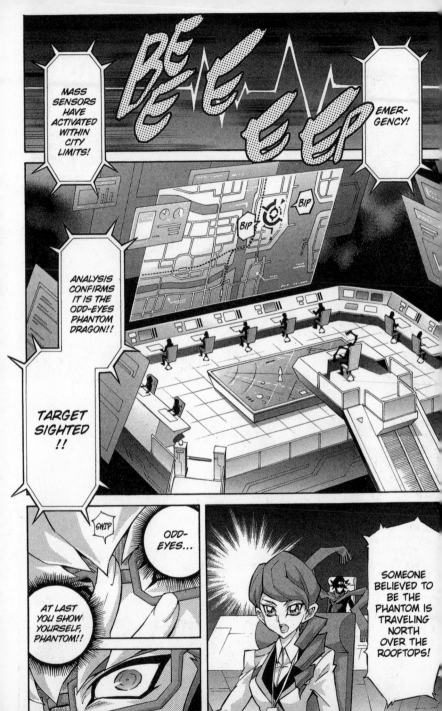

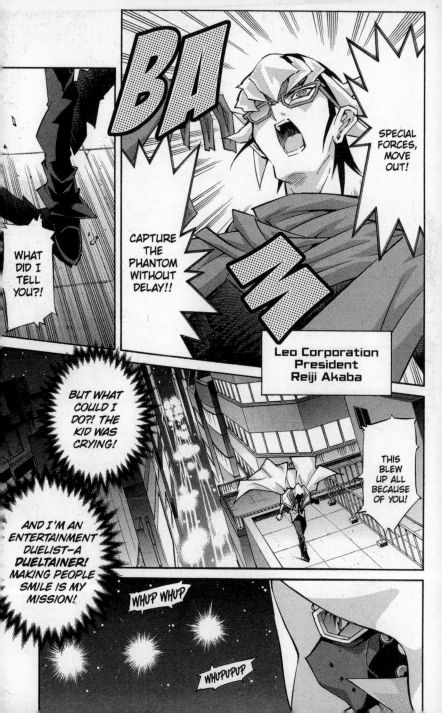

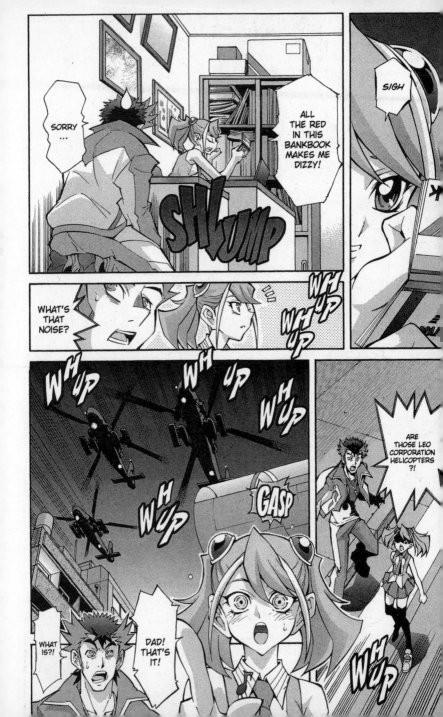

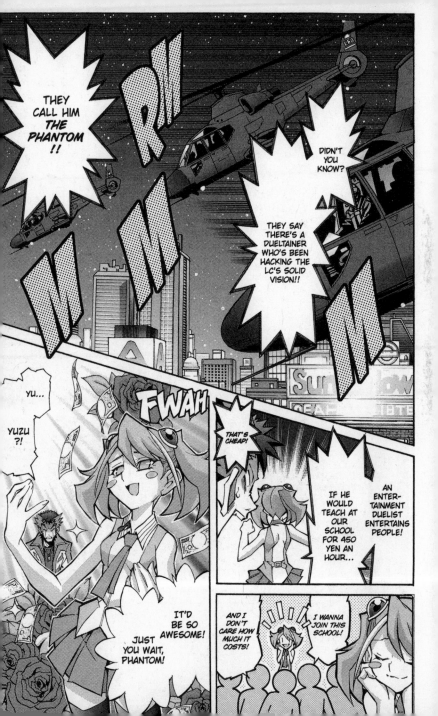

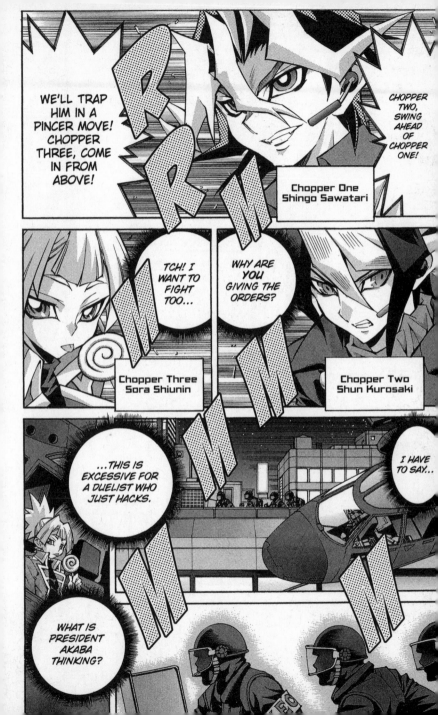

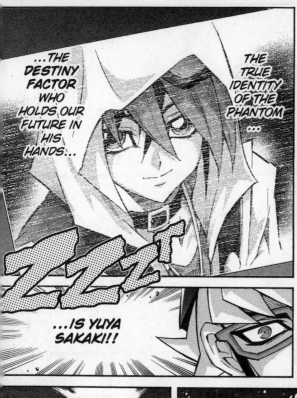

...THE DESTINY FACTOR WHO HOLDS OUR FUTURE IN HIS HANDS...

THE TRUE IDENTITY OF THE PHANTOM...

ZZZZT

...IS YUYA SAKAKI!!

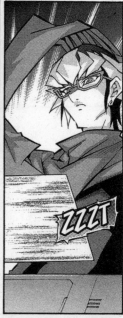

ZZZT

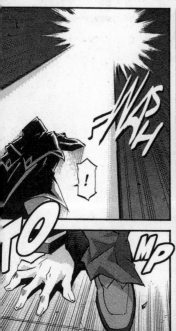

FWAH

!

TO

MP

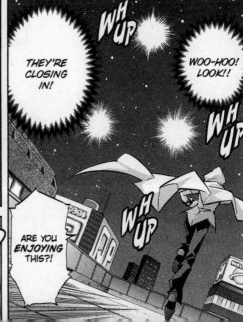

THEY'RE CLOSING IN!

WH UP

WOO-HOO! LOOK!!

WH UP

WH UP

ARE YOU ENJOYING THIS?!

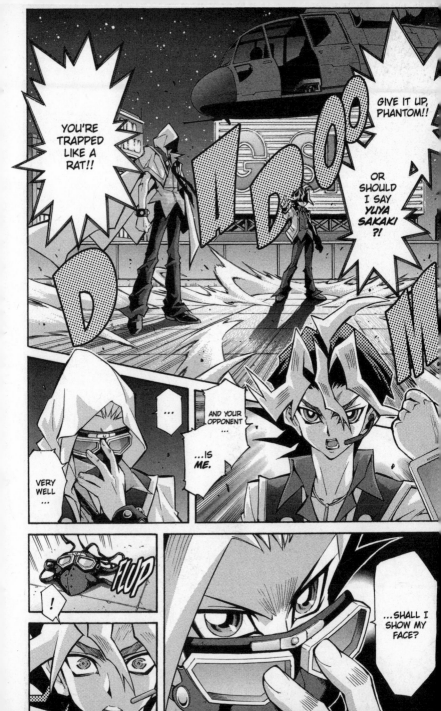

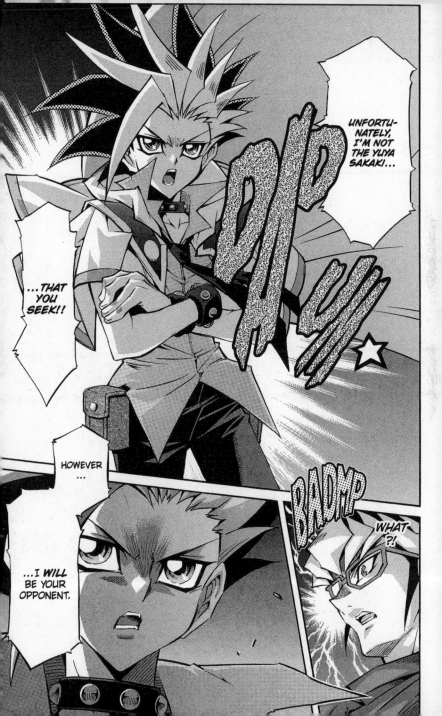

Yuya Sakaki

Everyday clothes

Duel school outfit 1

Yuya's early design had a younger feel to it than the one he has now. His clothes were sportier, and he looked mischievous.

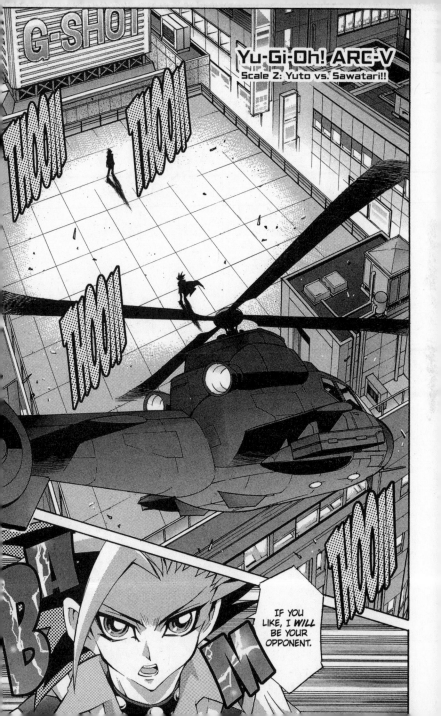

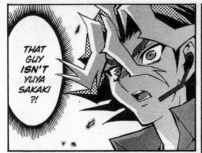

THAT GUY ISN'T YUYA SAKAKI?!

WEREN'T WE IN THE MIDDLE OF RUNNING AWAY?

HEY, YUTO!

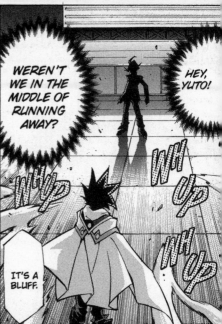

WHUP

WHUP

WHUP

AND THEY WOULDN'T TIP THEIR HAND SO EASILY EITHER.

IT'S A BLUFF.

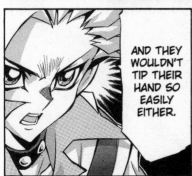

WHAT SHOULD WE DO, PRESIDENT AKABA?!

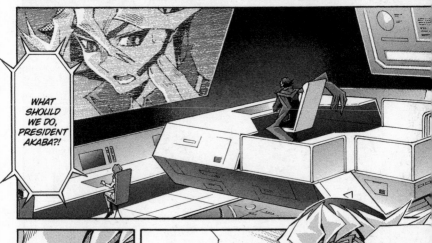

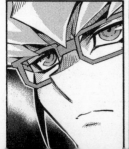

LIKE ME, HE IS ONE OF A KIND.

YUYA SAKAKI IS THE *DESTINY FACTOR*, THE ONE WHO WILL DETERMINE THE WORLD'S FUTURE.

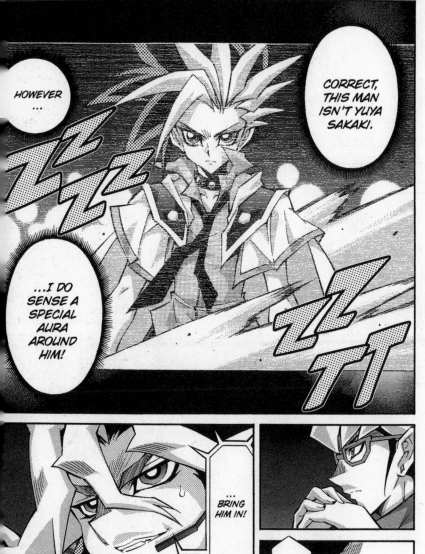

HOWEVER...

CORRECT, THIS MAN ISN'T YUYA SAKAKI.

...I DO SENSE A SPECIAL AURA AROUND HIM!

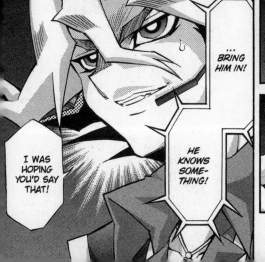

...BRING HIM IN!

I WAS HOPING YOU'D SAY THAT!

HE KNOWS SOMETHING!

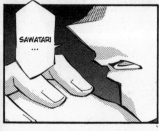

SAWATARI...

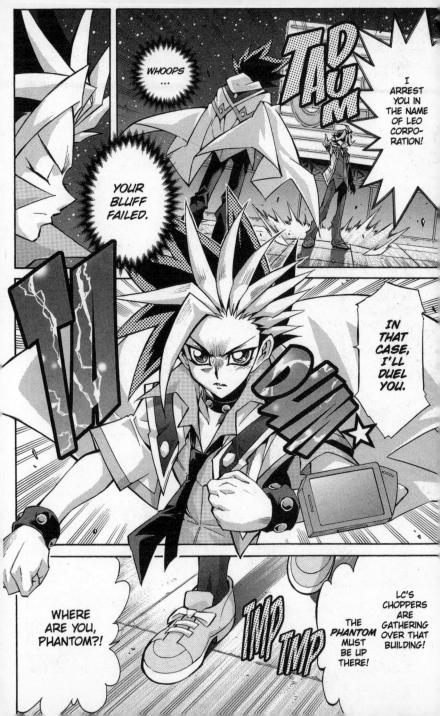

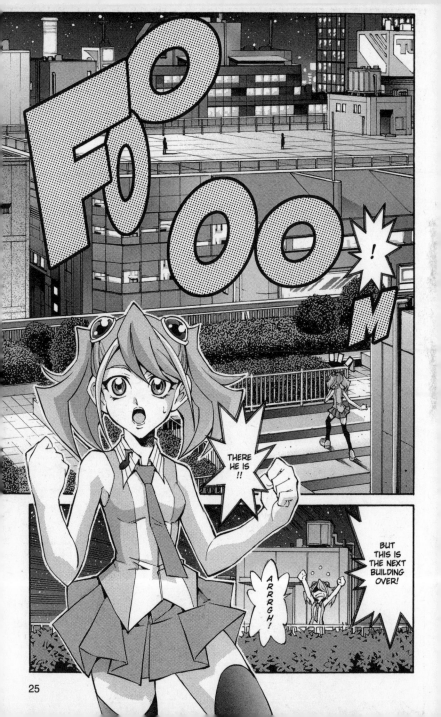

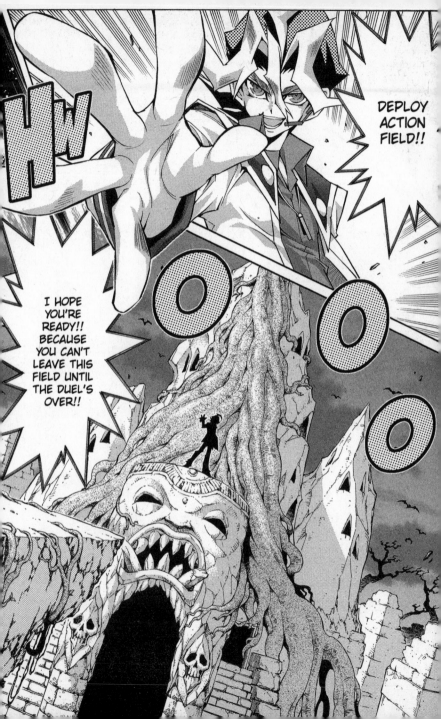

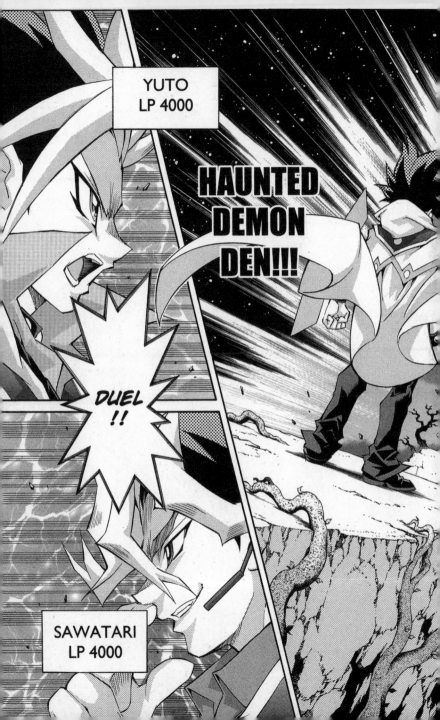

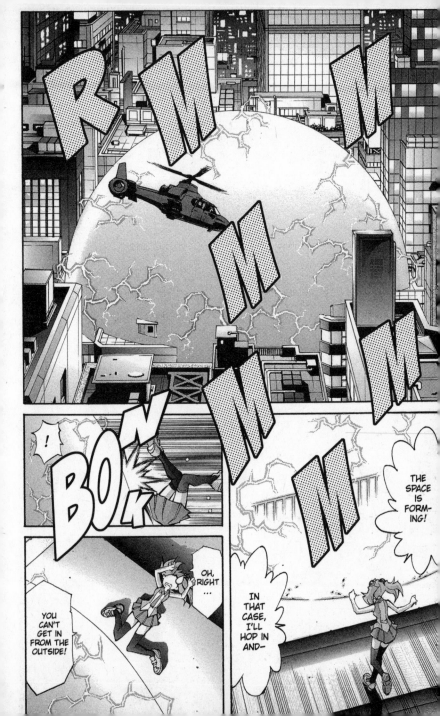

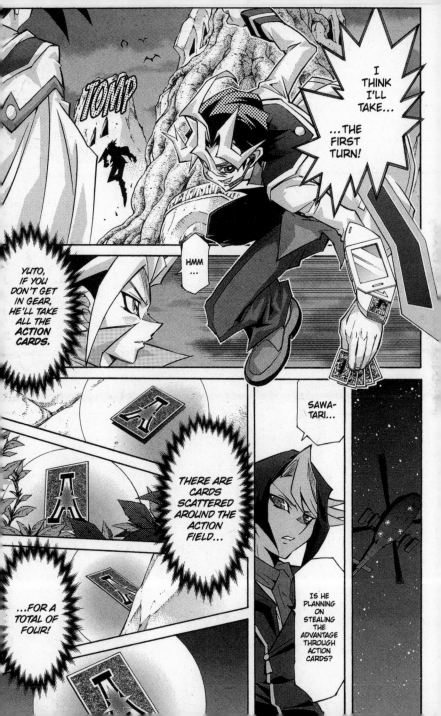

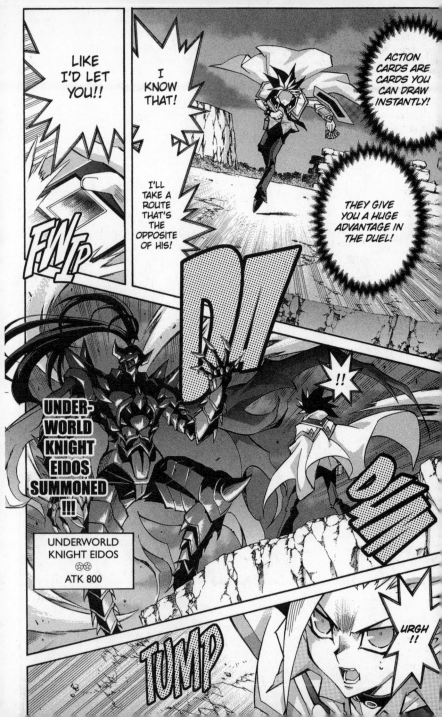

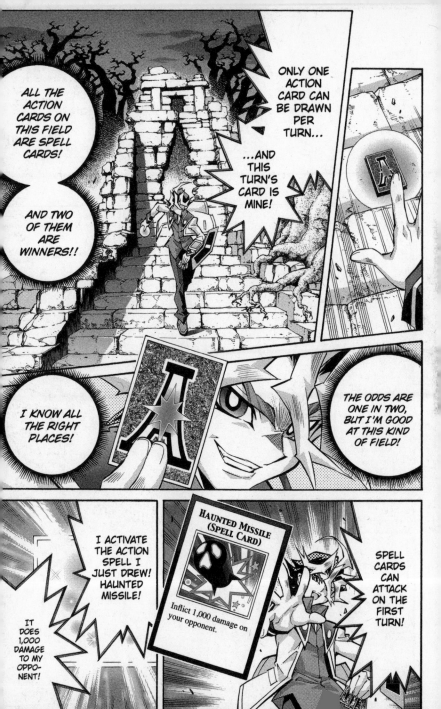

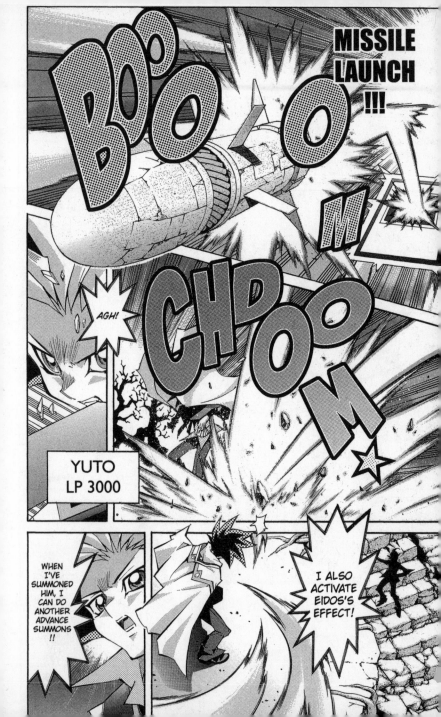

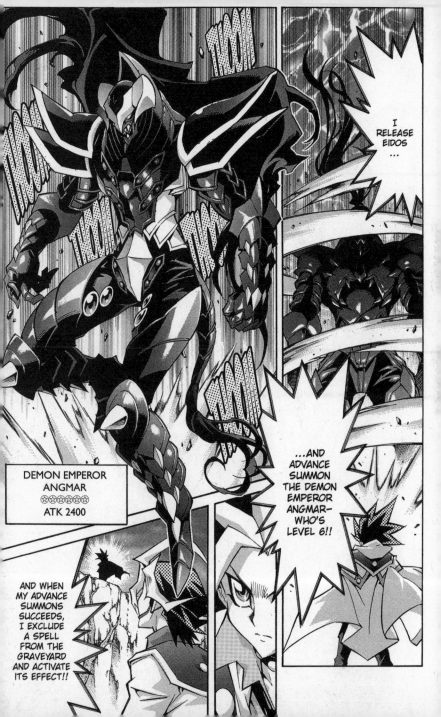

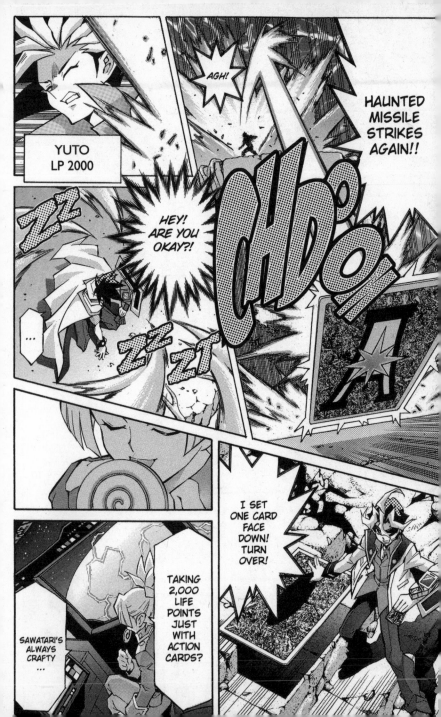

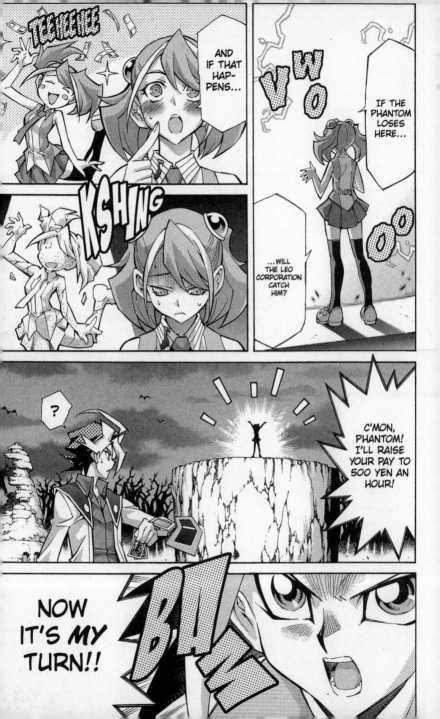

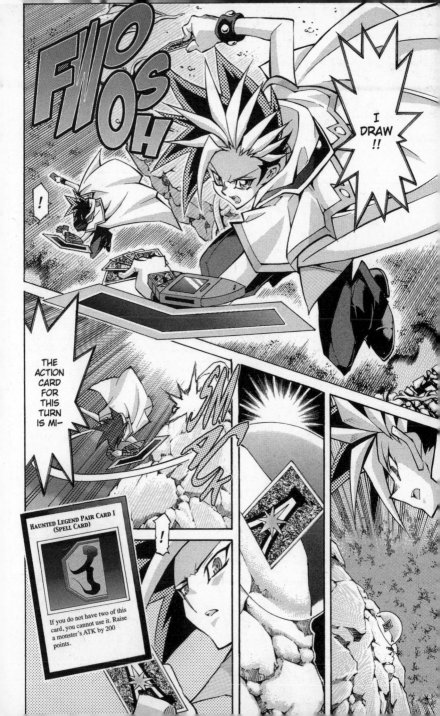

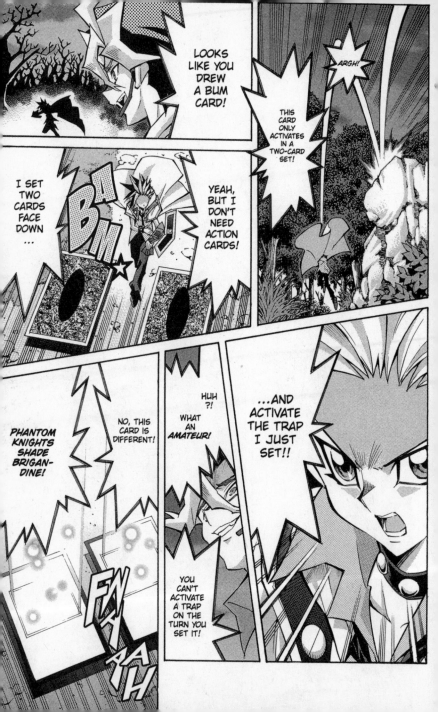

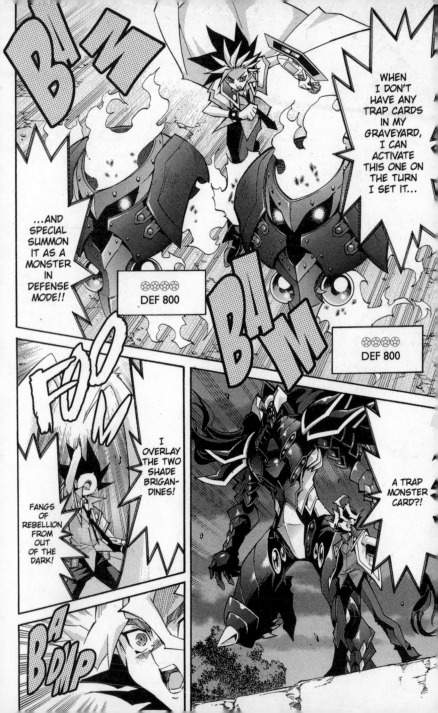

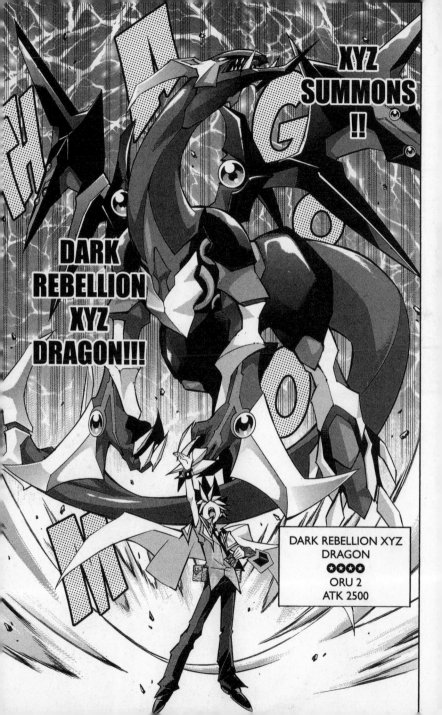

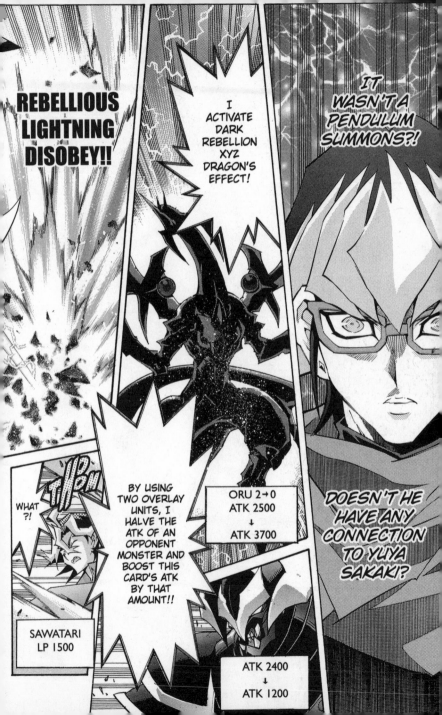

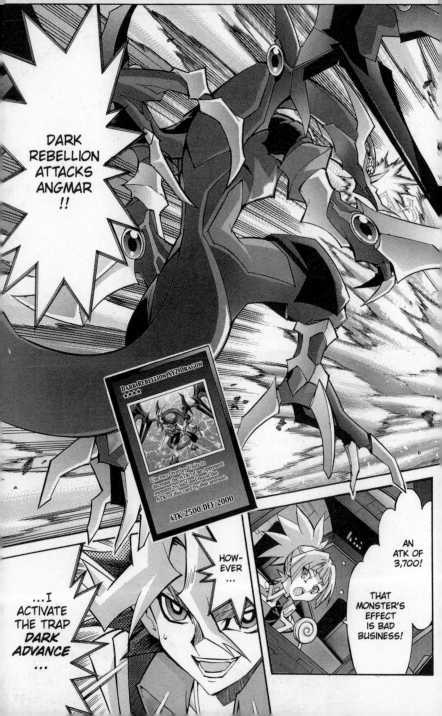

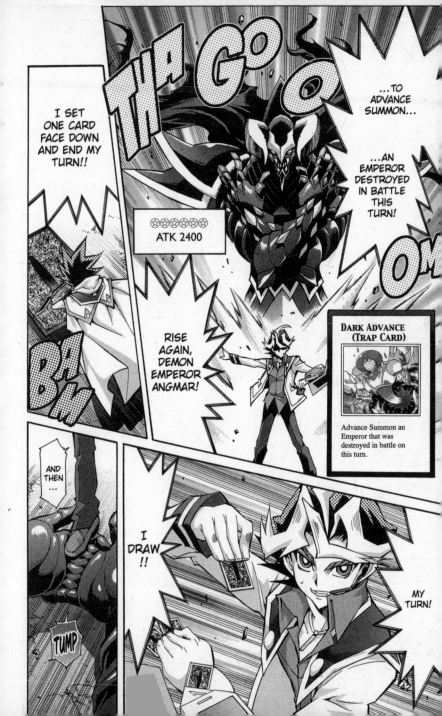

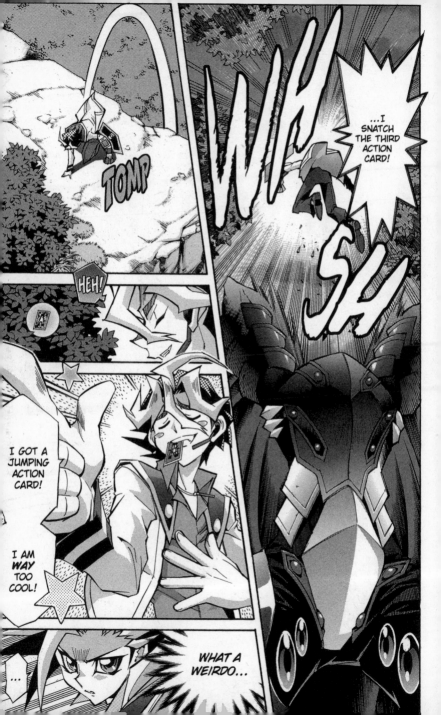

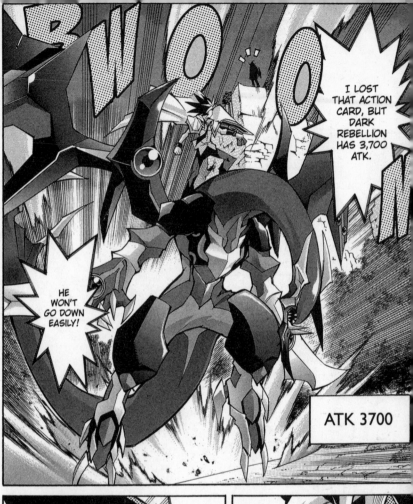

I LOST THAT ACTION CARD, BUT DARK REBELLION HAS 3,700 ATK.

HE WON'T GO DOWN EASILY!

ATK 3700

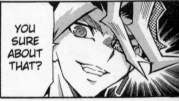

YOU SURE ABOUT THAT?

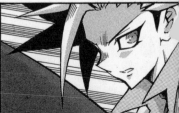

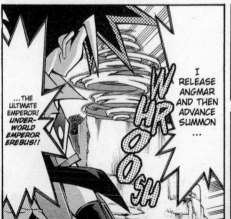

...THE ULTIMATE EMPEROR! UNDER-WORLD EMPEROR EREBUS!!

I RELEASE ANGMAR AND THEN ADVANCE SUMMON...

WHR OOSH

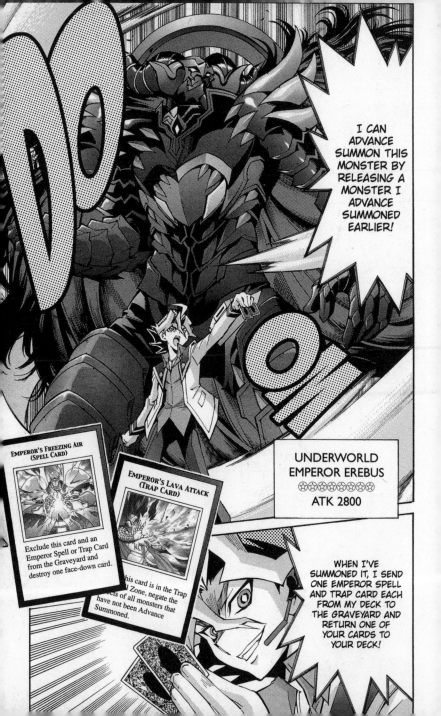

I CAN ADVANCE SUMMON THIS MONSTER BY RELEASING A MONSTER I ADVANCE SUMMONED EARLIER!

EMPEROR'S FREEZING AIR
(SPELL CARD)

Exclude this card and an Emperor Spell or Trap Card from the Graveyard and destroy one face-down card.

EMPEROR'S LAVA ATTACK
(TRAP CARD)

...his card is in the Trap ...d Zone, negate the ...cts of all monsters that have not been Advance Summoned.

UNDERWORLD EMPEROR EREBUS
☆☆☆☆☆☆☆☆☆☆
ATK 2800

WHEN I'VE SUMMONED IT, I SEND ONE EMPEROR SPELL AND TRAP CARD EACH FROM MY DECK TO THE GRAVEYARD AND RETURN ONE OF YOUR CARDS TO YOUR DECK!

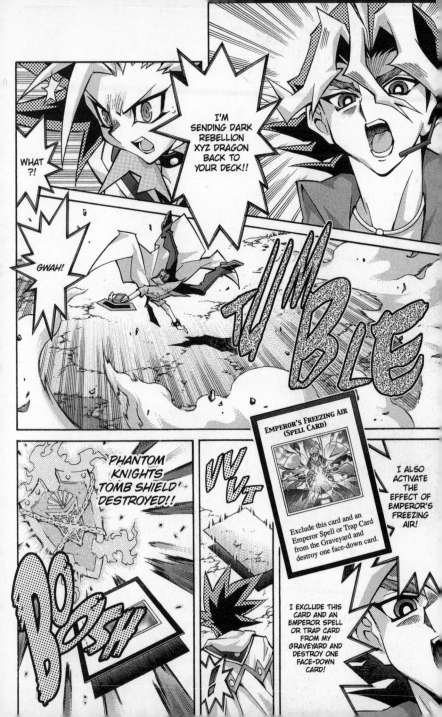

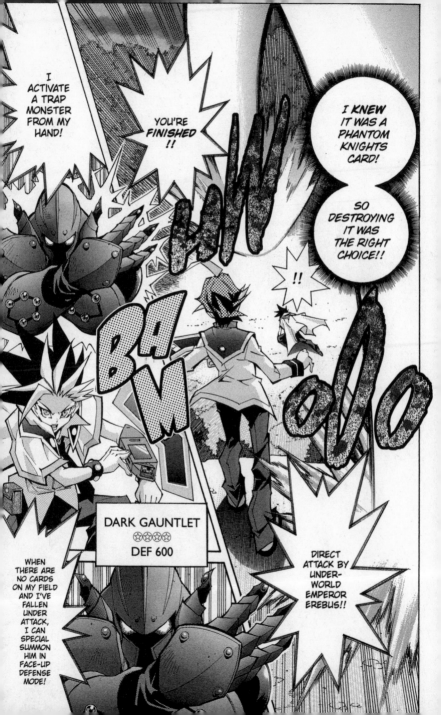

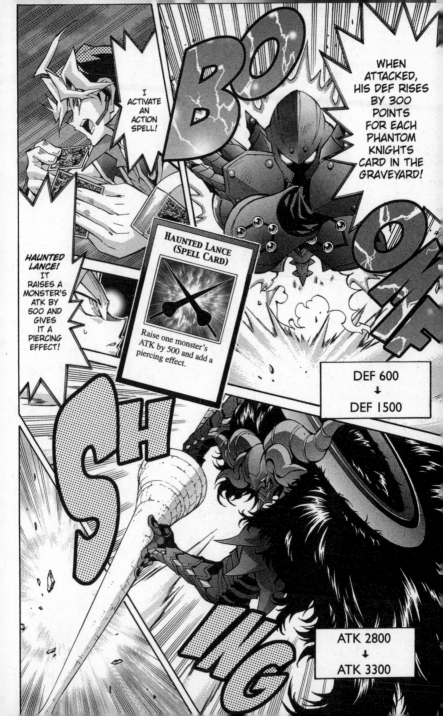

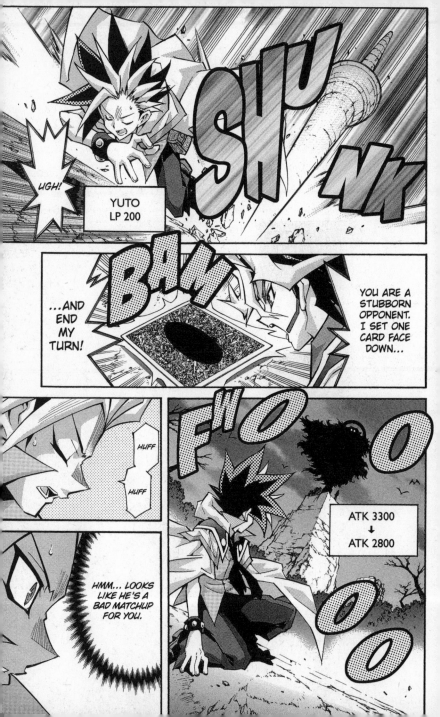

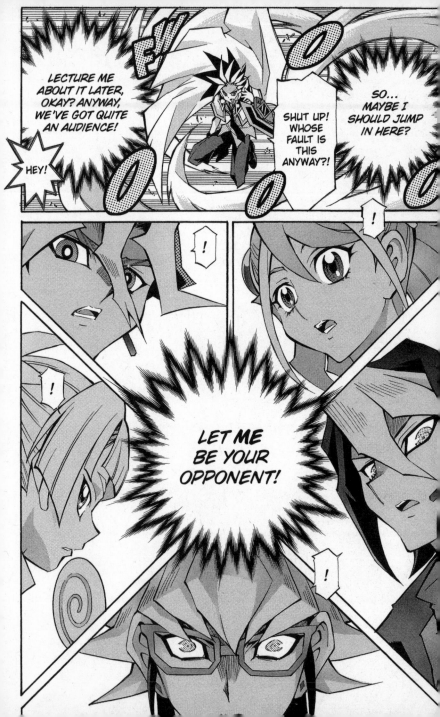

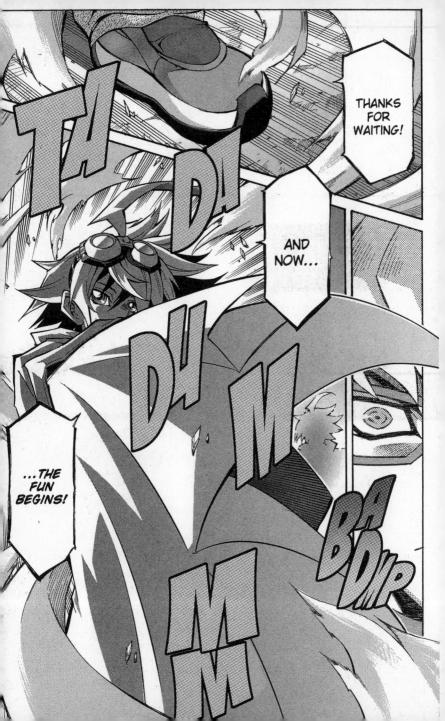

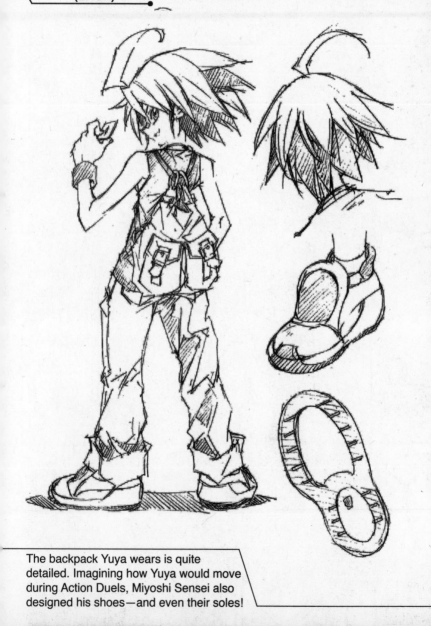

The backpack Yuya wears is quite detailed. Imagining how Yuya would move during Action Duels, Miyoshi Sensei also designed his shoes—and even their soles!

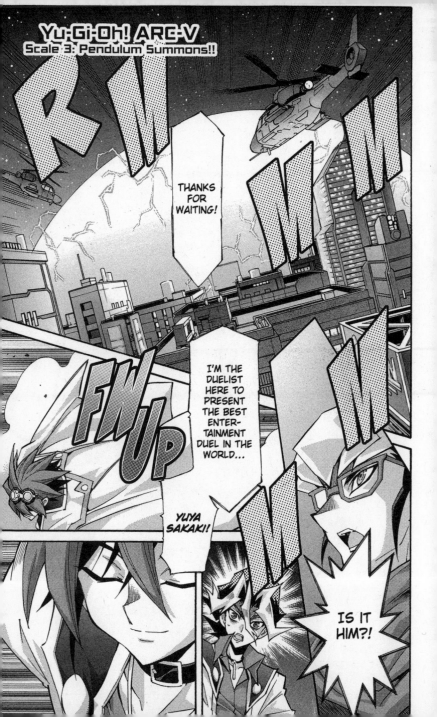

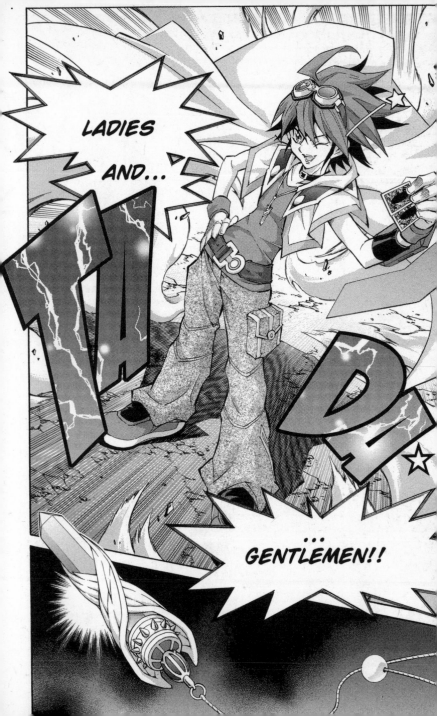

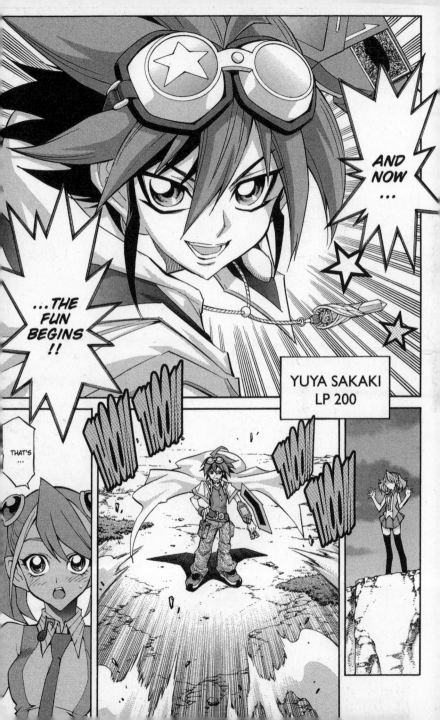

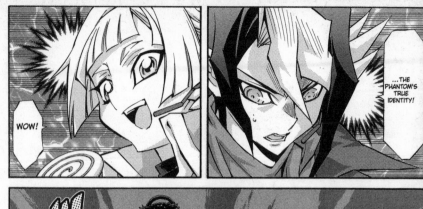

WOW!

...THE PHANTOM'S TRUE IDENTITY!

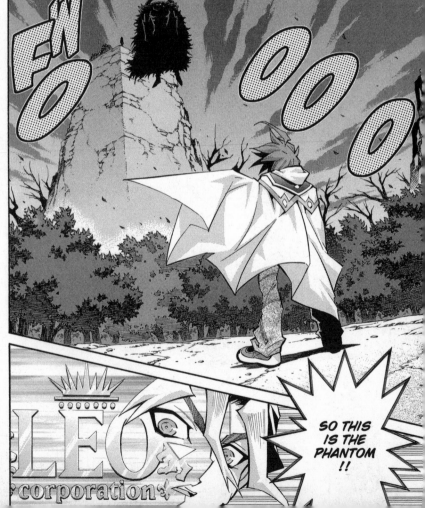

FN OOOO

LEO corporation

SO THIS IS THE PHANTOM!!

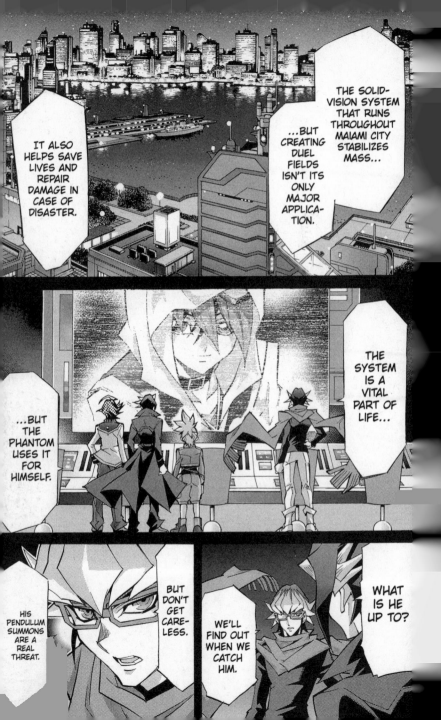

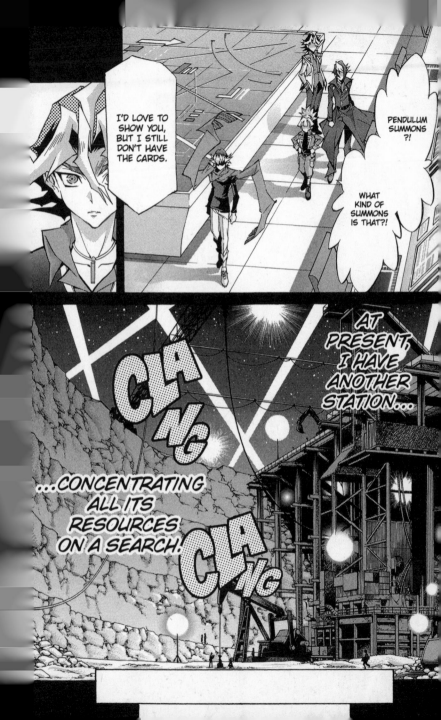

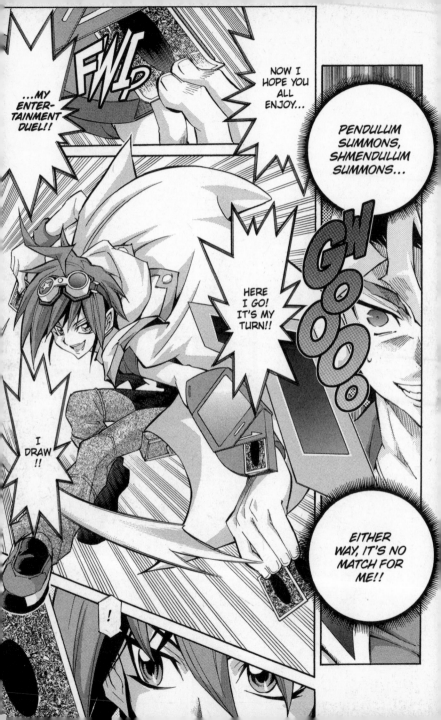

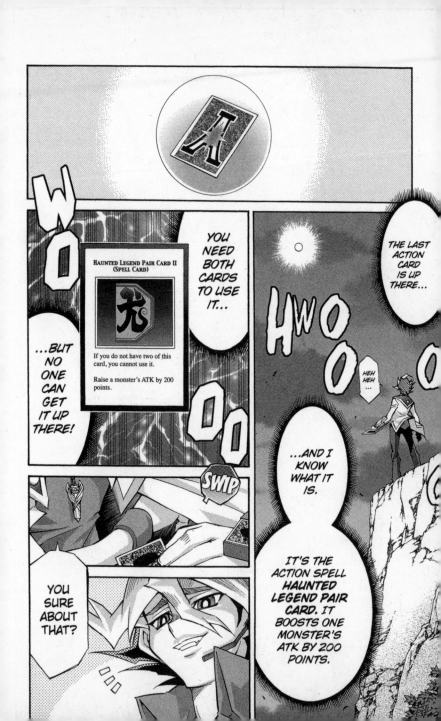

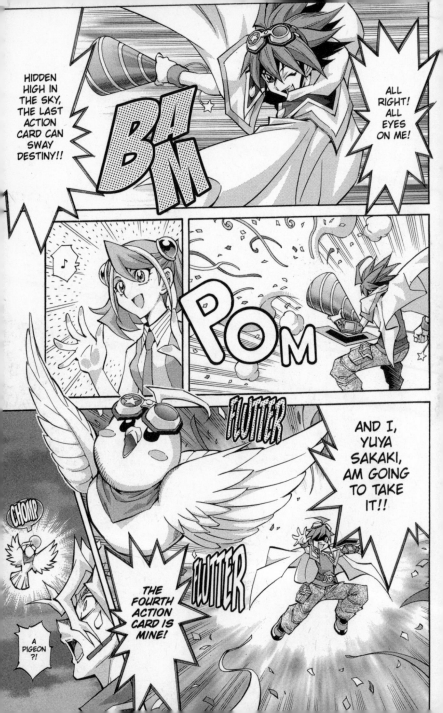

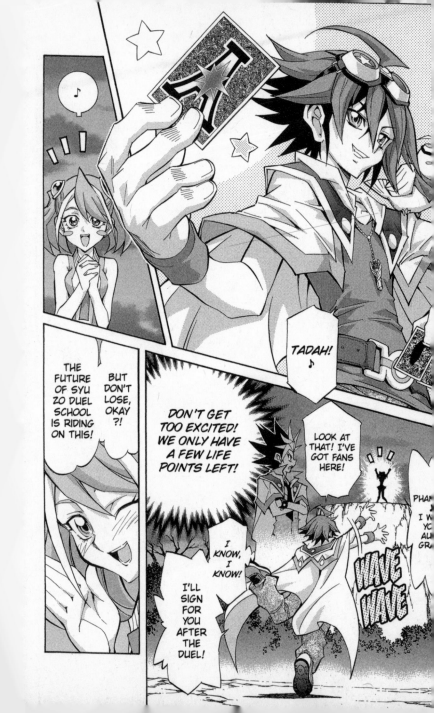

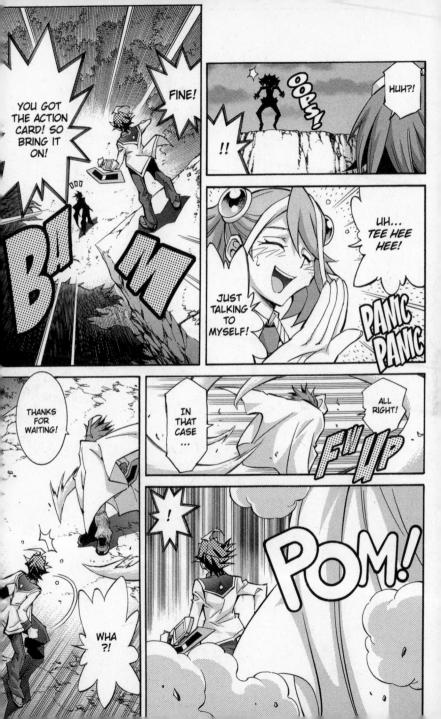

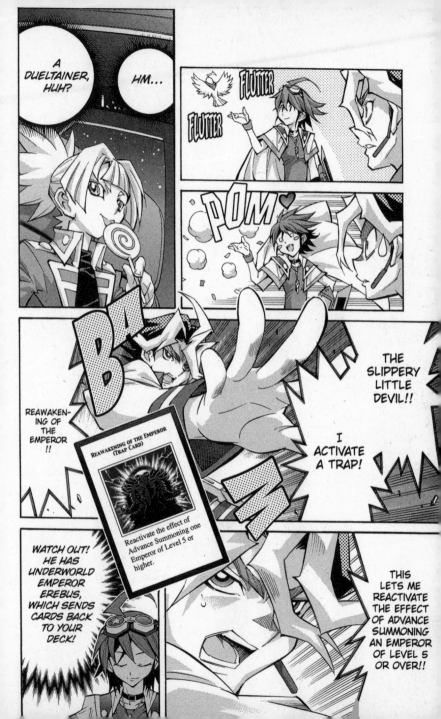

A DUELTAINER, HUH?

HM...

FLUTTER

FLUTTER

POM ♥

BA

REAWAKENING OF THE EMPEROR!!

THE SLIPPERY LITTLE DEVIL!!

I ACTIVATE A TRAP!

REAWAKENING OF THE EMPEROR
(TRAP CARD)

Reactivate the effect of Advance Summoning one Emperor of Level 5 or higher.

WATCH OUT! HE HAS UNDERWORLD EMPEROR EREBUS, WHICH SENDS CARDS BACK TO YOUR DECK!

THIS LETS ME REACTIVATE THE EFFECT OF ADVANCE SUMMONING AN EMPEROR OF LEVEL 5 OR OVER!!

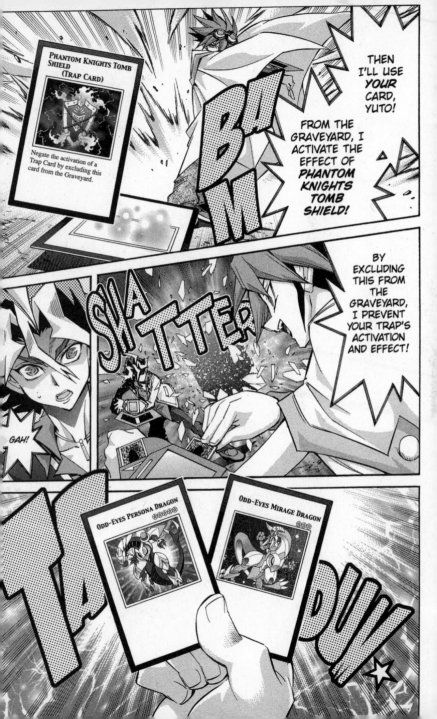

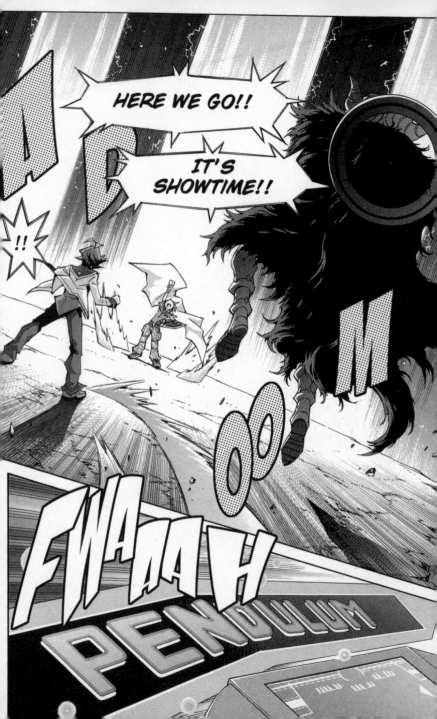

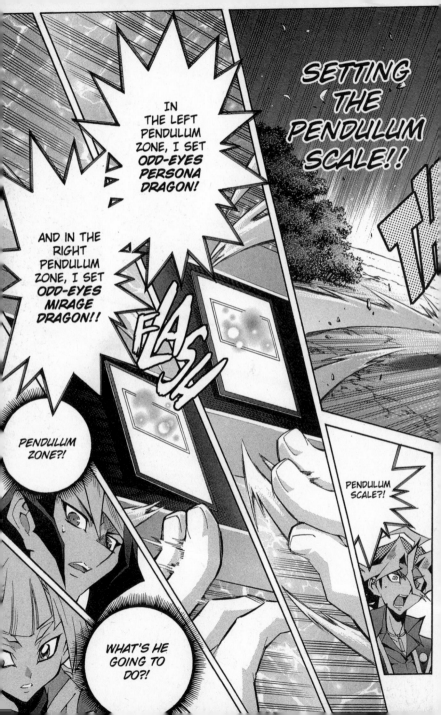

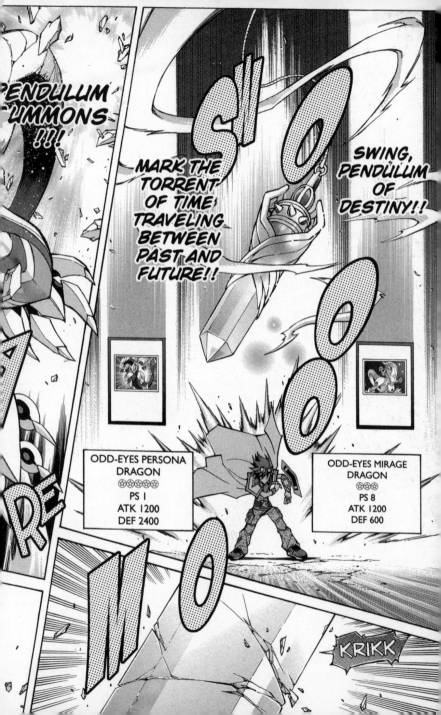

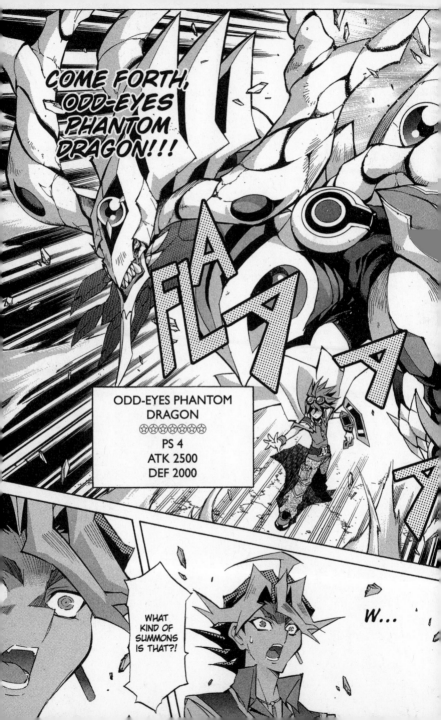

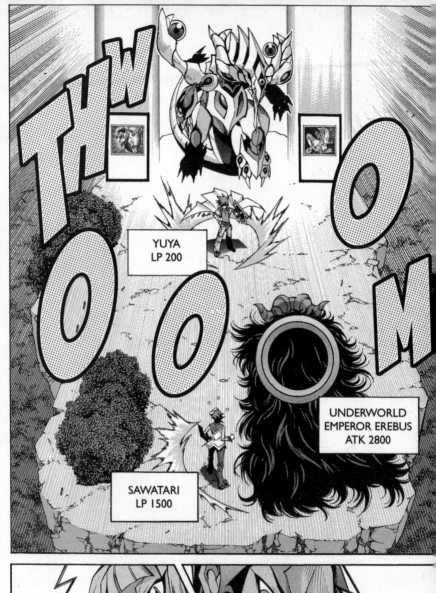

YUYA
LP 200

SAWATARI
LP 1500

UNDERWORLD
EMPEROR EREBUS
ATK 2800

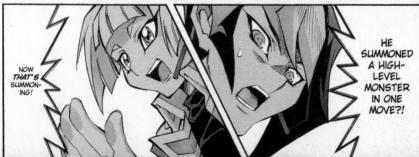

NOW *THAT'S* SUMMON-ING!

HE SUMMONED A HIGH-LEVEL MONSTER IN ONE MOVE?!

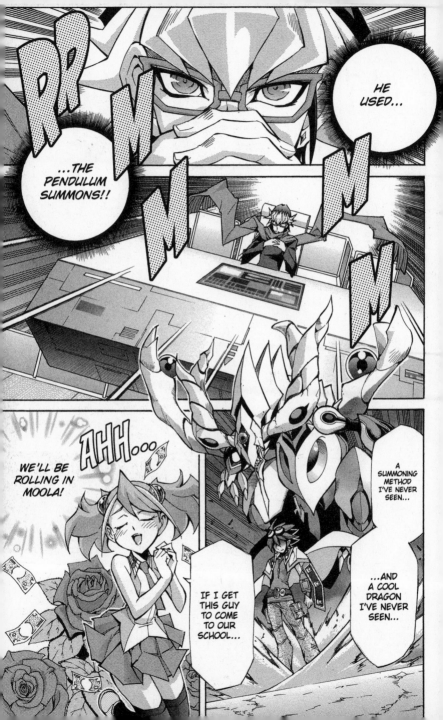

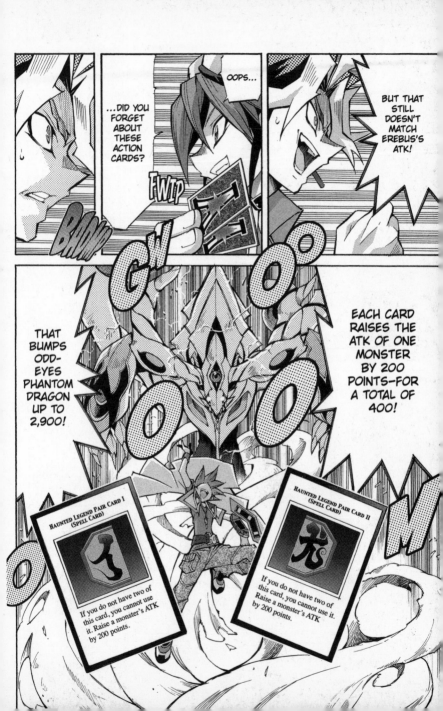

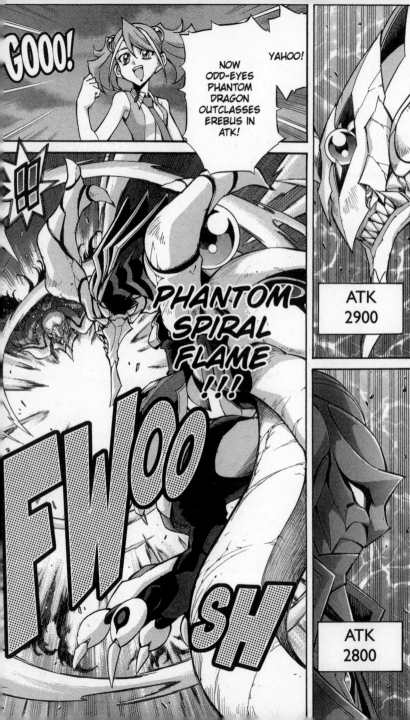

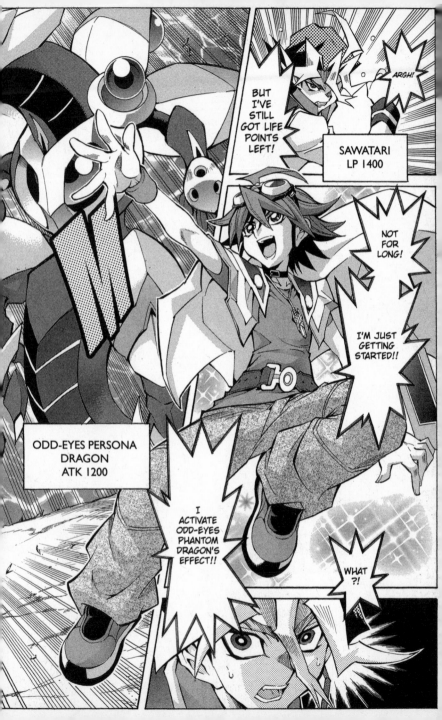

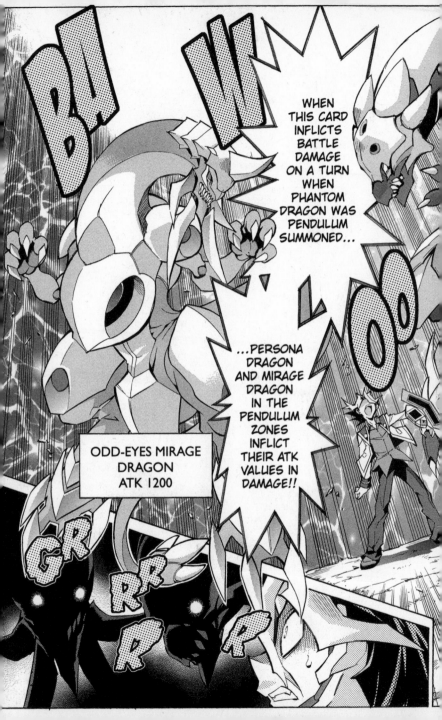

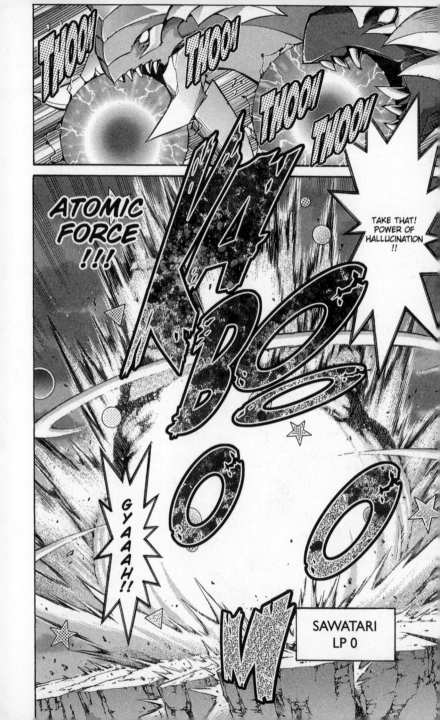

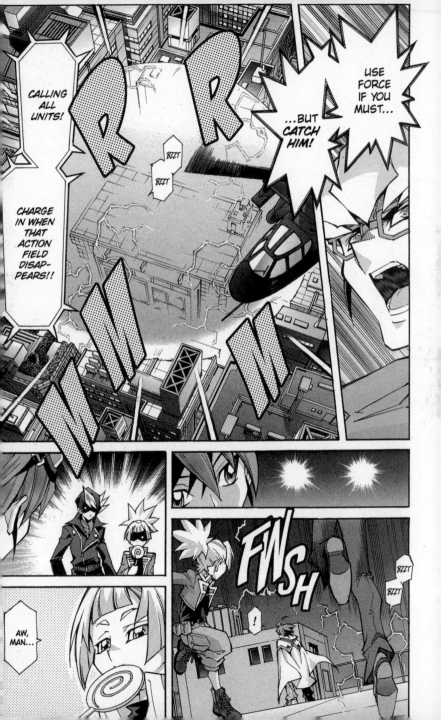

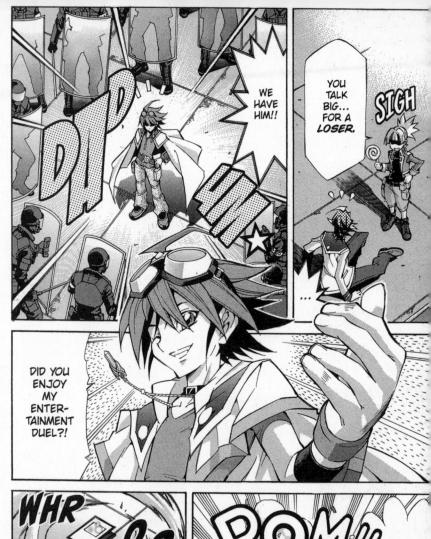

WE HAVE HIM!!

YOU TALK BIG... FOR A *LOSER*.

SIGH

...

DID YOU ENJOY MY ENTERTAINMENT DUEL?!

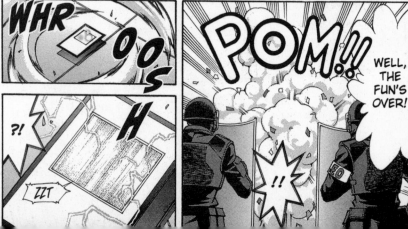

WHROOSH

?!

ZZT

POM!!

!!

WELL, THE FUN'S OVER!

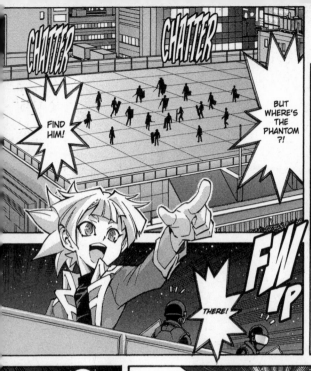

CHATTER CHATTER

FIND HIM!

BUT WHERE'S THE PHANTOM?!

THERE!

FW!P

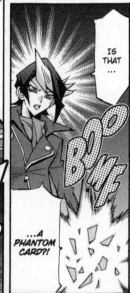

IS THAT...

...A PHANTOM CARD?!

BOO BAFF

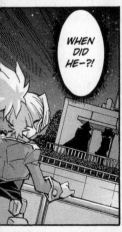

WHEN DID HE-?!

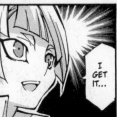

I GET IT...

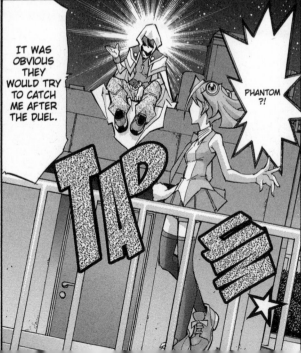

IT WAS OBVIOUS THEY WOULD TRY TO CATCH ME AFTER THE DUEL.

PHANTOM?!

TAP TMP

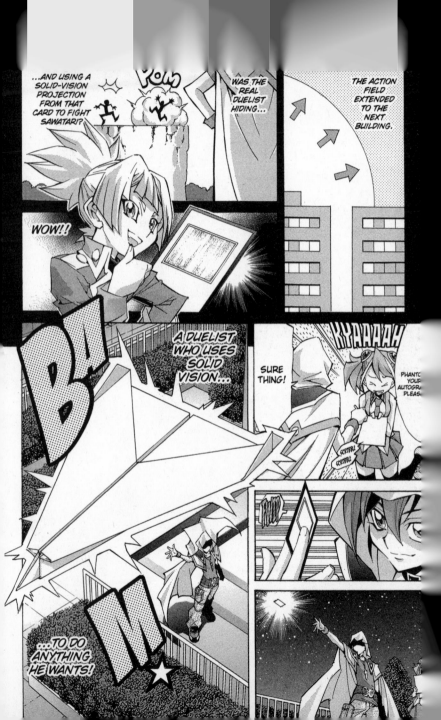

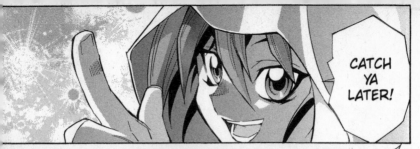

CATCH YA LATER!

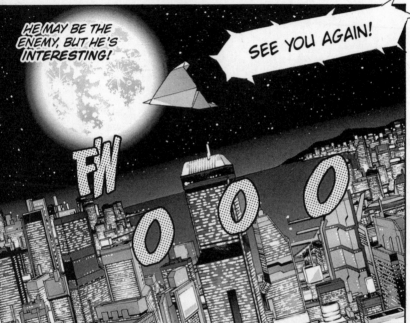

HE MAY BE THE ENEMY, BUT HE'S INTERESTING!

SEE YOU AGAIN!

FW OOO O

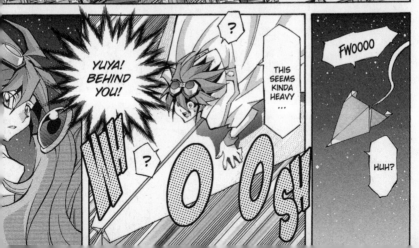

YUYA! BEHIND YOU!

?

THIS SEEMS KINDA HEAVY...

WHO O OSH

?

?

FWOOOO

HUH?

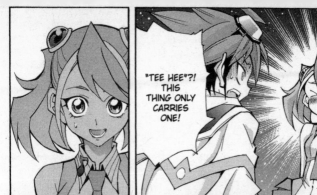

"TEE HEE"?! THIS THING ONLY CARRIES ONE!

I SORTA JUMPED ON! ♡

TEE HEE!

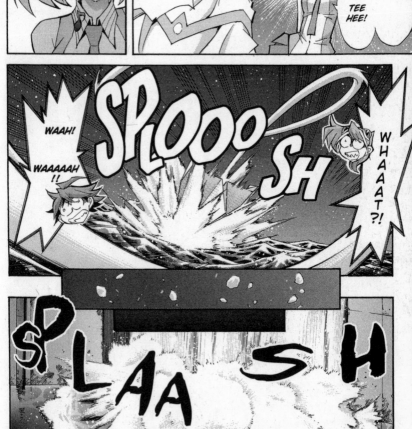

WAAH!

WAAAAAH!!

SPLOOOSH

WHAAAT?!

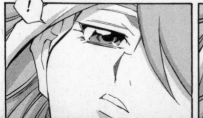

SPLAASH

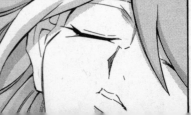

!

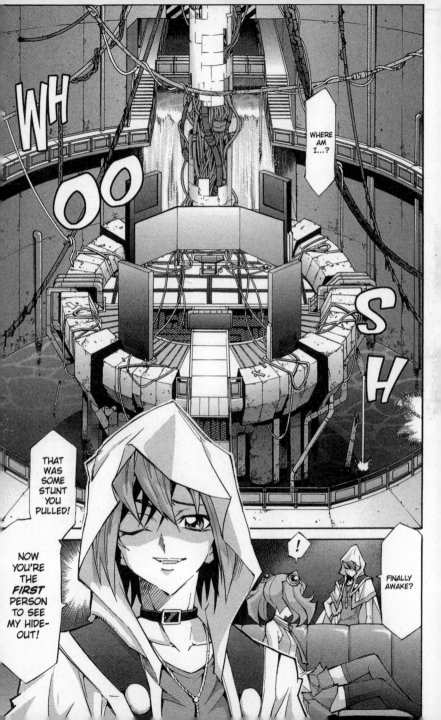

YUTO

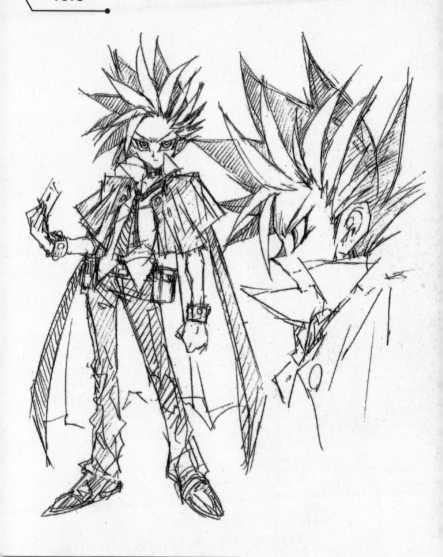

In the story, it's Yuto's job to lecture
Yuya, so he had sharp eyes in the early
designs. He's distinctive for his cloak and his
hairstyle, which is like Yuya's hair but spiked up.

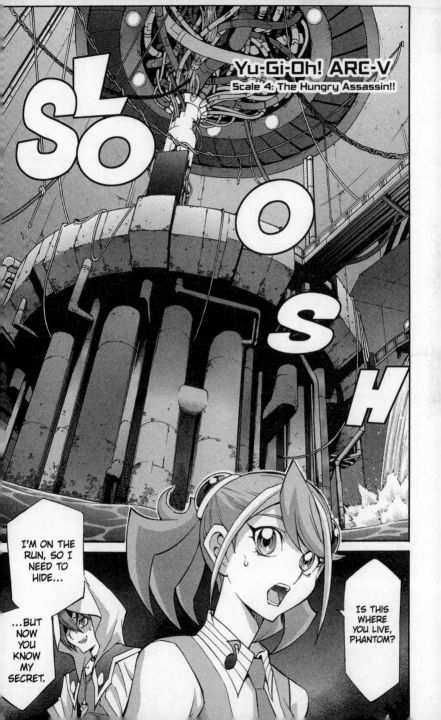

SLOSH

I'M ON THE RUN, SO I NEED TO HIDE...

...BUT NOW YOU KNOW MY SECRET.

IS THIS WHERE YOU LIVE, PHANTOM?

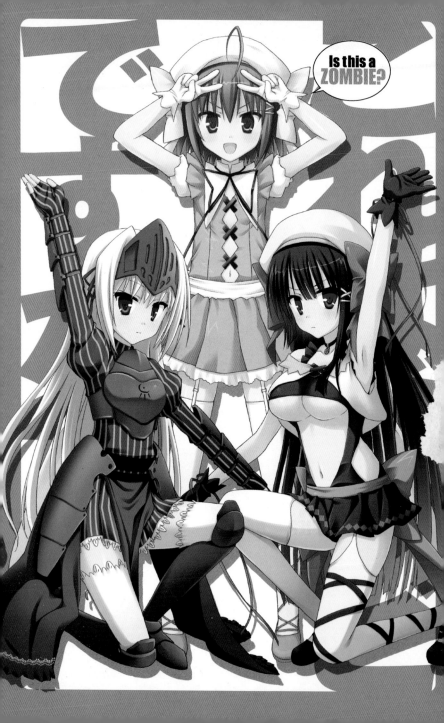

Is this a ZOMBIE?

CONTENTS

40 Stop It! Stop It, Joker! 009

035 **41**

What'll! It! Be! Aikawa~!?♪

F91!! **42**

053

43 Your Ass, in Particular, Is Too Much for Me.

071

44 113

I Thought for Sure You'd Taken Steps Against the Declining Birthrate!

I'm Number One!

135 **45**

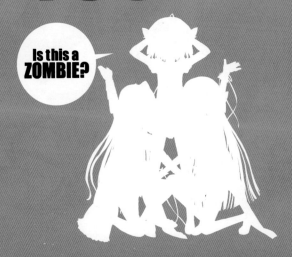

Is this a ZOMBIE?

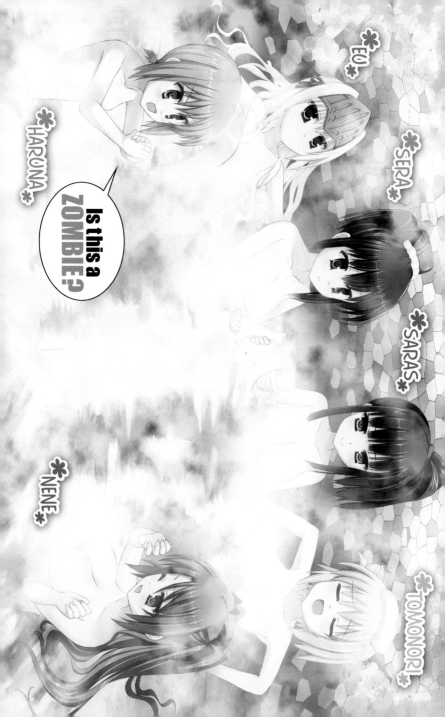

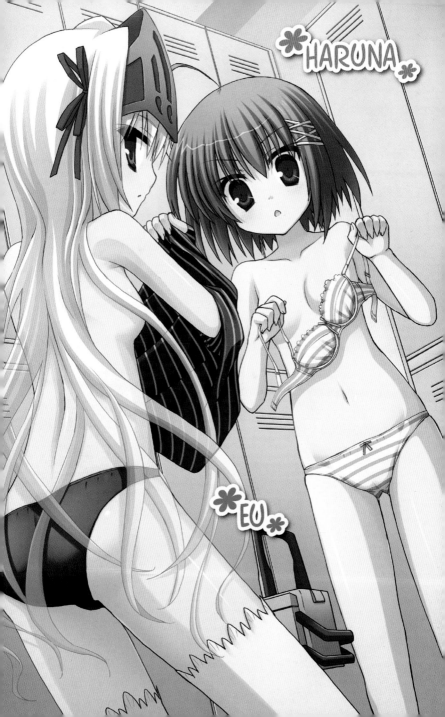

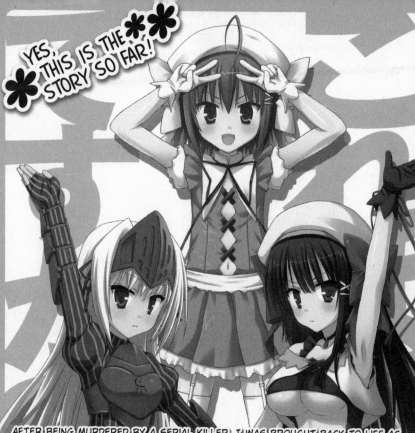

AFTER BEING MURDERED BY A SERIAL KILLER, I WAS BROUGHT BACK TO LIFE AS A ZOMBIE BY THE NECROMANCER EU, THEN ORDERED TO BE A MAGIKEWL GIRL BY A MAGIKEWL GIRL HERSELF, HARUNA, AND FINALLY HAD A VAMPIRE NINJA NAMED SERA SHOW UP, BEFORE I KNEW IT, THEY'D ALL STARTED LIVING WITH ME. FAREWELL, SWEET DAYS OF PEACE...

WE'VE GOTTA GET BACK THOSE POWERS THAT CHRIS STOLE AND SETTLE THIS ONCE AND FOR ALL! OR SO I THOUGHT! THEN THE MAGICAL POWERS GET TRANSFERRED TO EU!!
WHY IS THIS HAPPENING!?

TO MAKE MATTERS WORSE, THE QUEEN OF VILLIERS, LILIA, ATTACKS WITH HER EYES SET ON EU'S POWERS! THIS QUEEN HAS ITTY-BITTY BOOBIES!!

WHEN I TRY TO TAKE ON THAT FLAT-CHESTED GIRL, I GET CURSED WITH THE WORST THING EVER.

THIS IS WHAT EU SAYS TO ME: "WHO ARE YOU?"

HOW ON EARTH COULD EU HAVE FORGOTTEN HER MOST BELOVED AND ATTRACTIVE OLDER BROTHER!?

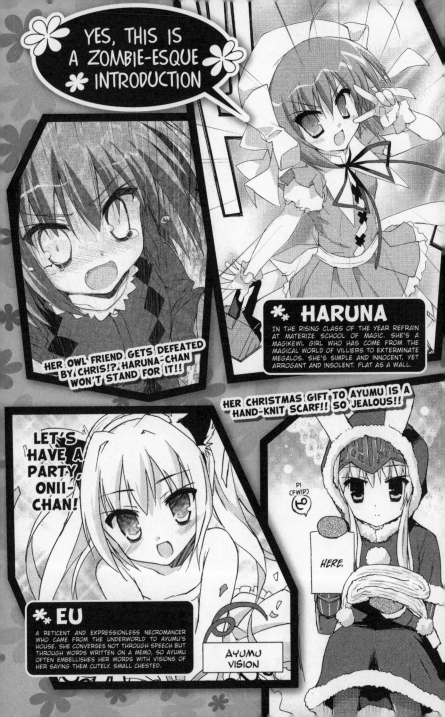

YES, THIS IS A ZOMBIE-ESQUE * INTRODUCTION

HER OWL FRIEND GETS DEFEATED BY CHRIS!? HARUNA-CHAN WON'T STAND FOR IT!!

✿ HARUNA

IN THE RISING CLASS OF THE YEAR REFRAIN AT MATERIZE SCHOOL OF MAGIC. SHE'S A MAGIKEWL GIRL WHO HAS COME FROM THE MAGICAL WORLD OF VILLIERS TO EXTERMINATE MEGALOS. SHE'S SIMPLE AND INNOCENT, YET ARROGANT AND INSOLENT. FLAT AS A WALL.

HER CHRISTMAS GIFT TO AYUMU IS A HAND-KNIT SCARF!! SO JEALOUS!!

LET'S HAVE A PARTY, ONII-CHAN!

PI (FWIP)

HERE.

AYUMU VISION

✿ EU

A RETICENT AND EXPRESSIONLESS NECROMANCER WHO CAME FROM THE UNDERWORLD TO AYUMU'S HOUSE. SHE CONVERSES NOT THROUGH SPEECH BUT THROUGH WORDS WRITTEN ON A MEMO, SO AYUMU OFTEN EMBELLISHES HER WORDS WITH VISIONS OF HER SAYING THEM CUTELY. SMALL CHESTED.

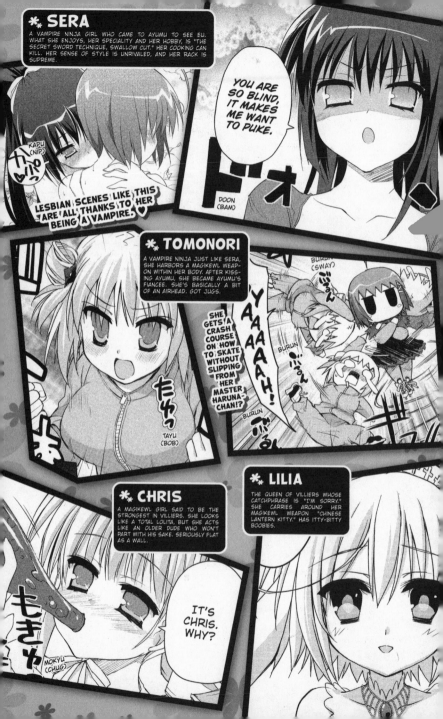

✳ SERA

A VAMPIRE NINJA GIRL WHO CAME TO AYUMU TO SEE EU. WHAT SHE ENJOYS, HER SPECIALITY AND HER HOBBY, IS "THE SECRET SWORD TECHNIQUE, SWALLOW CUT." HER COOKING CAN KILL. HER SENSE OF STYLE IS UNRIVALED, AND HER RACK IS SUPREME.

YOU ARE SO BLIND, IT MAKES ME WANT TO PUKE.

KAPU (NIP)

DOON (BAM)

LESBIAN SCENES LIKE THIS ARE ALL THANKS TO HER BEING A VAMPIRE.

✳ TOMONORI

A VAMPIRE NINJA JUST LIKE SERA, SHE HARBORS A MAGIKEWL WEAPON WITHIN HER BODY. AFTER KISSING AYUMU, SHE BECAME AYUMU'S FIANCEE. SHE'S BASICALLY A BIT OF AN AIRHEAD. GOT JUGS.

BURUN (SWAY)

SHE GETS A CRASH COURSE ON HOW TO SKATE WITHOUT SLIPPING FROM HER MASTER HARUNA-CHAN!?

YAAAAH!

BURUN

BURUN

TAYU (BOB)

✳ CHRIS

A MAGIKEWL GIRL SAID TO BE THE STRONGEST IN VILLIERS. SHE LOOKS LIKE A TOTAL LOLITA, BUT SHE ACTS LIKE AN OLDER DUDE WHO WON'T PART WITH HIS SAKE. SERIOUSLY FLAT AS A WALL.

✳ LILIA

THE QUEEN OF VILLIERS WHOSE CATCHPHRASE IS "I'M SORRY." SHE CARRIES AROUND HER MAGIKEWL WEAPON "CHINESE LANTERN KITTY." HAS ITTY-BITTY BOOBIES.

MOKYU (CHUG)

IT'S CHRIS. WHY?

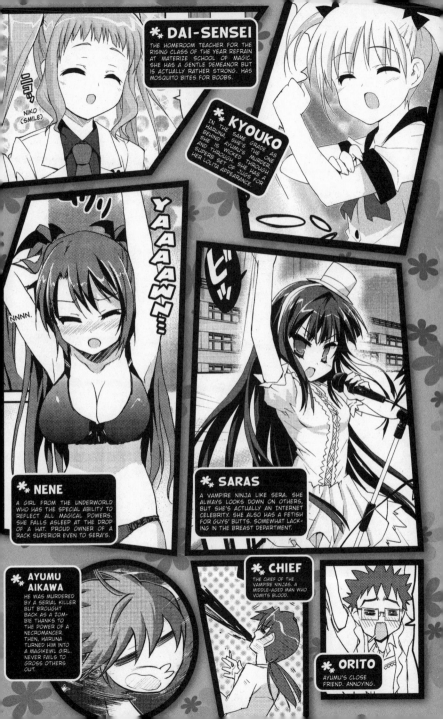

NIKO (SMILE)

✳ DAI-SENSEI

THE HOMEROOM TEACHER FOR THE RISING CLASS OF THE YEAR REFRAIN AT MATERIZE SCHOOL OF MAGIC. SHE HAS A GENTLE DEMEANOR BUT IS ACTUALLY RATHER STRONG. HAS MOSQUITO BITES FOR BOOBS.

✳ KYOUKO

IN THE SAME GRADE AS HARUNA, SHE'S THE ONE BEHIND AYUMU'S MURDER. SHE IS WICKED THROUGH AND THROUGH. SHE HAS A SUPERB SET OF JUGS FOR HER LOLITA APPEARANCE.

YAAAAWN...

NNNN.

✳ NENE

A GIRL FROM THE UNDERWORLD WHO HAS THE SPECIAL ABILITY TO REFLECT ALL MAGICAL POWERS. SHE FALLS ASLEEP AT THE DROP OF A HAT. PROUD OWNER OF A RACK SUPERIOR EVEN TO SERA'S.

✳ SARAS

A VAMPIRE NINJA LIKE SERA. SHE ALWAYS LOOKS DOWN ON OTHERS, BUT SHE'S ACTUALLY AN INTERNET CELEBRITY. SHE ALSO HAS A FETISH FOR GUYS' BUTTS. SOMEWHAT LACKING IN THE BREAST DEPARTMENT.

✳ AYUMU AIKAWA

HE WAS MURDERED BY A SERIAL KILLER BUT BROUGHT BACK AS A ZOMBIE THANKS TO THE POWER OF A NECROMANCER. THEN, HARUNA TURNED HIM INTO A MAGIKEWL GIRL. NEVER FAILS TO GROSS OTHERS OUT.

✳ CHIEF

THE CHIEF OF THE VAMPIRE NINJAS. A MIDDLE-AGED MAN WHO VOMITS BLOOD.

✳ ORITO

AYUMU'S CLOSE FRIEND. ANNOYING.

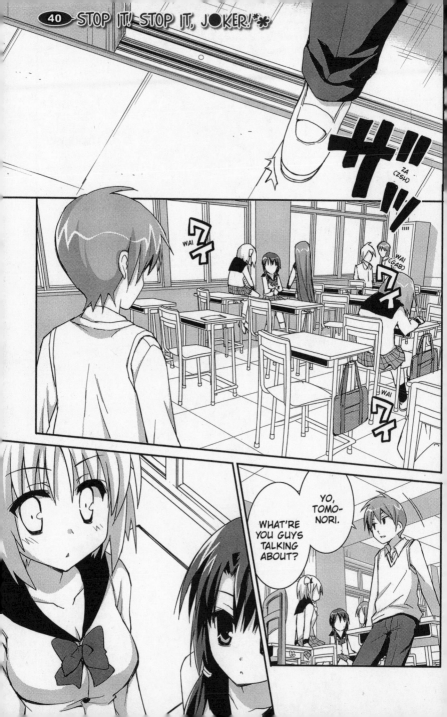

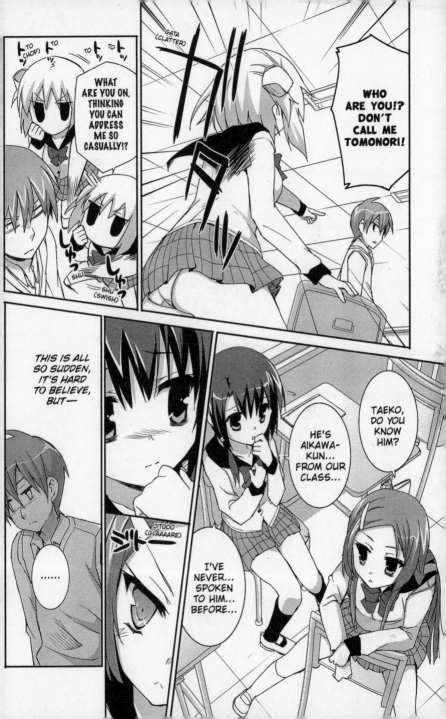

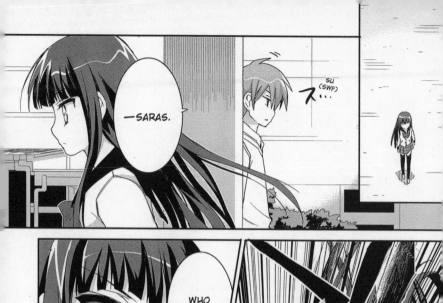

—SARAS.

SU
(SWF)

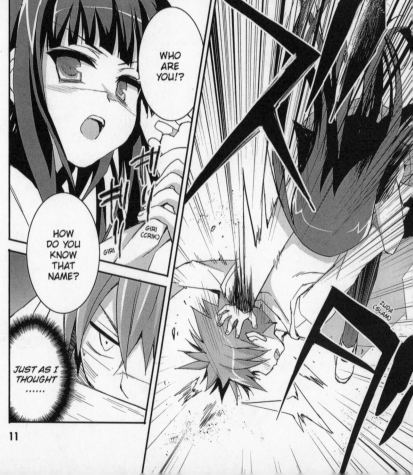

WHO ARE YOU!?

HOW DO YOU KNOW THAT NAME?

GIRI
(CRIK)

GIRI

ZUDA
(SLAM)

JUST AS I THOUGHT
......

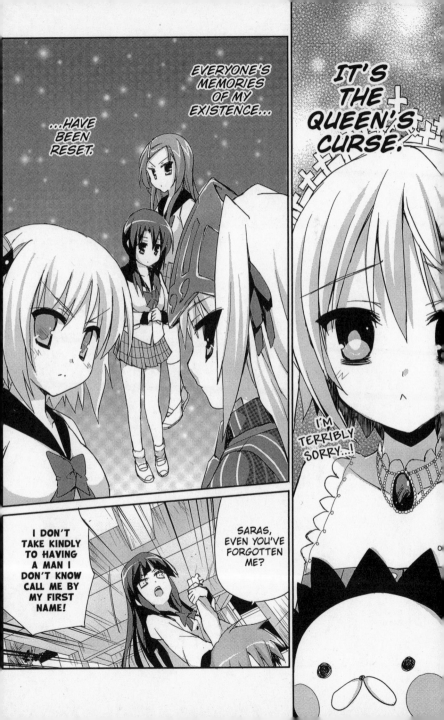

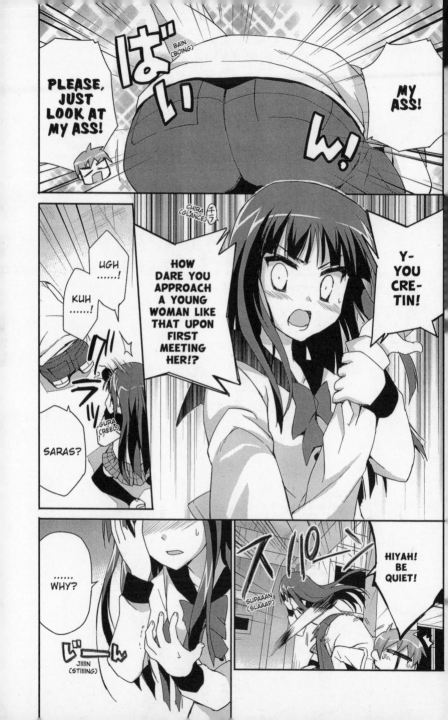

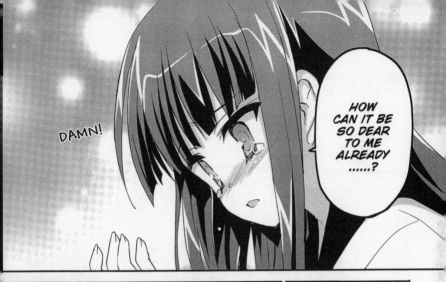

DAMN!

HOW CAN IT BE SO DEAR TO ME ALREADY ......?

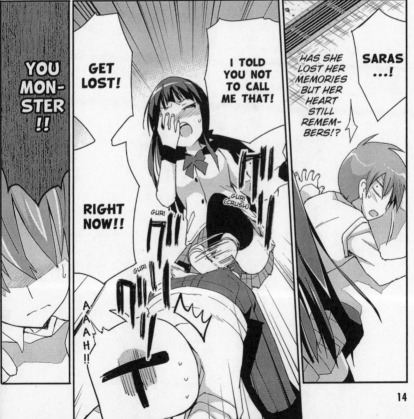

YOU MONSTER!!

GET LOST!

RIGHT NOW!!

I TOLD YOU NOT TO CALL ME THAT!

GURI

GURI

GURI (CRUSH)

AAAH!!

HAS SHE LOST HER MEMORIES BUT HER HEART STILL REMEMBERS!?

SARAS....!

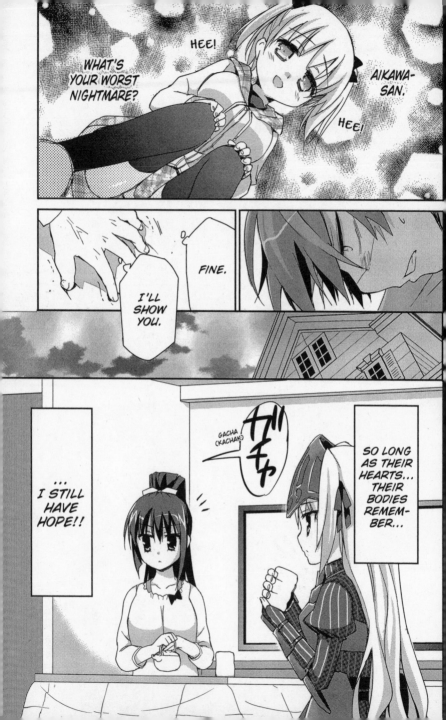

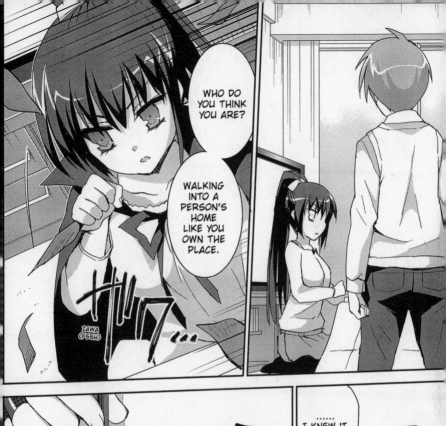

WHO DO YOU THINK YOU ARE?

WALKING INTO A PERSON'S HOME LIKE YOU OWN THE PLACE.

ZAWA (FSSH)

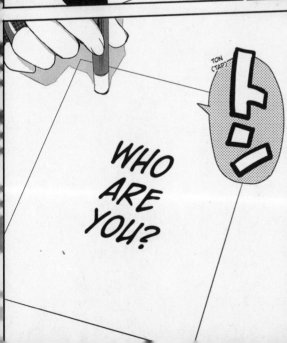

TON (TAP)

WHO ARE YOU?

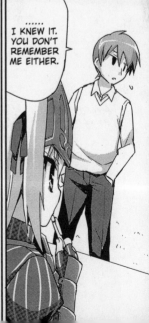

...... I KNEW IT. YOU DON'T REMEMBER ME EITHER.

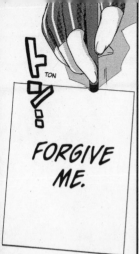

TON

FORGIVE ME.

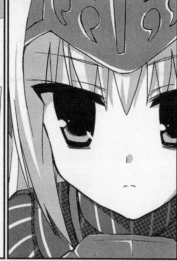

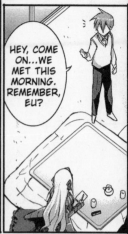

HEY, COME ON...WE MET THIS MORNING. REMEMBER, EU?

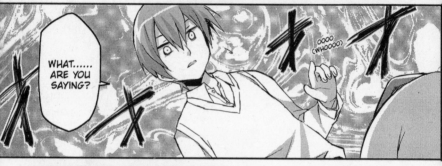

WHAT...... ARE YOU SAYING?

OOOO (WHOOOO)

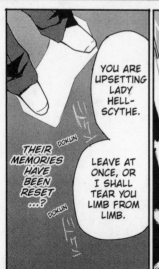

THEIR MEMORIES HAVE BEEN RESET ...?

DOKUN

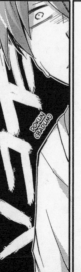

YOU ARE UPSETTING LADY HELL-SCYTHE.

LEAVE AT ONCE, OR I SHALL TEAR YOU LIMB FROM LIMB.

DOKUN (DADUM)

SHE CURSES YOU WITH YOUR WORST NIGHTMARE, A FATE WORSE THAN DEATH.

♥

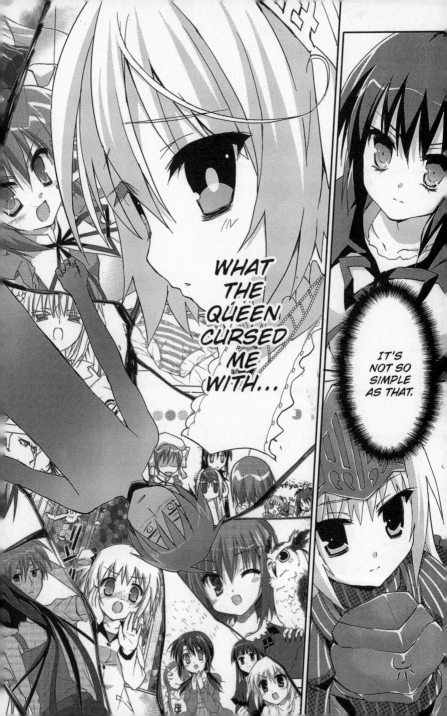

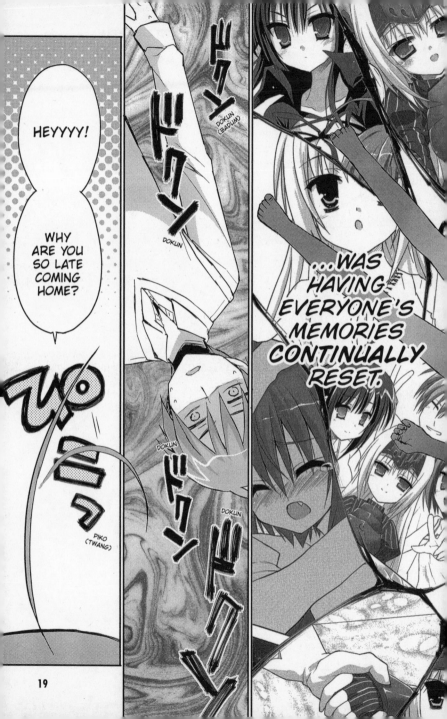

HEYYYY!

WHY ARE YOU SO LATE COMING HOME?

...WAS HAVING EVERYONE'S MEMORIES CONTINUALLY RESET.

PIKO (TWANG)

DOKUN

DOKUN (BADUM)

DOKUN

DOKUN

DOKUN

PIKO
ぴこ

PIKO
(TWANG)
ぴこ

カレーポルシェ

......DID...

...YOU JUST SPEAK TO ME?

キョトン

KYOTON
(BLINK)

I'M HUNGRY.

MUSUUU
(POUUUT)

ムスー

21

PIKKO
ピッコ

PIKKO (FWING)
ピッコ

KACCHI (STICK)
カッ

KOCCHI (TOCK)
コッチ

I SEE, MEOW!

HMM **MM.**

PI (FWIP)
ピッ

I CAN CONFIRM THAT HE AND I ARE BONDED BY MAGIC.

SO YOU ARE SAYING THAT THANKS TO THIS QUEEN'S CURSE OR SOMETHING, NOBODY REMEMBERS YOU.

TON (TAP)
トン

TON
トン

AND WHEN WE ARE AWAY FROM YOU FOR A LITTLE WHILE, WE RESET ALL OVER AGAIN.

I FEEL A FAMILIAR TRUST-WORTHI-NESS IN HIM.

IT'S TRUE. YES.

THERE IS SOMETHING REASSURING ABOUT HIM...

TOKUN トクン

TOKUN トクン

TOKUN (BADUM) トクン...

BUT WHY'S HARUNA THE ONLY ONE WHO REMEMBERS ME?

I'M SURE THAT YOU AND I WERE LOVERS.

MY HEART IS RACING...

HUH.........? I CAN'T EVEN BEGIN TO IMAGINE WHERE THAT'S COMING FROM.

'COS I'M A GENIUS, DUH.

PIKO ピコ

PIKO ピコ

GOOOON (SHOOOOCK)

IT'S TOO MUCH OF A PAIN TO HAVE YOU FORGOTTEN EACH AND EVERY TIME, SO...

IN ANY CASE!

...FROM NOW ON WE JUST GOTTA STAY IN AYUMU'S FIELD OF VISION AT ALL TIMES!

SKREEE!

ZORAAA! SKREEE!

ZAAA
(SSSHHH)

カポーン
ザァァァ
KAPOOON
(KERPLUUUUNN)

AWA
(SOAM)

AWA
アワ
アワ

IS THE
WATER
WARM
ENOUGH
FOR
YOU?

Y-
YEAH...

WHAT'S
THAT
NOISE?

DOKI
(BADUM)

DOKI

SFX: BASHA (SPLASH) BASHA BASHA

GOSHI

GOSHI

IT IS
BETTER
THAN HIM
BEING
DIRTY.

GOSHI
(SCRUB)

I DIDN'T
MEAN WE
OUGHTA
GET INTO
THE BATH
WITH HIM.

PYUN

PYUN
(FLING)

YOU
KNOW
THAT
IDIOT
AYUMU'S
A BEAST,
DON'T
YOU?

24

I KNOW THIS FEELING!

DOKI!

DOKI!

DOKI!

DOKI!

WAAH!

MUNI (MOOSH)

GOSHI

GOSHI

NOW TO WASH YOUR FRONT.

JAAAA (SSHH)

AWA

AWA

AWA

AYUMU VISION

YOUR TURN NEXT.

I WANT TO TEASE ONII-CHAN'S HIROSHI.

WITH MY EYES COVERED, MY IMAGINATION'S GOING FULL SPEED!

KUH!

YOU CAN DO IT...STAY STRONG, HIROSHI!

MUKU (POKE)

↑ HIROSHI (AGE 16)

↑ HIROSHI (AGE 16)

CHIKKA
(TICK)

CHIKKA

CHIKKA

CHIKKA

CHIKKA

THESE TWO... SURE MOVE AROUND A LOT IN THEIR SLEEP.

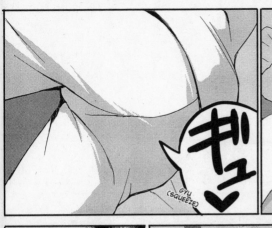

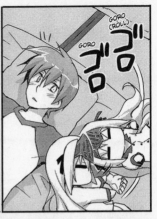

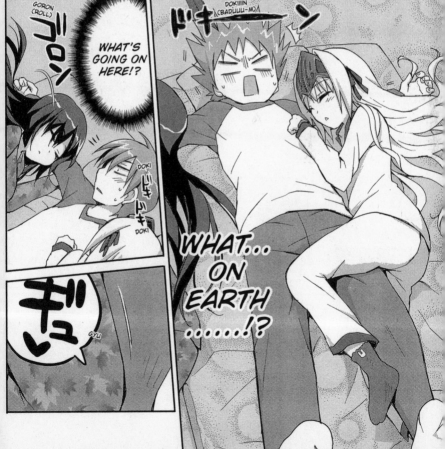

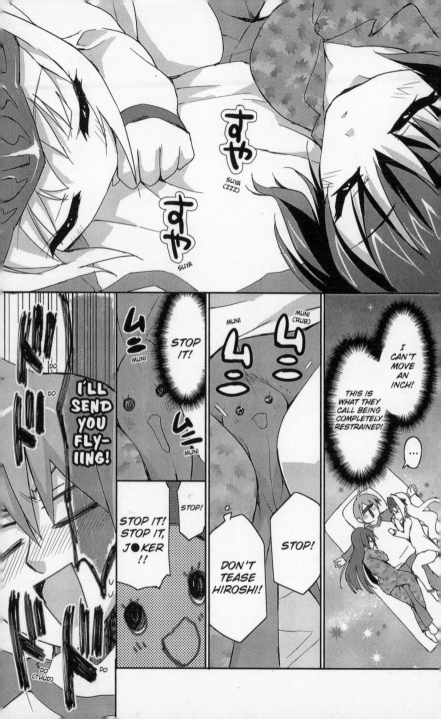

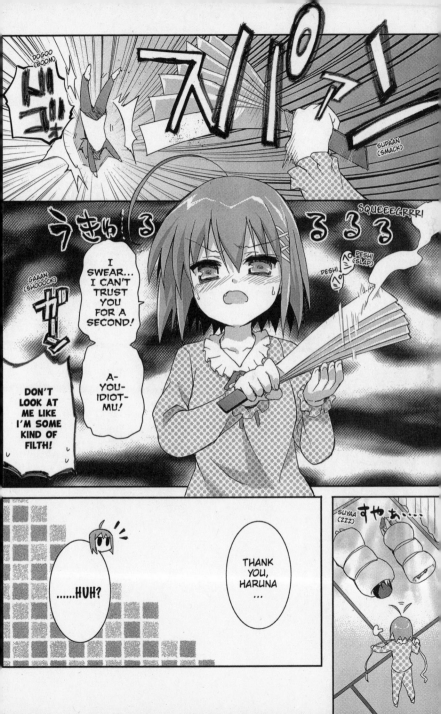

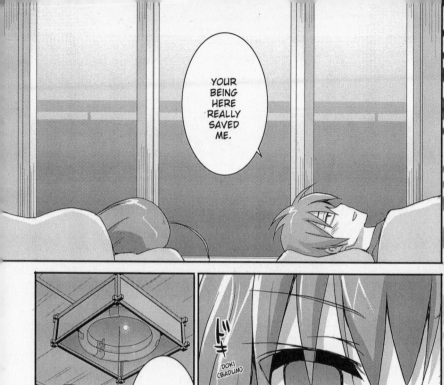

YOUR BEING HERE REALLY SAVED ME.

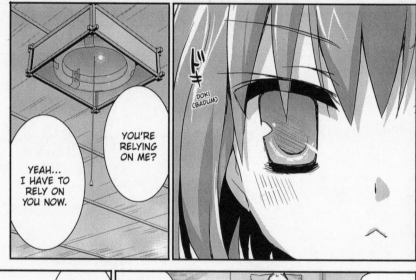

YOU'RE RELYING ON ME?

YEAH... I HAVE TO RELY ON YOU NOW.

DOKI (BADUM)

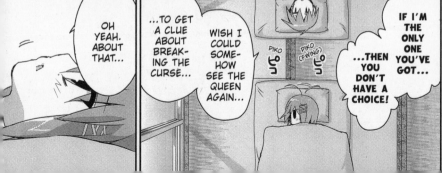

OH YEAH. ABOUT THAT...

...TO GET A CLUE ABOUT BREAKING THE CURSE...

WISH I COULD SOMEHOW SEE THE QUEEN AGAIN...

PIKO

PIKO (FWING)

IF I'M THE ONLY ONE YOU'VE GOT...

...THEN YOU DON'T HAVE A CHOICE!

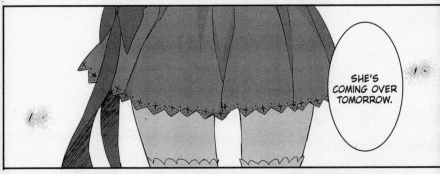

SHE'S COMING OVER TOMORROW.

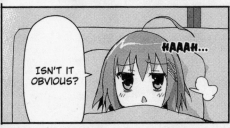

ISN'T IT OBVIOUS?

HAAAH...

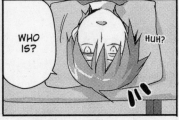

WHO IS?

HUH?

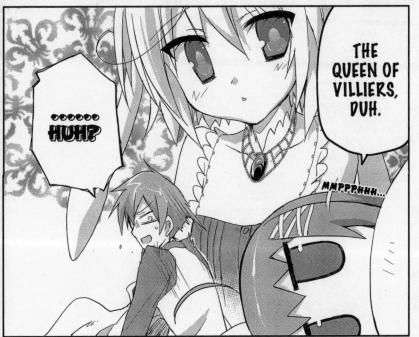

HUH?

THE QUEEN OF VILLIERS, DUH.

MMPPPPHHH...

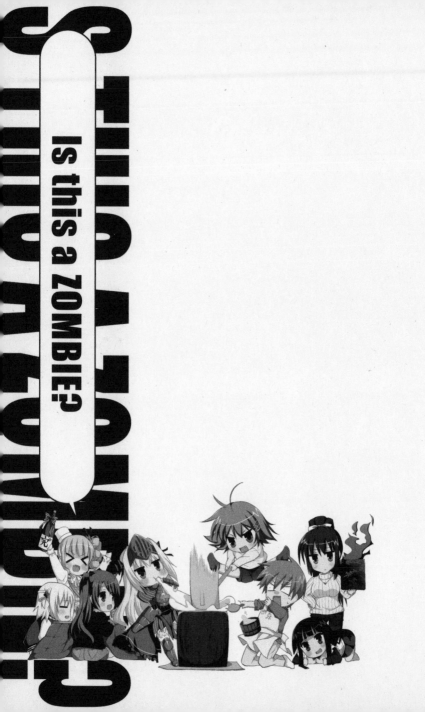

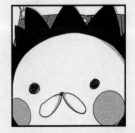

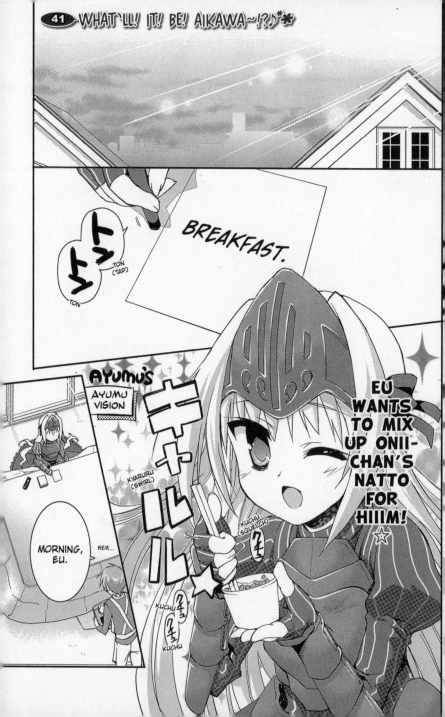

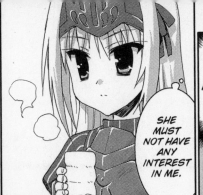

SHE MUST NOT HAVE ANY INTEREST IN ME.

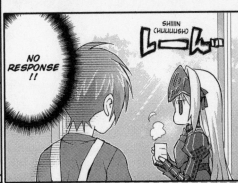

NO RESPONSE!!

SHIIIN (HUUUUSH)

SHIO (DROOP)

SHIO

FUAA (YAWN)

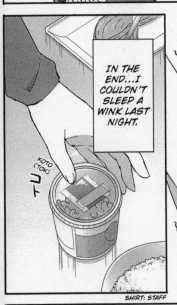

IN THE END...I COULDN'T SLEEP A WINK LAST NIGHT.

KOTO (TOK)

SHIRT: STAFF

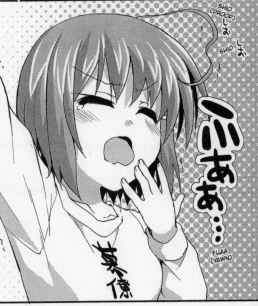

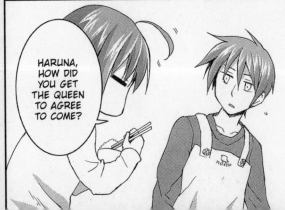

HARUNA, HOW DID YOU GET THE QUEEN TO AGREE TO COME?

...THE PROBLEM IS HOW TO UNDO IT.

I GET THE NATURE OF THE QUEEN'S CURSE, BUT...

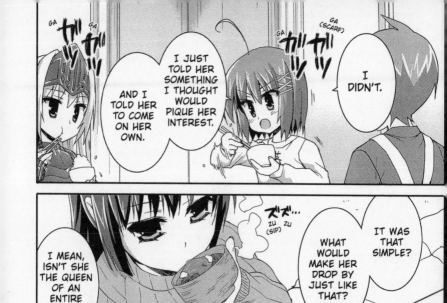

GA ガリ ガリッ (SCARF)

AND I TOLD HER TO COME ON HER OWN.

I JUST TOLD HER SOMETHING I THOUGHT WOULD PIQUE HER INTEREST.

GA ガリ ガリッ (SCARF)

I DIDN'T.

ズズ... ZU ZU (SIP)

I MEAN, ISN'T SHE THE QUEEN OF AN ENTIRE COUNTRY?

WHAT WOULD MAKE HER DROP BY JUST LIKE THAT?

IT WAS THAT SIMPLE?

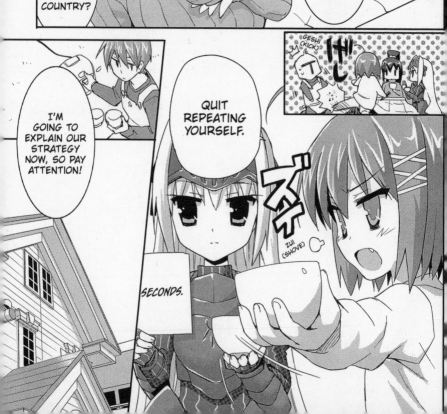

GESHI (KICK)

I'M GOING TO EXPLAIN OUR STRATEGY NOW, SO PAY ATTENTION!

QUIT REPEATING YOURSELF.

ズイ ZUI (SHOVE)

SECONDS.

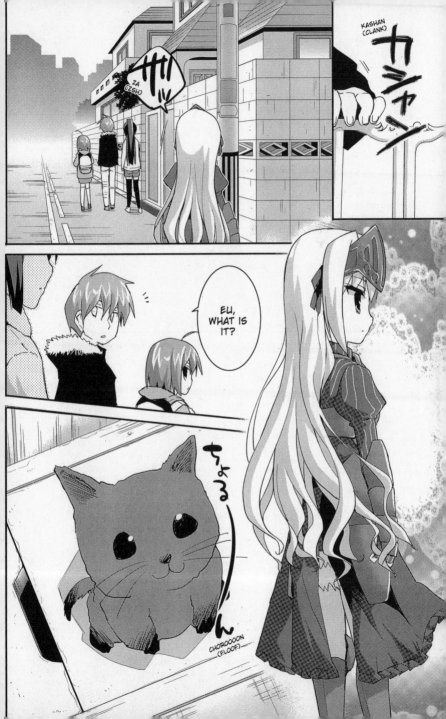

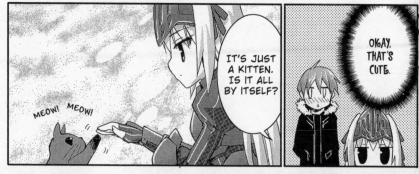

IT'S JUST A KITTEN. IS IT ALL BY ITSELF?

MEOW! MEOW!

OKAY, THAT'S CUTE.

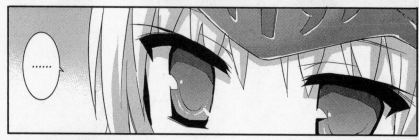

......

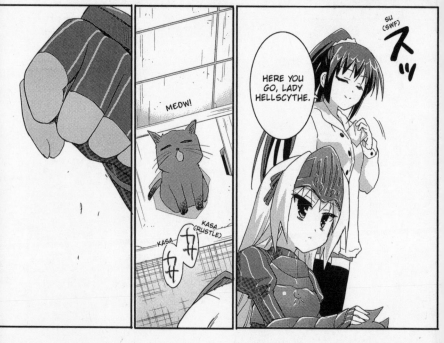

MEOW!

KASA (RUSTLE)

KASA

HERE YOU GO, LADY HELLSCYTHE.

SU (SWF)

スッ

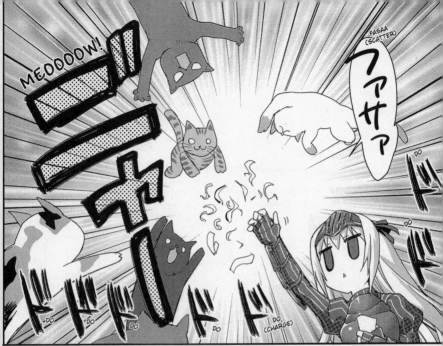

MEOOOOW!!

FASAA (SCATTER)

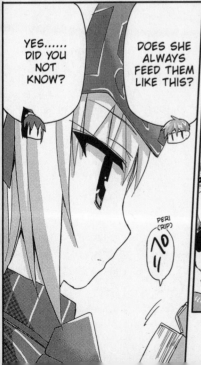

YES...... DID YOU NOT KNOW?

DOES SHE ALWAYS FEED THEM LIKE THIS?

PERI (RIP)

GA!

GA! (SCARF)

GA!

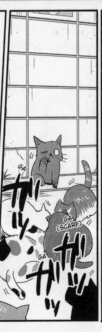

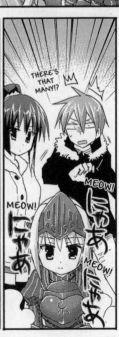

THERE'S THAT MANY!?

MEOW!

MEOW!

MEOW!

40

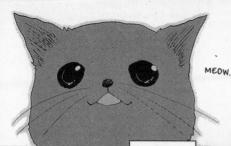

MEOW.

THIS KITTEN IS ME.

SHE MAKES HERSELF THE BAIT IN ORDER TO GET FED.

ONE OF THESE DAYS, SHE WILL REALIZE SHE IS ALL ALONE.

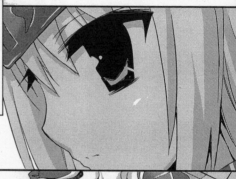

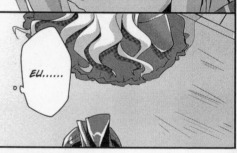

EU......

THEN...

...SHE'LL PROBABLY FIND WHERE SHE BELONGS TOO.

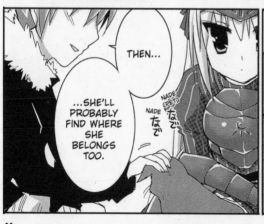

NADE (PAT)
なで

NADE
なで

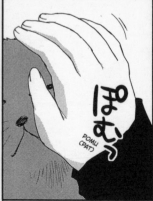

POMU (PAT)

41

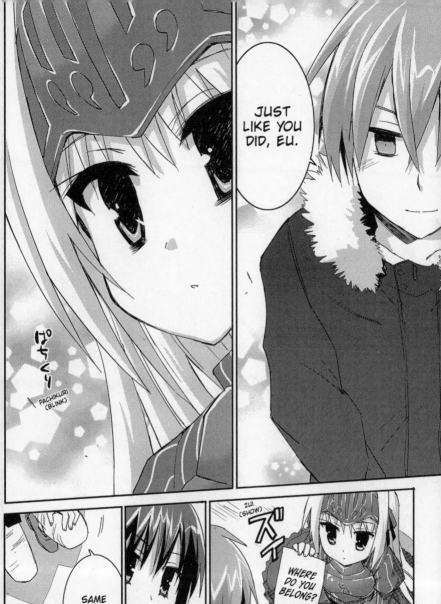

JUST LIKE YOU DID, EU.

パちくり
PACHIKURI
(BLINK)

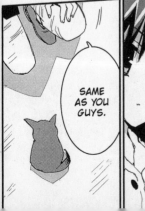

SAME AS YOU GUYS.

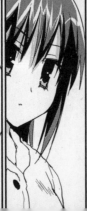

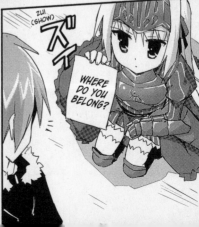

ズイ
(ZUI)
(SHOW)

WHERE DO YOU BELONG?

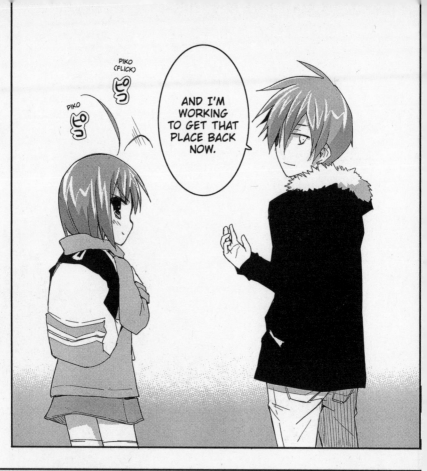

PIKO
(FLICK)

PIKO

AND I'M WORKING TO GET THAT PLACE BACK NOW.

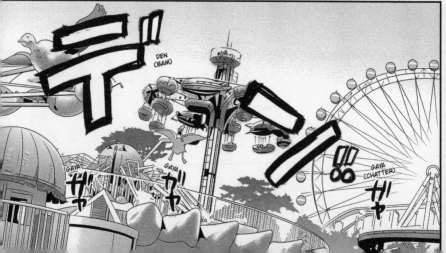

DEN
(BAM)

GAYA

GAYA

GAYA
(CHATTER)

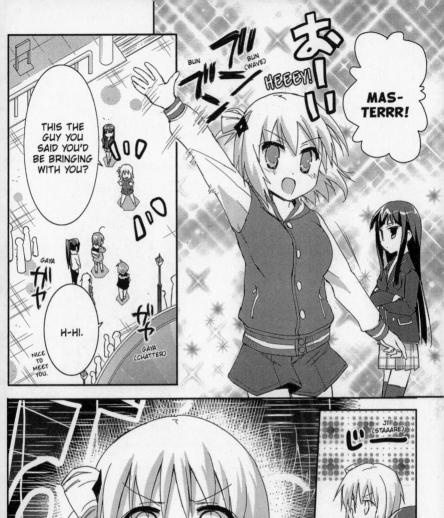
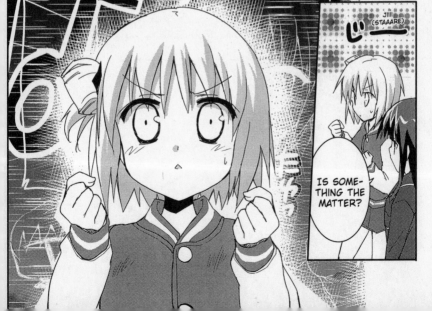

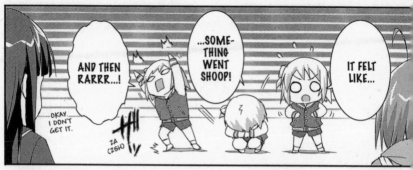

AND THEN RARRR...!

...SOME-THING WENT SHOOP!

IT FELT LIKE...

OKAY. I DON'T GET IT.

ZA CZSH

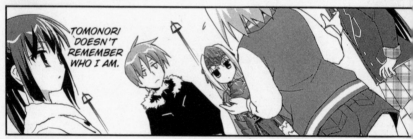

TOMONORI DOESN'T REMEMBER WHO I AM.

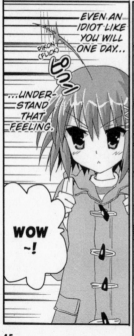

EVEN AN IDIOT LIKE YOU WILL ONE DAY...

PIKON (FLICK)

...UNDER-STAND THAT FEELING.

WOW ~!

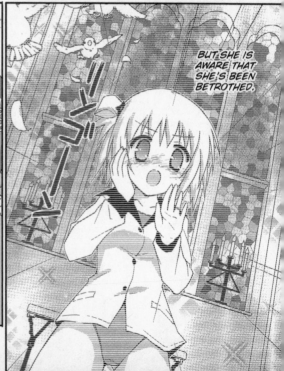

BUT SHE IS AWARE THAT SHE'S BEEN BETROTHED.

45

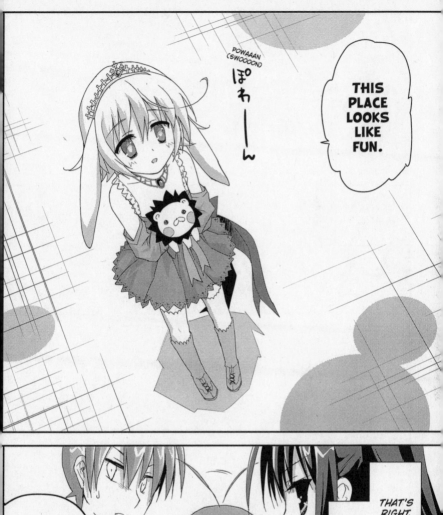

POWAAAN
(SWOOOON)
ぽわーん

THIS PLACE LOOKS LIKE FUN.

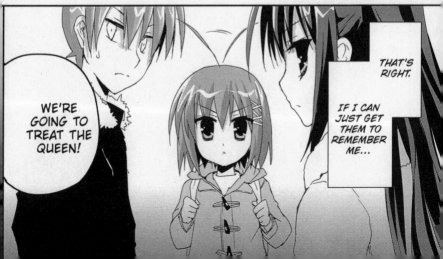

WE'RE GOING TO TREAT THE QUEEN!

THAT'S RIGHT.

IF I CAN JUST GET THEM TO REMEMBER ME...

AT THE AQUA SOMETHING OR OTHER?

IT'S A GIANT NEW THEME PARK.

ば

ん

BAN (BAM)

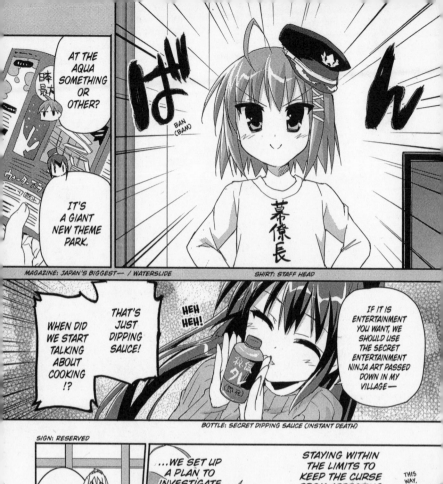

MAGAZINE: JAPAN'S BIGGEST— / WATERSLIDE

SHIRT: STAFF HEAD

WHEN DID WE START TALKING ABOUT COOKING!?

THAT'S JUST DIPPING SAUCE!

HEH HEH!

IF IT IS ENTERTAINMENT YOU WANT, WE SHOULD USE THE SECRET ENTERTAINMENT NINJA ART PASSED DOWN IN MY VILLAGE—

BOTTLE: SECRET DIPPING SAUCE (INSTANT DEATH)

SIGN: RESERVED

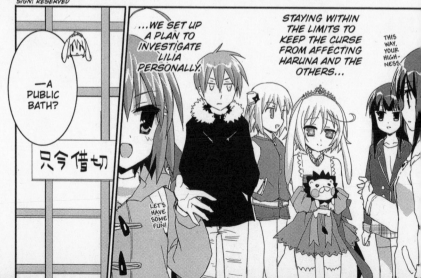

...WE SET UP A PLAN TO INVESTIGATE LILIA PERSONALLY.

STAYING WITHIN THE LIMITS TO KEEP THE CURSE FROM AFFECTING HARUNA AND THE OTHERS...

THIS WAY, YOUR HIGHNESS.

—A PUBLIC BATH?

LET'S HAVE SOME FUN!

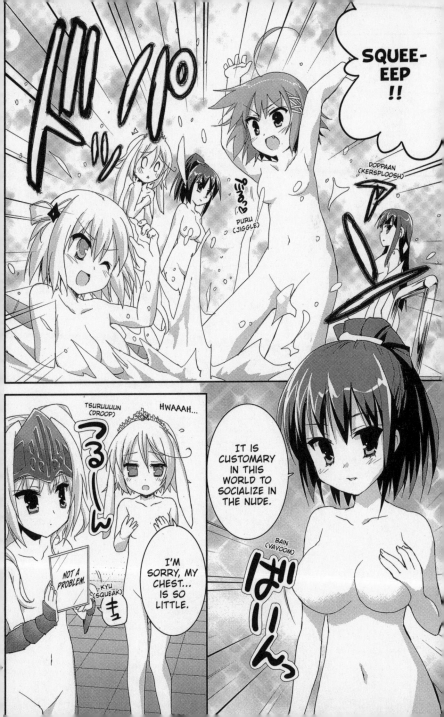

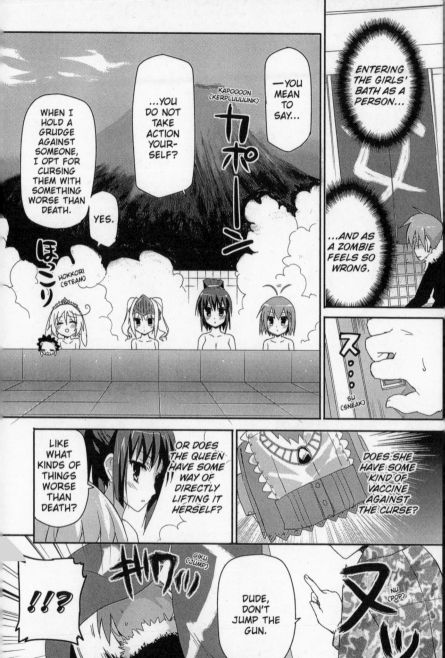

WHEN I HOLD A GRUDGE AGAINST SOMEONE, I OPT FOR CURSING THEM WITH SOMETHING WORSE THAN DEATH.

YES.

...YOU DO NOT TAKE ACTION YOUR-SELF?

—YOU MEAN TO SAY...

KAPOOOON (KERPLUUUUNK)

カポーン

ほっこり
HOKKORI (STEAM)

ENTERING THE GIRLS' BATH AS A PERSON...

...AND AS A ZOMBIE FEELS SO WRONG.

ス
SU (SNEAK)

LIKE WHAT KINDS OF THINGS WORSE THAN DEATH?

OR DOES THE QUEEN HAVE SOME WAY OF DIRECTLY LIFTING IT HERSELF?

DOES SHE HAVE SOME KIND OF VACCINE AGAINST THE CURSE?

!!!?

GIKU (JUMP)
ギクッ

DUDE, DON'T JUMP THE GUN.

NU (POP)
ヌッ

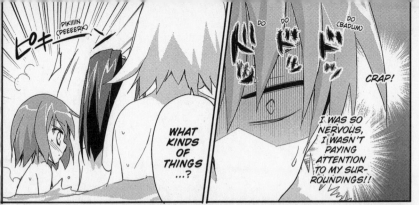

WHAT KINDS OF THINGS...?

CRAP! I WAS SO NERVOUS, I WASN'T PAYING ATTENTION TO MY SURROUNDINGS!!

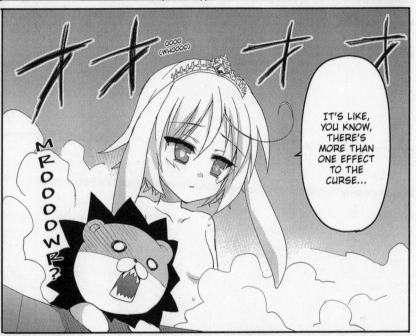

IT'S LIKE, YOU KNOW, THERE'S MORE THAN ONE EFFECT TO THE CURSE...

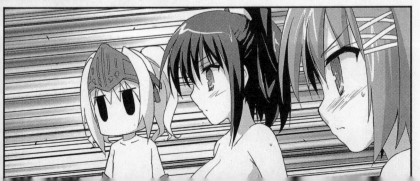

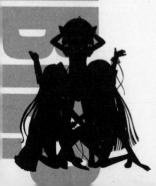

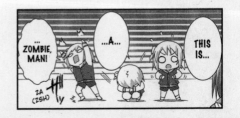

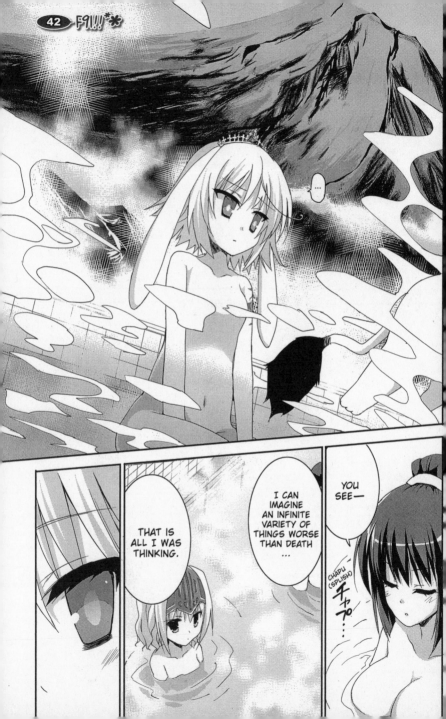

...

THAT IS ALL I WAS THINKING.

I CAN IMAGINE AN INFINITE VARIETY OF THINGS WORSE THAN DEATH ...

YOU SEE—

CHAPU (SPLISH)

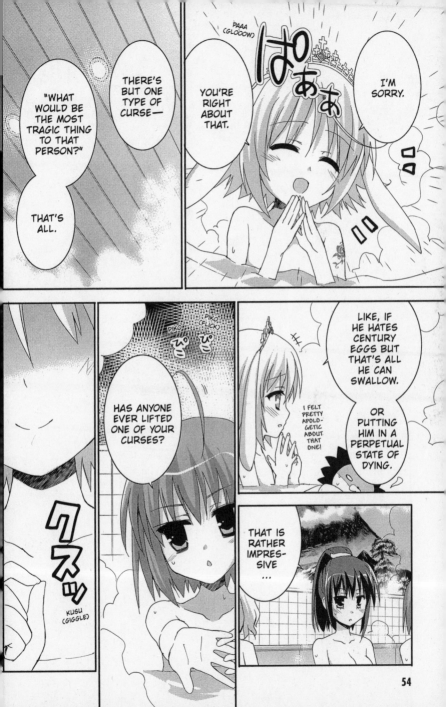

"WHAT WOULD BE THE MOST TRAGIC THING TO THAT PERSON?"

THERE'S BUT ONE TYPE OF CURSE—

THAT'S ALL.

YOU'RE RIGHT ABOUT THAT.

PAAA (GLOOOW)

はあ

I'M SORRY.

LIKE, IF HE HATES CENTURY EGGS BUT THAT'S ALL HE CAN SWALLOW.

OR PUTTING HIM IN A PERPETUAL STATE OF DYING.

I FELT PRETTY APOLO-GETIC ABOUT THAT ONE!

PIKO (FLICK)
PIKO

HAS ANYONE EVER LIFTED ONE OF YOUR CURSES?

クスッ

KUSU (GIGGLE)

THAT IS RATHER IMPRESSIVE...

54

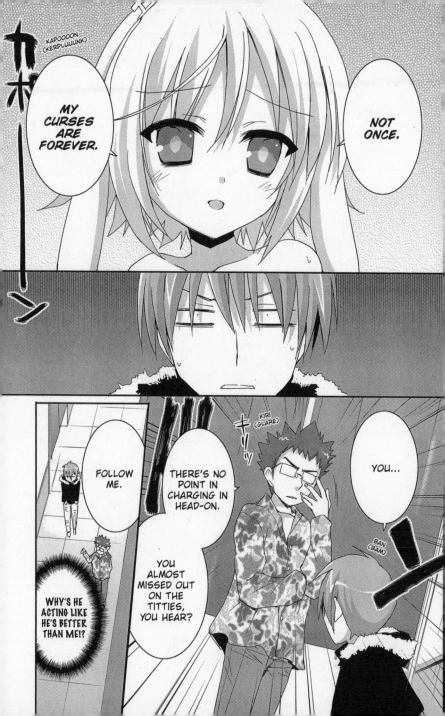

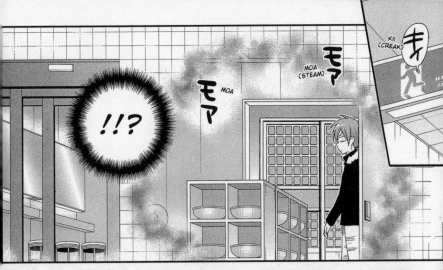

KII
(CREAK)

!!?

MOA

MOA
(STEAM)

モア

モア

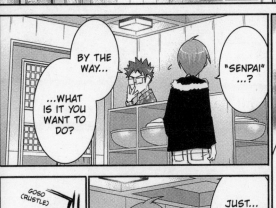

BY THE WAY...

...WHAT IS IT YOU WANT TO DO?

"SENPAI" ...?

THE WALL'S SEE-THROUGH...

MOA

モア

THIS IS MY SENPAI'S SPECIAL ABILITY.

IT'S A TRICK TO MAKE IT SO ONLY WE CAN SEE THROUGH

MOA

モア

MOA

モア

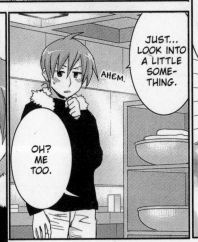

GOSO
(RUSTLE)

JUST... LOOK INTO A LITTLE SOMETHING.

AHEM.

OH? ME TOO.

56

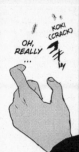

OH, REALLY... KOKI (CRACK)

HAAH...... I CAN'T GET ENOUGH OF THIS.

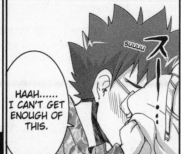

SUUUU

HAAAH!

SUUUU (SNIIIIFF)

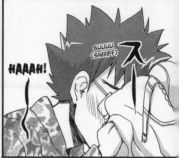

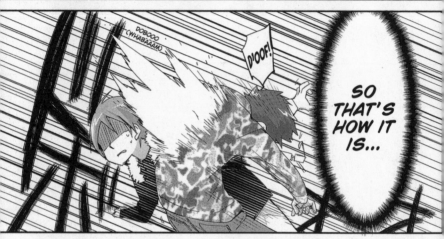

DOBOOO (WHABAAAM)

D'OOF!!

SO THAT'S HOW IT IS...

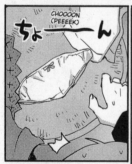

CHOOOON (PEEEEK)

THERE'S NOTHING HERE THAT LOOKS LIKE IT HAS TO DO WITH CURSES.

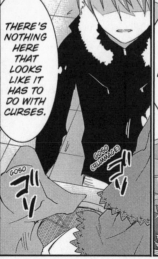

GOSO (RUMMAGE)

GOSO

UH-OH...

I DON'T HAVE TIME TO BE BOTHERING WITH ORITO.

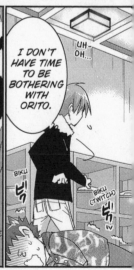

BIKU

BIKU (TWITCH)

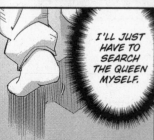

I'LL JUST HAVE TO SEARCH THE QUEEN MYSELF.

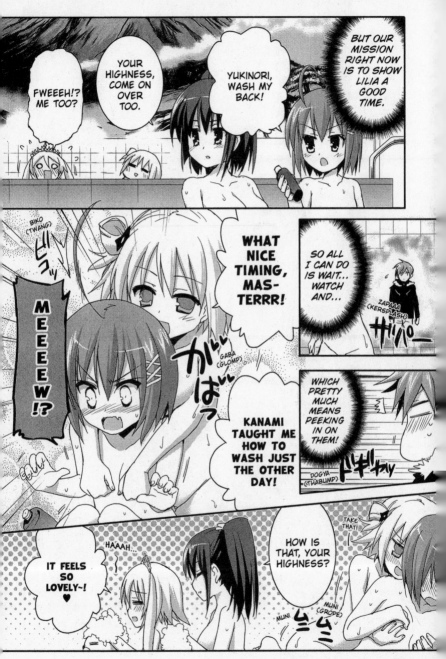

FWEEEH!? ME TOO?

YOUR HIGHNESS, COME ON OVER TOO.

YUKINORI, WASH MY BACK!

BUT OUR MISSION RIGHT NOW IS TO SHOW LILIA A GOOD TIME.

BIKO (TWANG)

WHAT NICE TIMING, MAS- TERRR!

SO ALL I CAN DO IS WAIT... WATCH AND...

ZAPAAA (KERSPLASH)

MEEEEW!?

GABA (GLOMP)

KANAMI TAUGHT ME HOW TO WASH JUST THE OTHER DAY!

WHICH PRETTY MUCH MEANS PEEKING IN ON THEM!

DOGYA (THABUMP)

IT FEELS SO LOVELY~! ♥

HAAAH...

HOW IS THAT, YOUR HIGHNESS?

TAKE THAT!

MUNI (GROPE)

MUNI (GROPE)

58

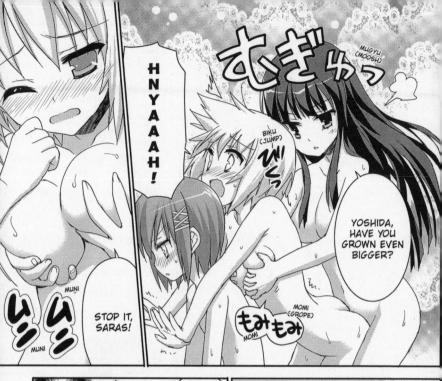

MUGYU (MOOSH)

HNYAAAH!

BIKU (JUMP)

YOSHIDA, HAVE YOU GROWN EVEN BIGGER?

MUNI

MUNI

STOP IT, SARAS!

MOMI (GROPE)

MOMI MOMI

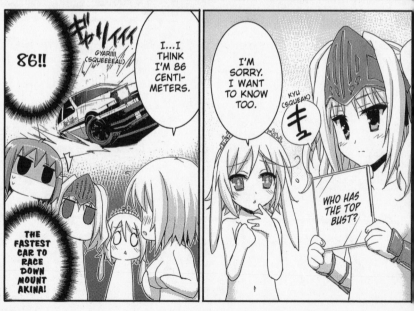

86!!

GYARIIIII (SQUEEEEEAL)

I...I THINK I'M 86 CENTI- METERS.

I'M SORRY. I WANT TO KNOW TOO.

KYU (SQUEAK)

WHO HAS THE TOP BUST?

THE FASTEST CAR TO RACE DOWN MOUNT AKINA!

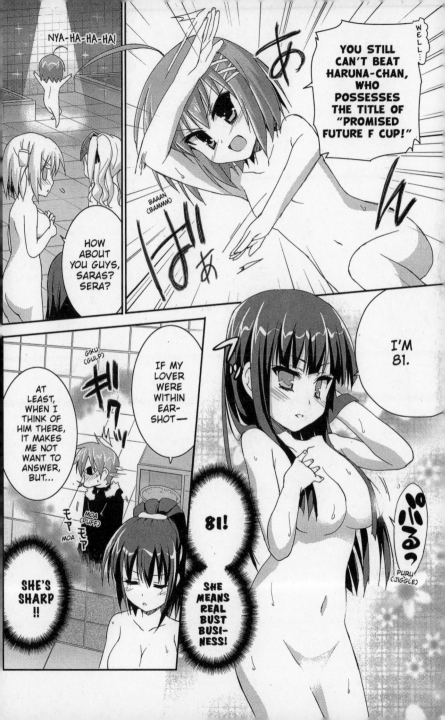

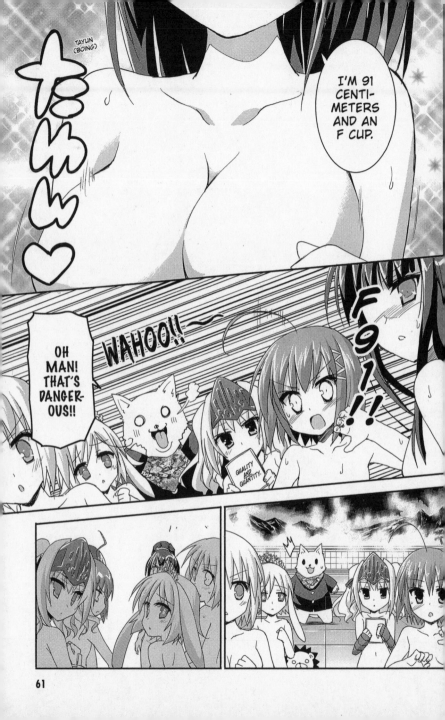

61

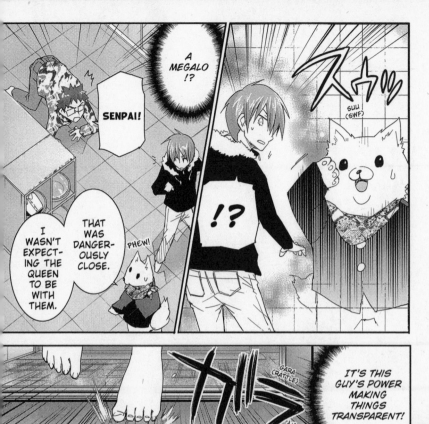

SENPAI!

A MEGALO!?

スゥゥ
SUU
(SWF)

!?

I WASN'T EXPECTING THE QUEEN TO BE WITH THEM.

THAT WAS DANGEROUSLY CLOSE.

PHEW!

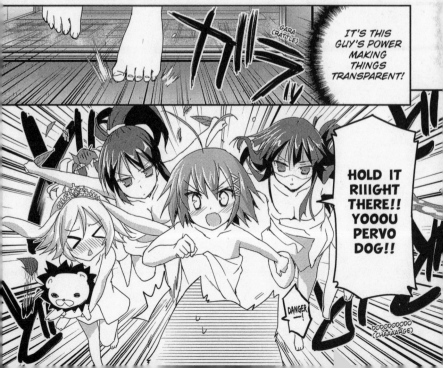

GARA
(RATTLE)

IT'S THIS GUY'S POWER MAKING THINGS TRANSPARENT!

HOLD IT RIIIGHT THERE!! YOOOU PERVO DOG!!

DANGER

DODODODODO
(CHAAAARGE)

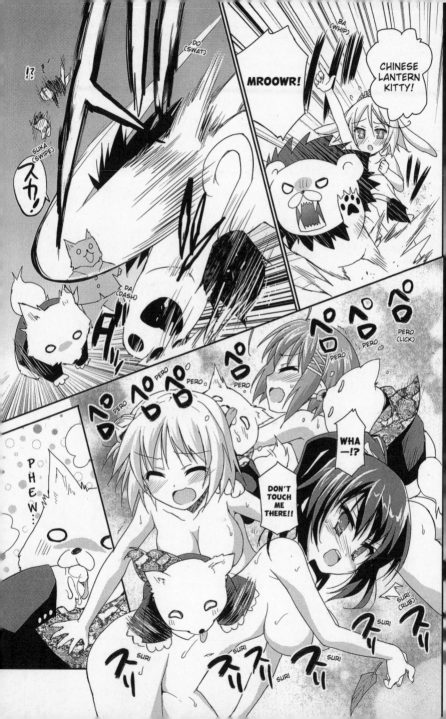

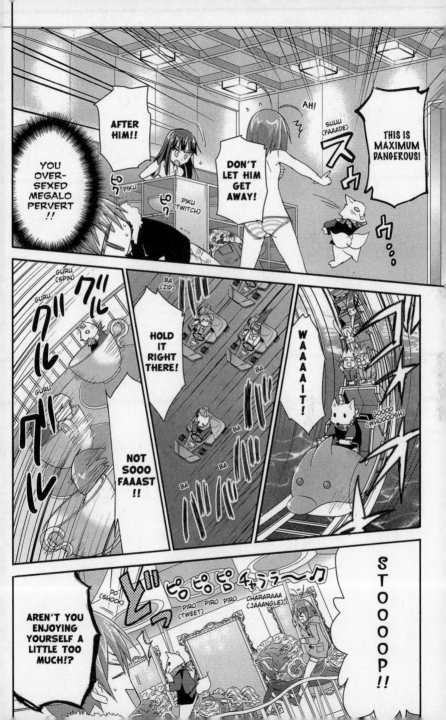

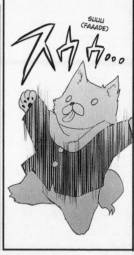

SUUU
(FAAADE)

WHEN I FIND HIM, I SHALL TEAR HIM TO RIBBONS!

YOU DISGRACE OF A DEMON!

HE DISAPPEARED AGAIN!

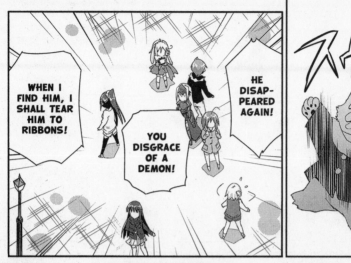

THAT'S A MOUTHFUL!!

ARNOLD CHIHUAHUARZENEGGER!

HE'S AN AAA-CLASS MEGALO AND THE GOVERNOR OF COMMANDO STATE.

OOO (WHOOO)

HARUNA...

WHO IS THAT MEGALO?

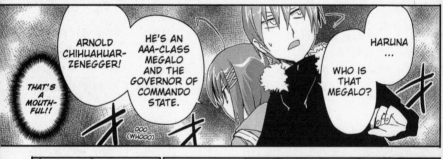

ISN'T DAI-SENSEI SUPPOSED TO BE THE STRONGEST MAGIKEWL GIRL THERE IS?

—HE'S THE ONE MEGALO DAI-SENSEI COULDN'T DEFEAT.

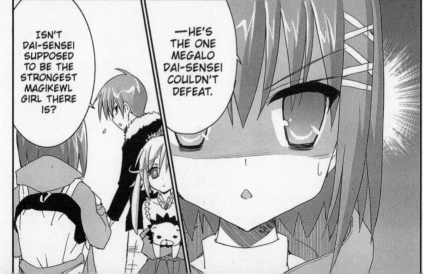

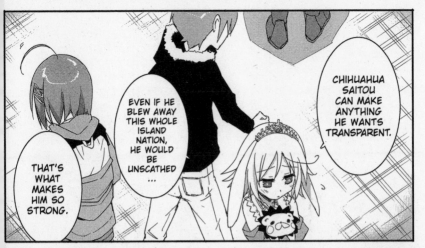

THAT'S WHAT MAKES HIM SO STRONG.

EVEN IF HE BLEW AWAY THIS WHOLE ISLAND NATION, HE WOULD BE UNSCATHED ...

CHIHUAHUA SAITOU CAN MAKE ANYTHING HE WANTS TRANSPARENT.

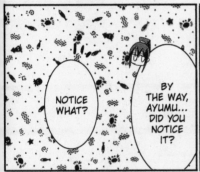

NOTICE WHAT?

BY THE WAY, AYUMU... DID YOU NOTICE IT?

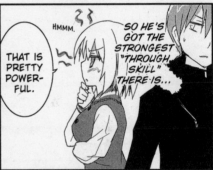

HMMM.

THAT IS PRETTY POWERFUL.

SO HE'S GOT THE STRONGEST "THROUGH SKILL" THERE IS...

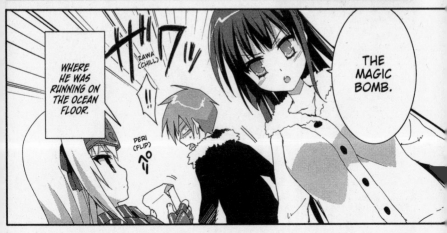

WHERE HE WAS RUNNING ON THE OCEAN FLOOR.

THE MAGIC BOMB.

ZAWA (CHILL)

PERI (FLIP)

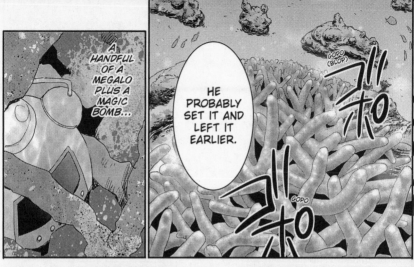

A HANDFUL OF A MEGALO PLUS A MAGIC BOMB...

HE PROBABLY SET IT AND LEFT IT EARLIER.

ゴリポ
GOPO (BLOP)

ゴリポ
GOPO

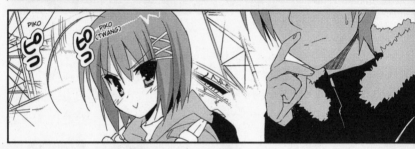

ピコ
PIKO

ピコ
PIKO (TWANG)

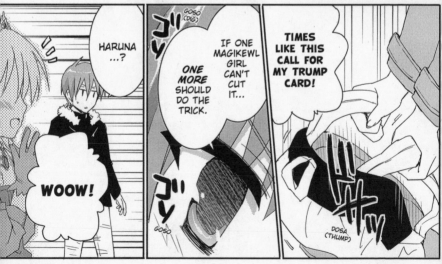

HARUNA...?

WOOW!

ゴソ
GOSO (DIG)

ゴソ
GOSO

ONE MORE SHOULD DO THE TRICK.

IF ONE MAGIKEWL GIRL CAN'T CUT IT...

TIMES LIKE THIS CALL FOR MY TRUMP CARD!

ドサ
DOSA (THUMP)

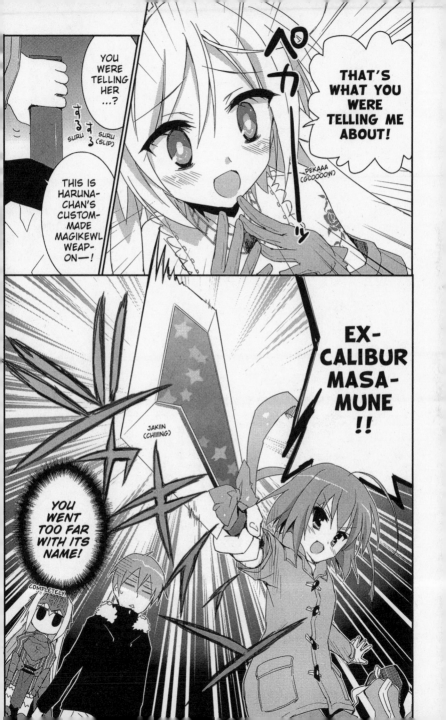

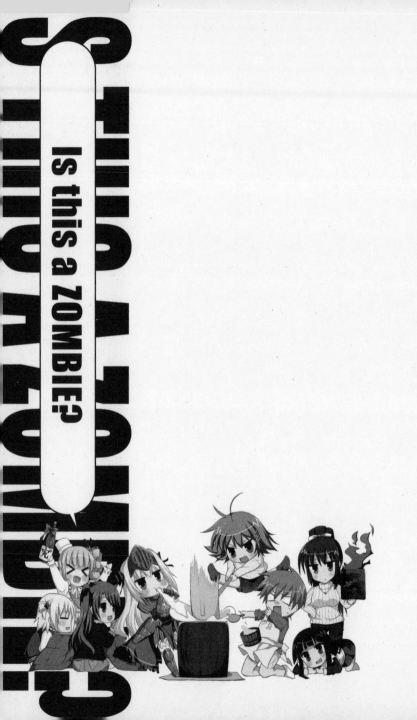

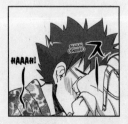

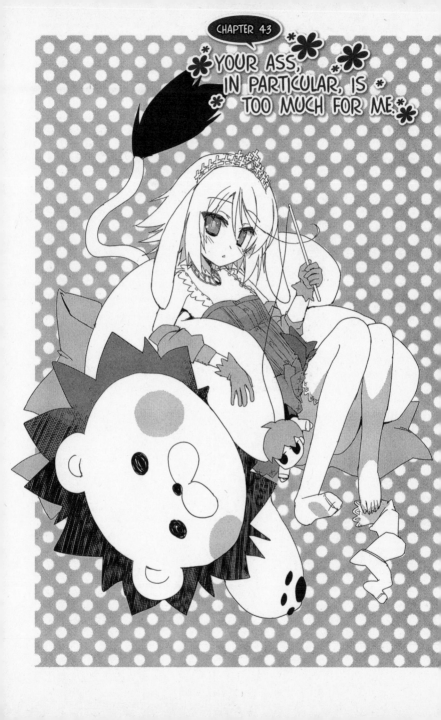

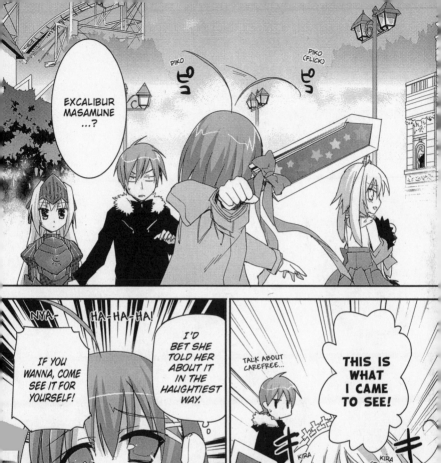

EXCALIBUR MASAMUNE...?

PIKO

PIKO (FLICK)

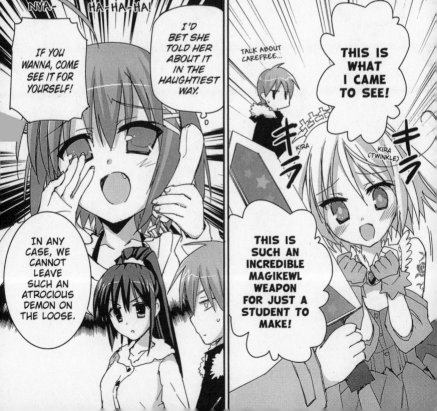

NYA— HA-HA-HA!

IF YOU WANNA, COME SEE IT FOR YOURSELF!

I'D BET SHE TOLD HER ABOUT IT IN THE HAUGHTIEST WAY.

IN ANY CASE, WE CANNOT LEAVE SUCH AN ATROCIOUS DEMON ON THE LOOSE.

TALK ABOUT CAREFREE...

THIS IS WHAT I CAME TO SEE!

KIRA

KIRA (TWINKLE)

THIS IS SUCH AN INCREDIBLE MAGIKEWL WEAPON FOR JUST A STUDENT TO MAKE!

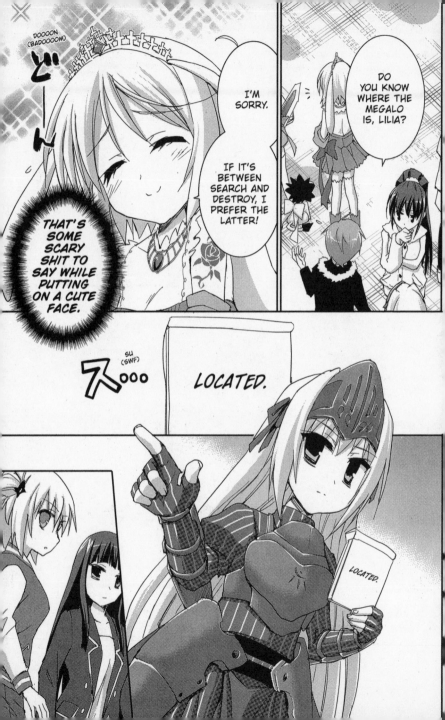

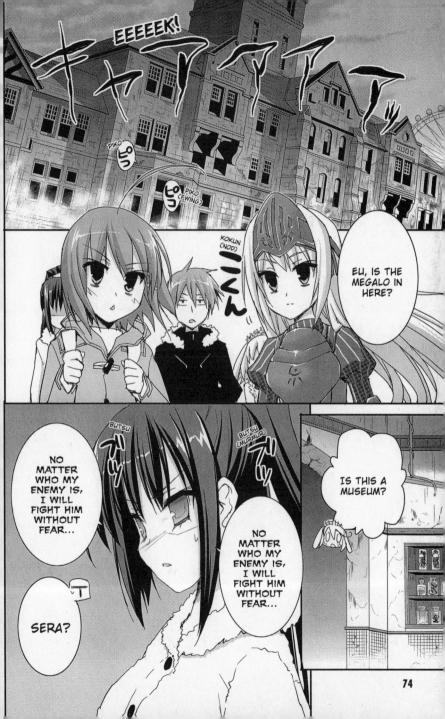

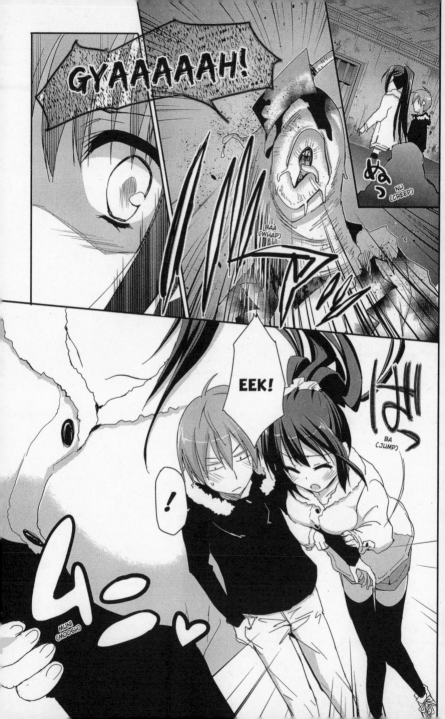

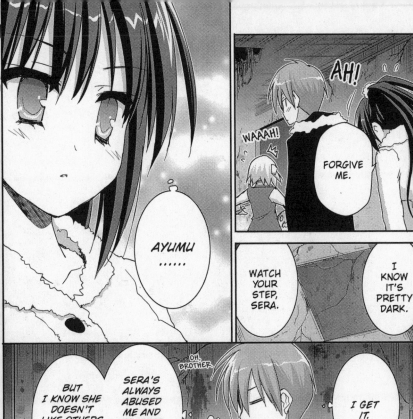

AYUMU ......

AH!

WAAAH!

FORGIVE ME.

WATCH YOUR STEP, SERA.

I KNOW IT'S PRETTY DARK.

OH, BROTHER.

BUT I KNOW SHE DOESN'T LIKE OTHERS TO SEE HER BEING WEAK...

SERA'S ALWAYS ABUSED ME AND TREATED ME LIKE TRASH.

I GET IT.

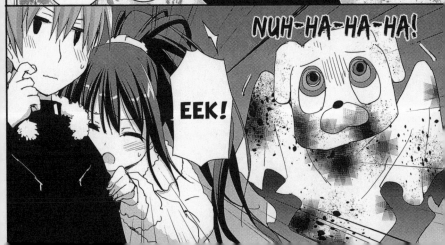

NUH-HA-HA-HA!

EEK!

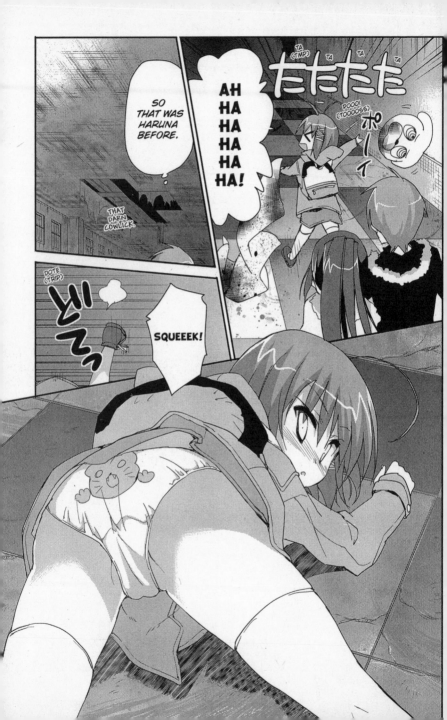

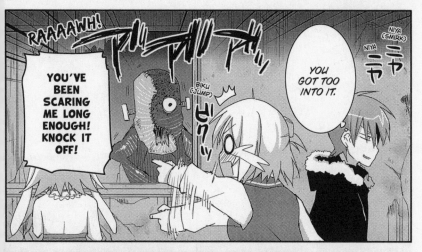

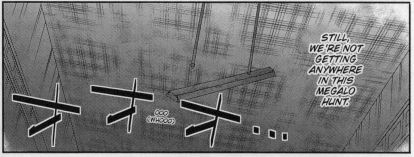

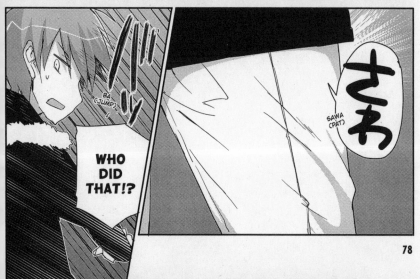

78

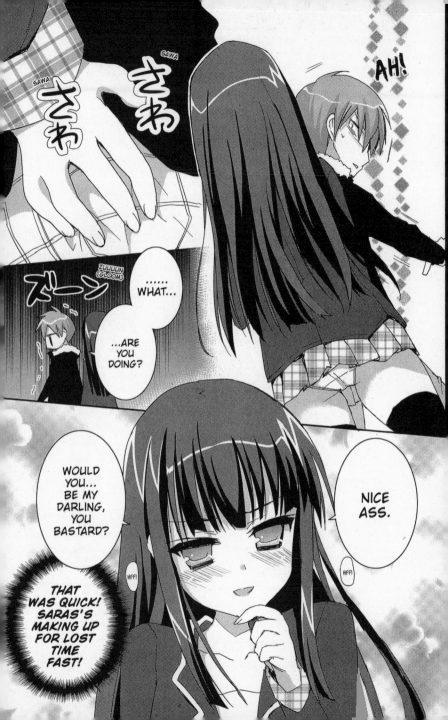

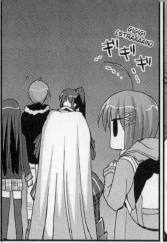

GIGIGI
(STRAAAIN)
ギリギリ

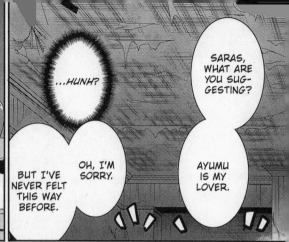

...HUNH?

SARAS, WHAT ARE YOU SUGGESTING?

BUT I'VE NEVER FELT THIS WAY BEFORE.

OH, I'M SORRY.

AYUMU IS MY LOVER.

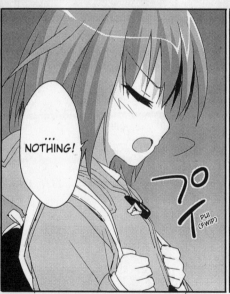

...NOTHING!

プイ
(F.WIP)

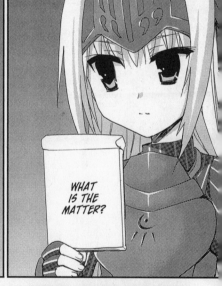

WHAT IS THE MATTER?

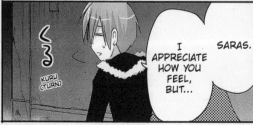

くる
(KURU
(TURN))

I APPRECIATE HOW YOU FEEL, BUT...

SARAS.

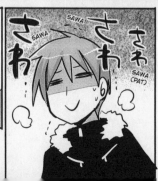

さわ
(SAWA)
さわ
SAWA
さわ
SAWA
さわ
SAWA (PAT)

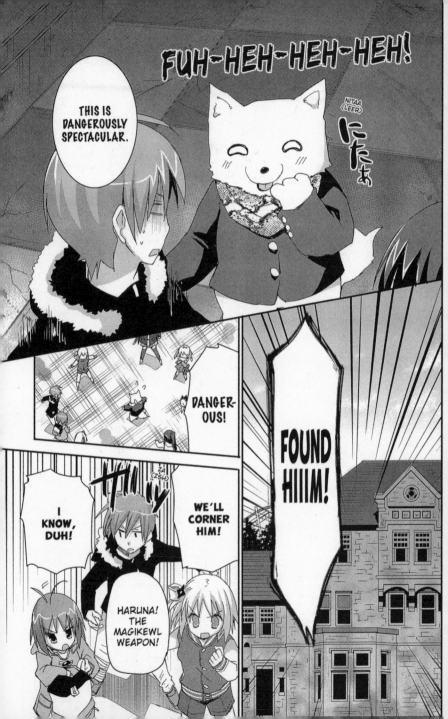

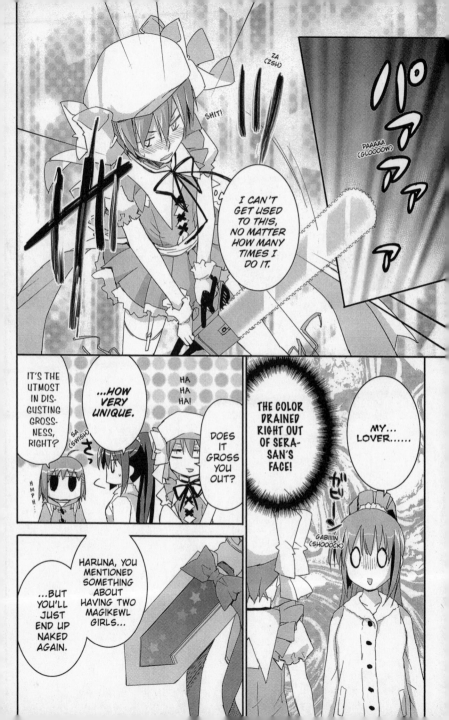

SHIT!

ZA (ZSH)

PAAAA (GLOOOOW)

PAAAAAA (GLOOOOW)

I CAN'T GET USED TO THIS, NO MATTER HOW MANY TIMES I DO IT.

IT'S THE UTMOST IN DIS-GUSTING GROSS-NESS, RIGHT?

HMPH...

...HOW VERY UNIQUE.

SA (SWISH)

HA HA HA!

DOES IT GROSS YOU OUT?

THE COLOR DRAINED RIGHT OUT OF SERA-SAN'S FACE!

MY... LOVER......

GABIIIIN (SHOOOCK)

...BUT YOU'LL JUST END UP NAKED AGAIN.

HARUNA, YOU MENTIONED SOMETHING ABOUT HAVING TWO MAGIKEWL GIRLS...

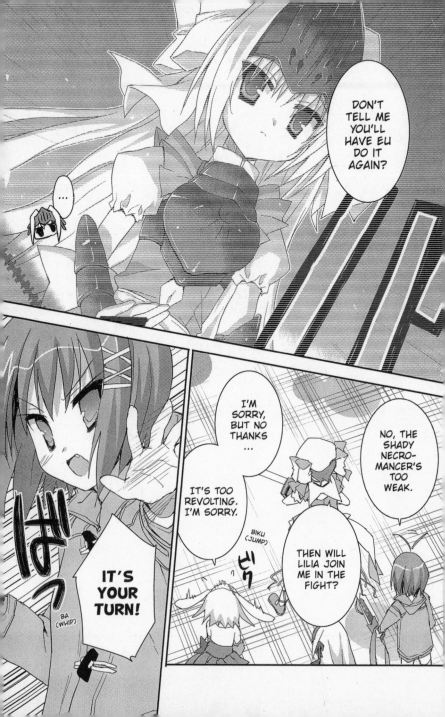

DON'T TELL ME YOU'LL HAVE EU DO IT AGAIN?

...

I'M SORRY, BUT NO THANKS...

IT'S TOO REVOLTING. I'M SORRY.

NO, THE SHADY NECROMANCER'S TOO WEAK.

BIKU (JUMP)

THEN WILL LILIA JOIN ME IN THE FIGHT?

IT'S YOUR TURN!

BA (WHIP)

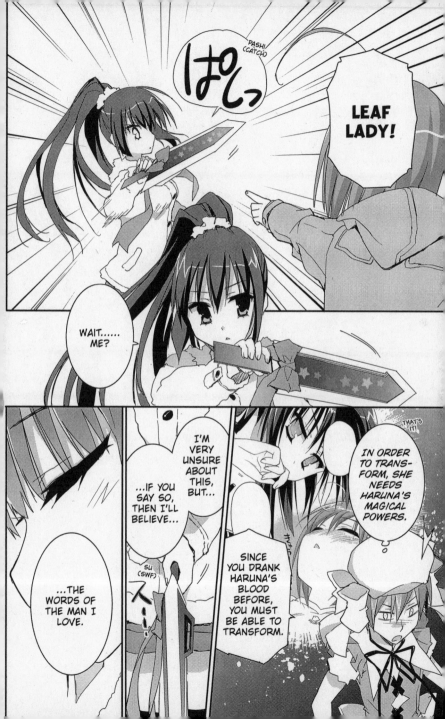

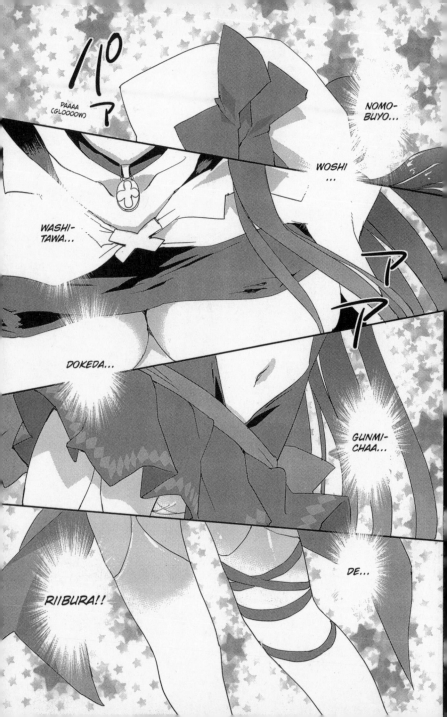

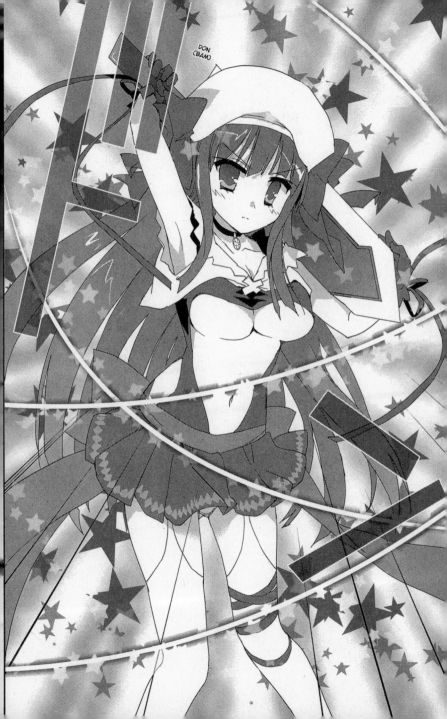

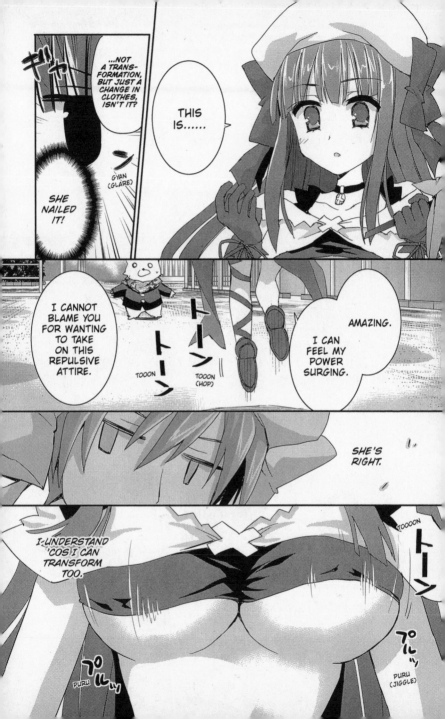

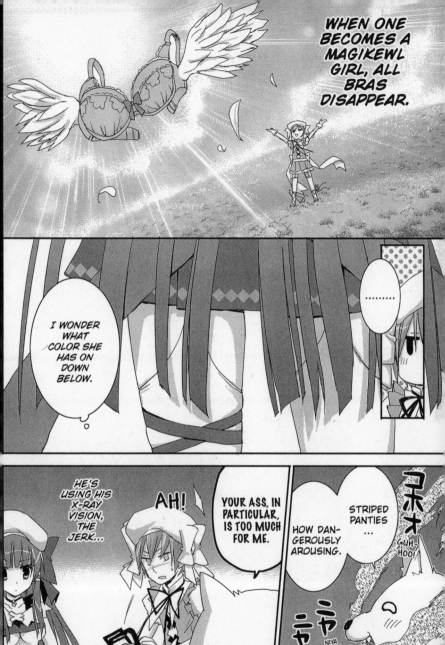

WHEN ONE BECOMES A MAGIKEWL GIRL, ALL BRAS DISAPPEAR.

I WONDER WHAT COLOR SHE HAS ON DOWN BELOW.

....

HE'S USING HIS X-RAY VISION, THE JERK...

AH!

YOUR ASS, IN PARTICULAR, IS TOO MUCH FOR ME.

HOW DAN-GEROUSLY AROUSING.

STRIPED PANTIES...

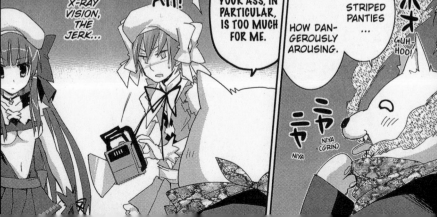

GUH-HOO!

NIYA

NIYA (GRIN)

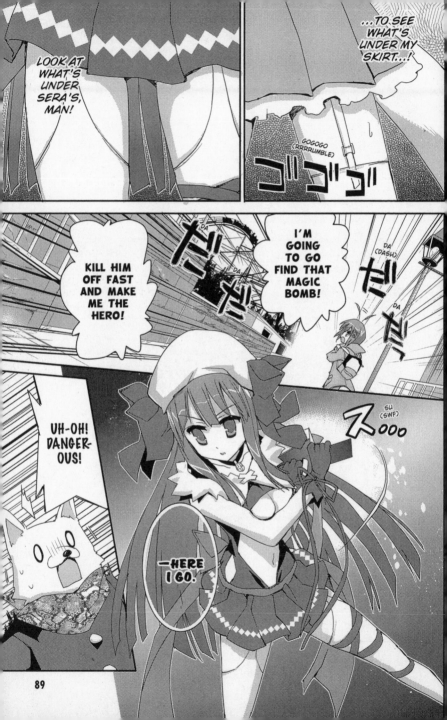

89

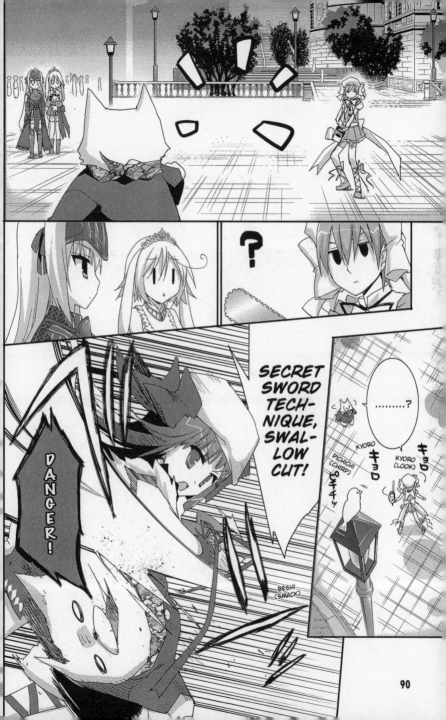

SECRET SWORD TECH-NIQUE, SWALLOW CUT!

DANGER!

BESHI
(SMACK)

.........?

KYORO
キョロ

KYORO
(LOOK)
キョロ

PICHICHI
(CHIRP)
ピチチ

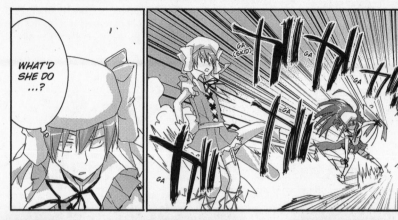

WHAT'D SHE DO ...?

GA (SKID)

GA

GA

GA

GA

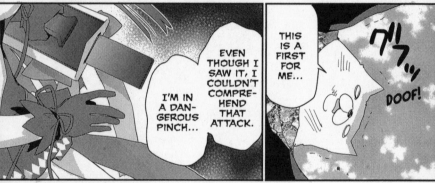

I'M IN A DANGEROUS PINCH...

EVEN THOUGH I SAW IT, I COULDN'T COMPREHEND THAT ATTACK.

THIS IS A FIRST FOR ME...

DOOF!

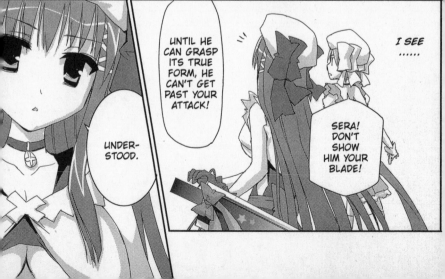

UNTIL HE CAN GRASP ITS TRUE FORM, HE CAN'T GET PAST YOUR ATTACK!

UNDERSTOOD.

I SEE ......

SERA! DON'T SHOW HIM YOUR BLADE!

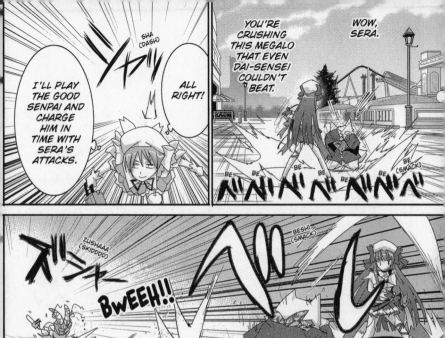

I'LL PLAY THE GOOD SENPAI AND CHARGE HIM IN TIME WITH SERA'S ATTACKS.

ALL RIGHT!

SHA (DASH)

YOU'RE CRUSHING THIS MEGALO THAT EVEN DAI-SENSEI COULDN'T BEAT.

WOW, SERA.

BE BE BE BE BE BE (SMACK)

ZUSHAAA (SKIDDDD)

BwEEH!!

BESHI (SMACK)

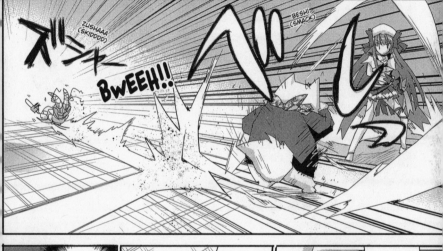

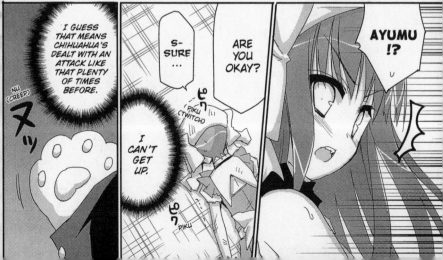

I GUESS THAT MEANS CHIHUAHUA'S DEALT WITH AN ATTACK LIKE THAT PLENTY OF TIMES BEFORE.

NU (CREEP)

ヌッ

S-SURE...

ARE YOU OKAY?

AYUMU!?

I CAN'T GET UP.

ピク PIKU (TWITCH)

ピク PIKU

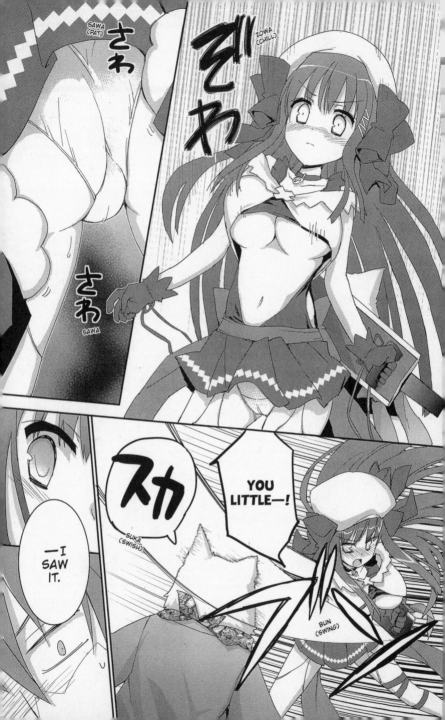

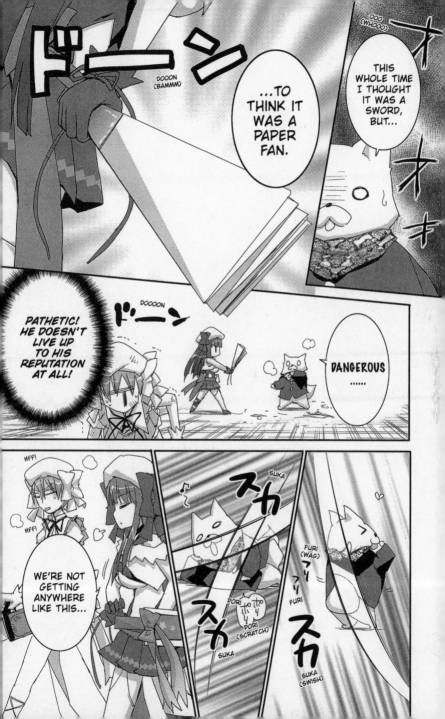

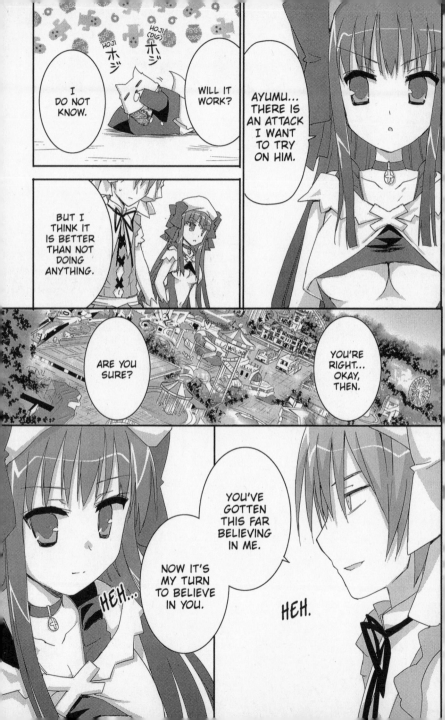

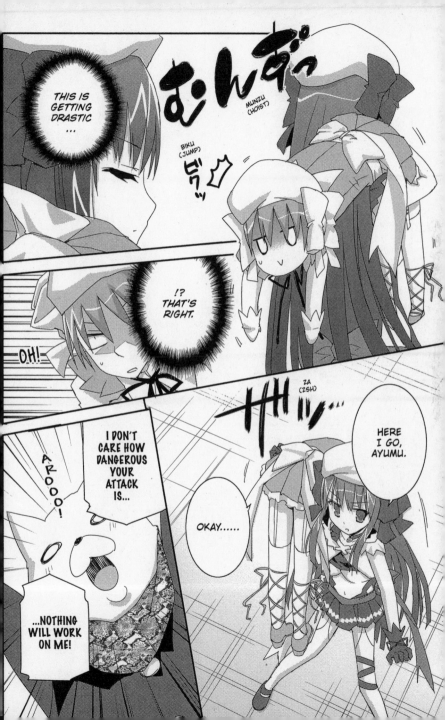

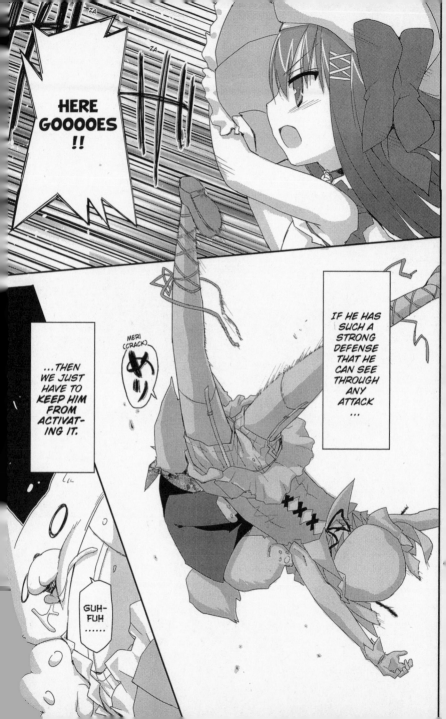

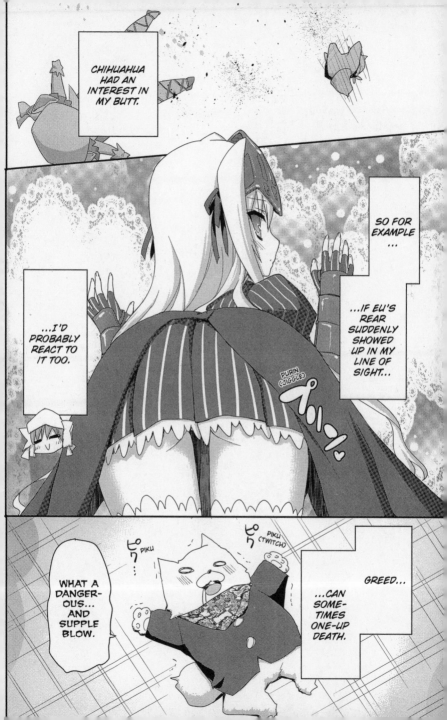

CHIHUAHUA HAD AN INTEREST IN MY BUTT.

SO FOR EXAMPLE...

...IF EU'S REAR SUDDENLY SHOWED UP IN MY LINE OF SIGHT...

...I'D PROBABLY REACT TO IT TOO.

PURIN (JIGGLE)

WHAT A DANGEROUS... AND SUPPLE BLOW.

PIKU

ピク PIKU (TWITCH)

GREED...

...CAN SOMETIMES ONE-UP DEATH.

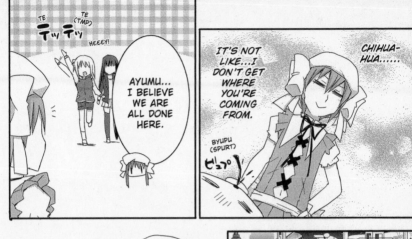

TE
TE
(TMP)
テッテッ

HEEEY!!

AYUMU... I BELIEVE WE ARE ALL DONE HERE.

IT'S NOT LIKE...I DON'T GET WHERE YOU'RE COMING FROM.

CHIHUA-HUA......

BYUPU
(SPURT)
ビュプッ

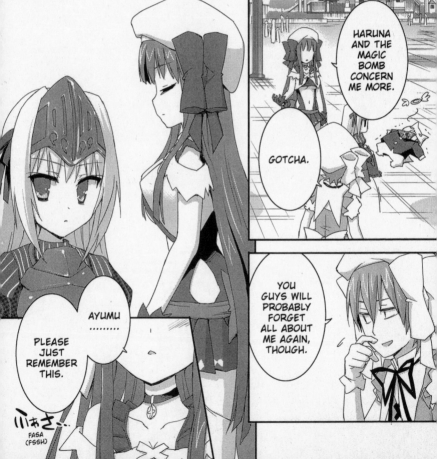

HARUNA AND THE MAGIC BOMB CONCERN ME MORE.

GOTCHA.

YOU GUYS WILL PROBABLY FORGET ALL ABOUT ME AGAIN, THOUGH.

AYUMU.........

PLEASE JUST REMEMBER THIS.

FASA
(FSSH)
しゃさ...

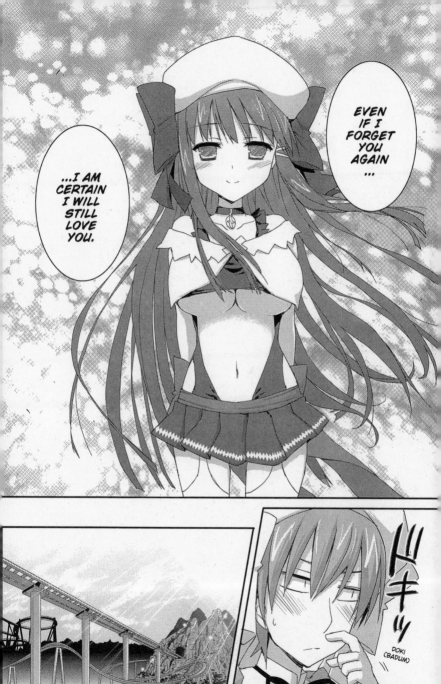

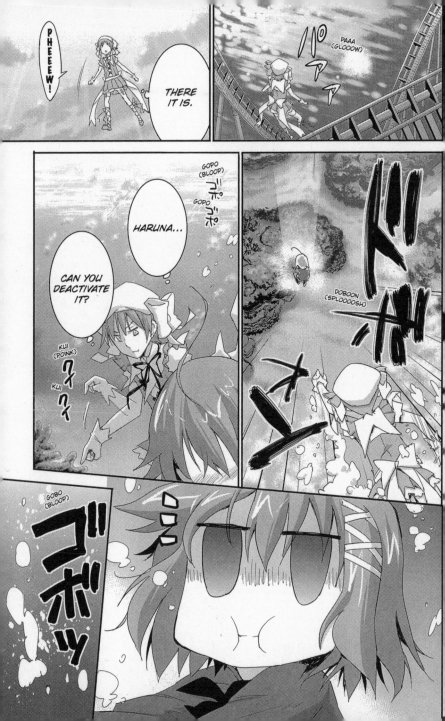

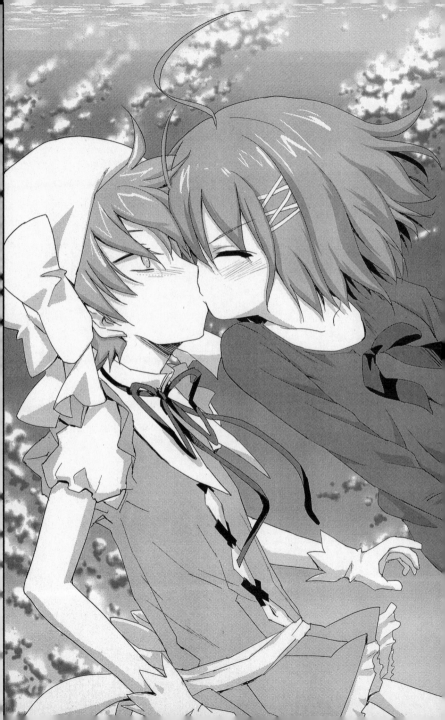

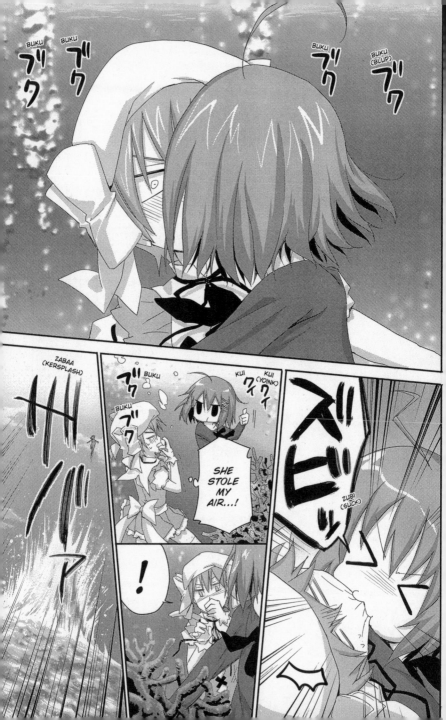

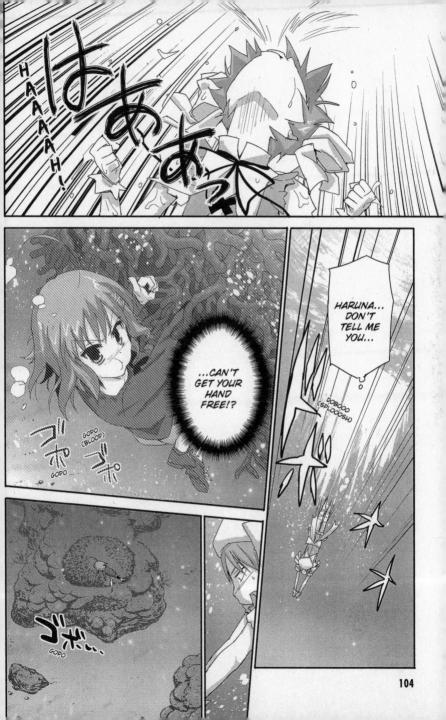

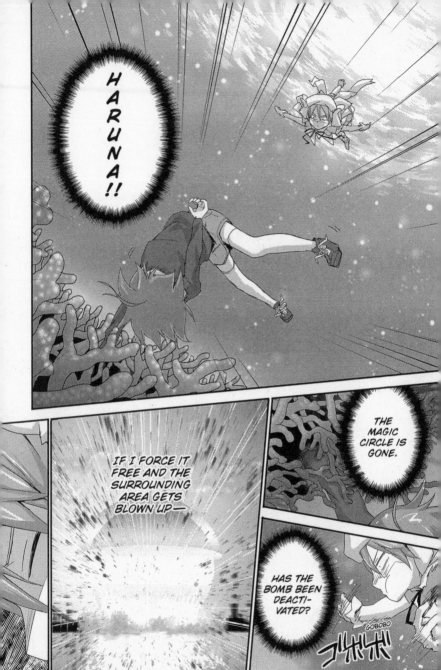

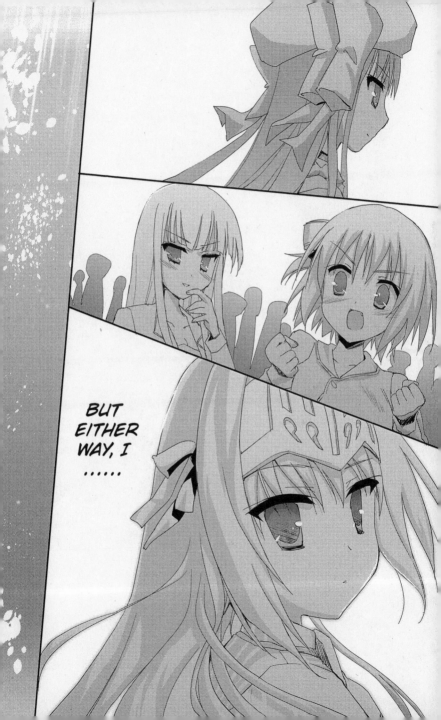

BUT
EITHER
WAY, I
......

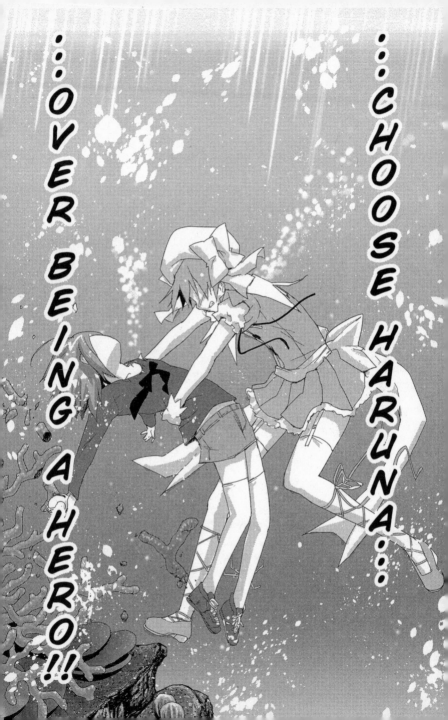

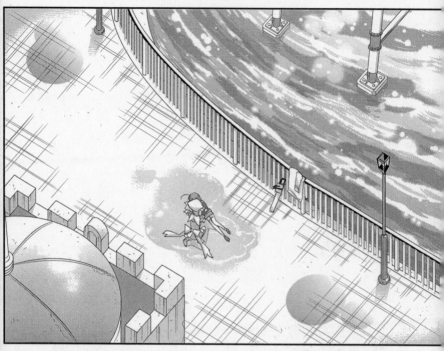

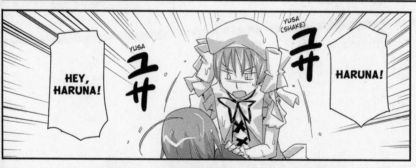

HEY, HARUNA!

YUSA

YUSA (SHAKE)

HARUNA!

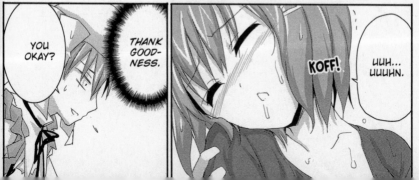

YOU OKAY?

THANK GOOD- NESS.

KOFF!

UUH... UUUHN.

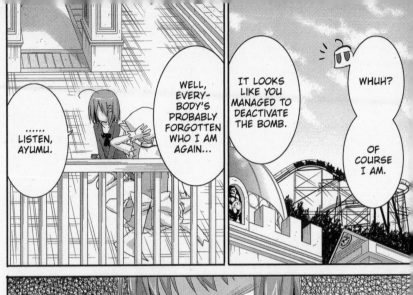

...... LISTEN, AYUMU.

WELL, EVERY-BODY'S PROBABLY FORGOTTEN WHO I AM AGAIN...

IT LOOKS LIKE YOU MANAGED TO DEACTIVATE THE BOMB.

WHUH?

OF COURSE I AM.

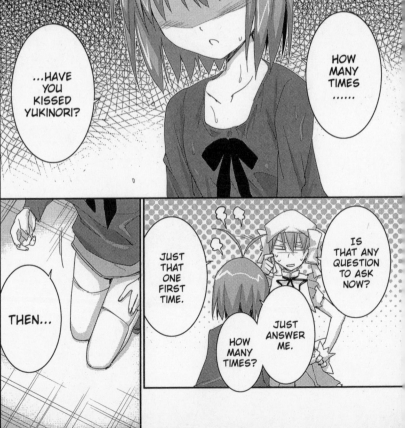

...HAVE YOU KISSED YUKINORI?

HOW MANY TIMES ......

THEN...

JUST THAT ONE FIRST TIME.

IS THAT ANY QUESTION TO ASK NOW?

JUST ANSWER ME.

HOW MANY TIMES?

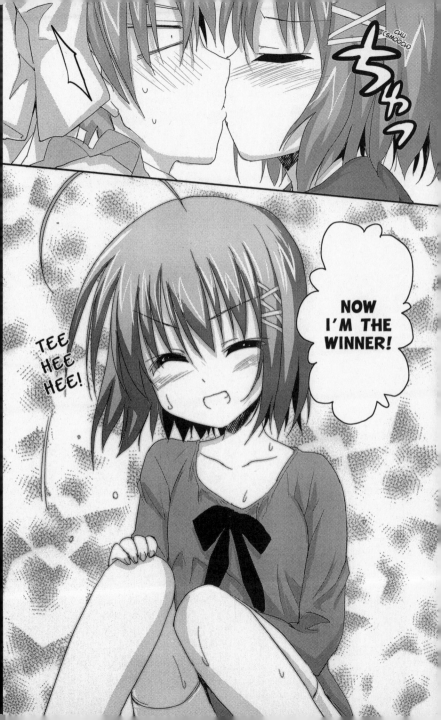

IS THIS A ZOMBIE?

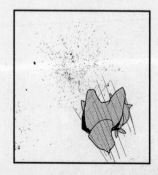

I THOUGHT FOR SURE YOU'D TAKEN STEPS AGAINST THE DECLINING BIRTHRATE!*

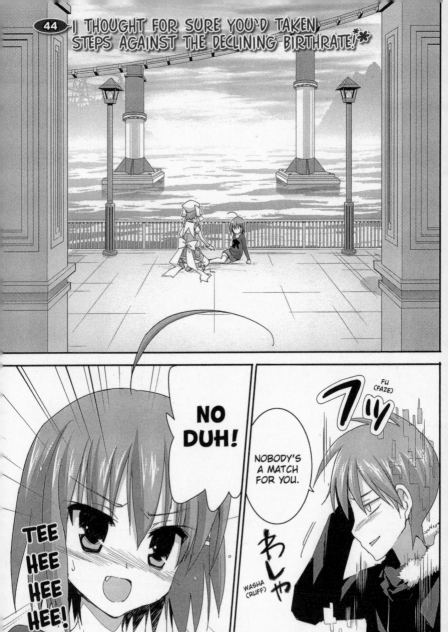

NO DUH!

NOBODY'S A MATCH FOR YOU.

FU (FAZE)

TEE HEE HEE HEE!

WASHA (RUFF)

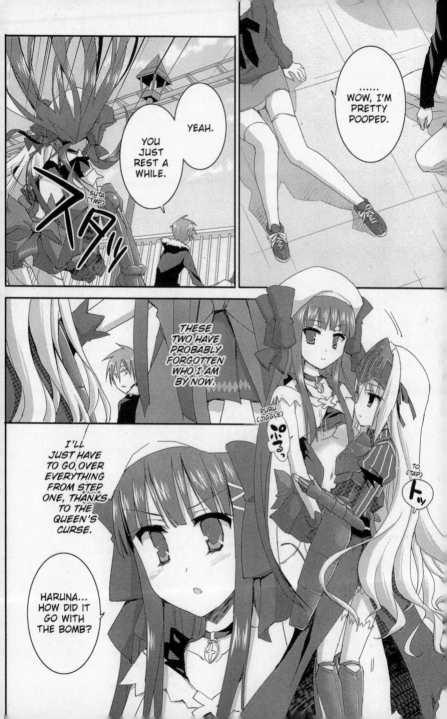

YEAH.

YOU JUST REST A WHILE.

スタッ
(TMP)

...... WOW, I'M PRETTY POOPED.

THESE TWO HAVE PROBABLY FORGOTTEN WHO I AM BY NOW.

PURU (JIGGLE)

TO (TAP)
トッ

I'LL JUST HAVE TO GO OVER EVERYTHING FROM STEP ONE, THANKS TO THE QUEEN'S CURSE.

HARUNA... HOW DID IT GO WITH THE BOMB?

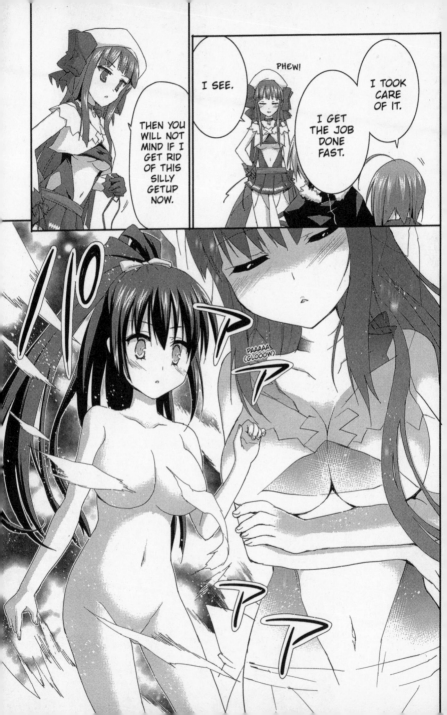

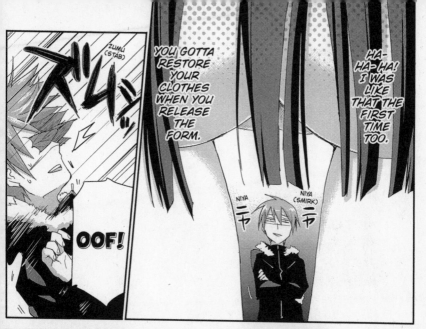

ZUMU (STAB)

OOF!

YOU GOTTA RESTORE YOUR CLOTHES WHEN YOU RELEASE THE FORM.

HA-HA-HA! I WAS LIKE THAT THE FIRST TIME TOO.

NIYA

NIYA (SMIRK)

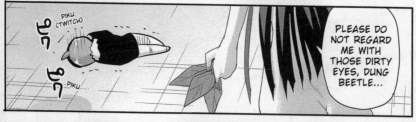

PIKU (TWITCH)

PIKU

PLEASE DO NOT REGARD ME WITH THOSE DIRTY EYES, DUNG BEETLE...

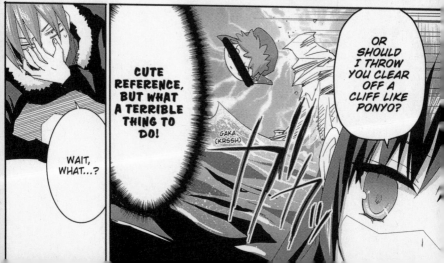

CUTE REFERENCE, BUT WHAT A TERRIBLE THING TO DO!

WAIT, WHAT...?

GAKA (KRSSH)

OR SHOULD I THROW YOU CLEAR OFF A CLIFF LIKE PONYO?

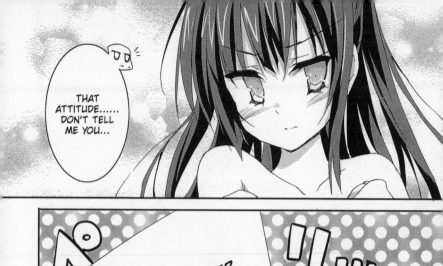

THAT ATTITUDE...... DON'T TELL ME YOU...

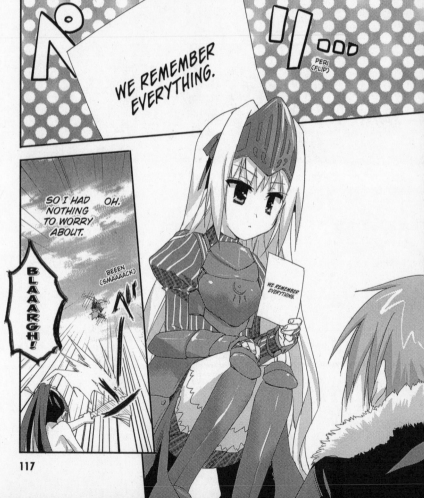

WE REMEMBER EVERYTHING.

PERI
(FLIP)

SO I HAD NOTHING TO WORRY ABOUT.

OH.

BEEEN
(SMAAAACK)

BLAAARGH!

WE REMEMBER EVERYTHING.

117

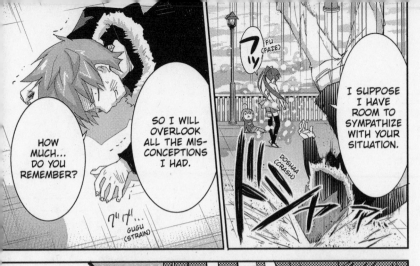

HOW MUCH... DO YOU REMEMBER?

SO I WILL OVERLOOK ALL THE MIS-CONCEPTIONS I HAD.

I SUPPOSE I HAVE ROOM TO SYMPATHIZE WITH YOUR SITUATION.

フリ
(FAZE)

ドシャァ
(CRASH)

グ゛グ゛...
GUGU (STRAIN)

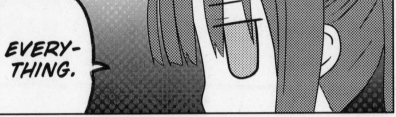

EVERY-THING.

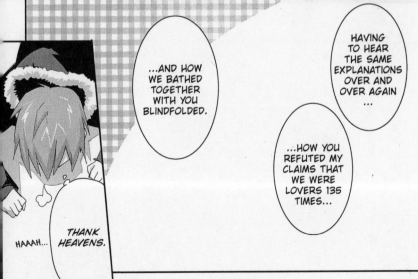

HAVING TO HEAR THE SAME EXPLANATIONS OVER AND OVER AGAIN...

...AND HOW WE BATHED TOGETHER WITH YOU BLINDFOLDED.

...HOW YOU REFUTED MY CLAIMS THAT WE WERE LOVERS 135 TIMES...

HAAAH...

THANK HEAVENS.

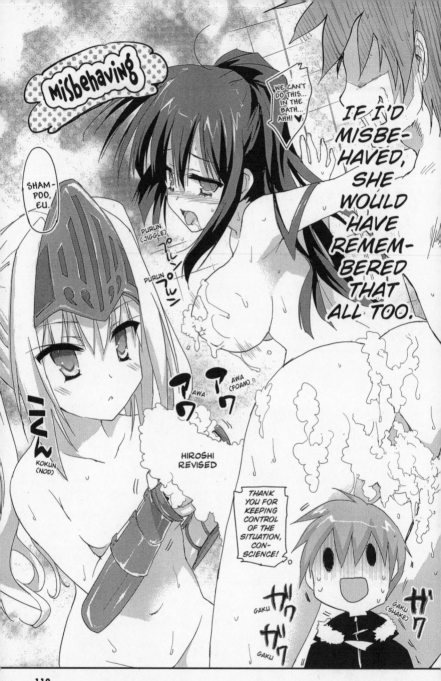

Misbehaving

WE CAN'T DO THIS... IN THE BATH... AHH! ♥

IF I'D MISBEHAVED, SHE WOULD HAVE REMEMBERED THAT ALL TOO.

SHAMPOO, EU.

PURUN (JIGGLE)

PURUN

AWA
AWA (FOAM)

KOKUN (NOD)

HIROSHI REVISED

THANK YOU FOR KEEPING CONTROL OF THE SITUATION, CONSCIENCE!

GAKU (SHAKE)

GAKU

GAKU

119

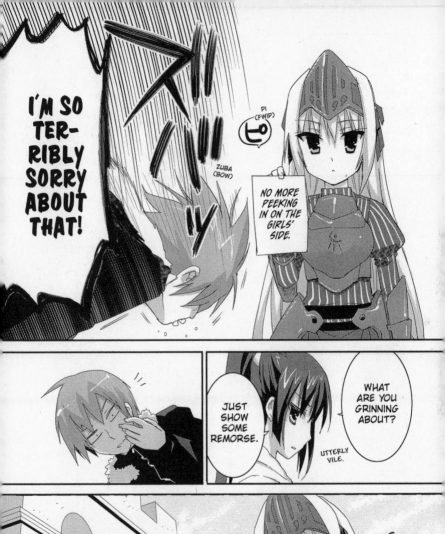

I'M SO TERRIBLY SORRY ABOUT THAT!

PI (FWIP)

ZUBA (BOW)

NO MORE PEEKING IN ON THE GIRLS' SIDE.

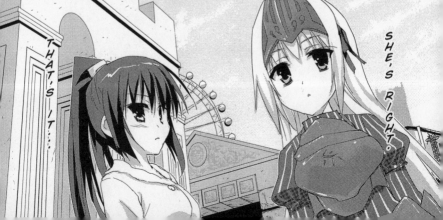

JUST SHOW SOME REMORSE.

WHAT ARE YOU GRINNING ABOUT?

UTTERLY VILE.

THAT'S IT...

SHE'S RIGHT.

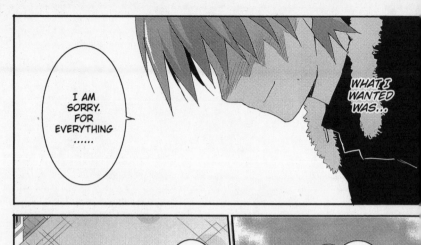

I AM SORRY. FOR EVERYTHING ......

WHAT I WANTED WAS...

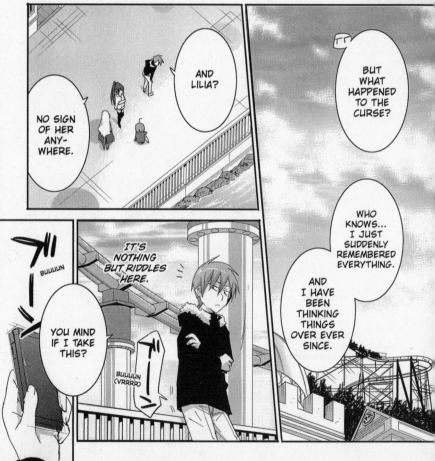

AND LILIA?

NO SIGN OF HER ANY-WHERE.

BUT WHAT HAPPENED TO THE CURSE?

WHO KNOWS... I JUST SUDDENLY REMEMBERED EVERYTHING.

AND I HAVE BEEN THINKING THINGS OVER EVER SINCE.

IT'S NOTHING BUT RIDDLES HERE.

YOU MIND IF I TAKE THIS?

BUUUUN

BUUUUN
(VRRRR)

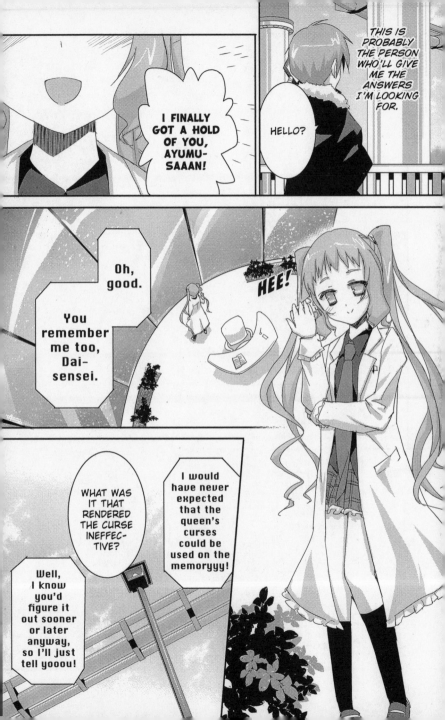

THIS IS PROBABLY THE PERSON WHO'LL GIVE ME THE ANSWERS I'M LOOKING FOR.

I FINALLY GOT A HOLD OF YOU, AYUMU-SAAAN!

HELLO?

Oh, good.

You remember me too, Dai-sensei.

HEE!

WHAT WAS IT THAT RENDERED THE CURSE INEFFEC-TIVE?

I would have never expected that the queen's curses could be used on the memoryyy!

Well, I know you'd figure it out sooner or later anyway, so I'll just tell yoooou!

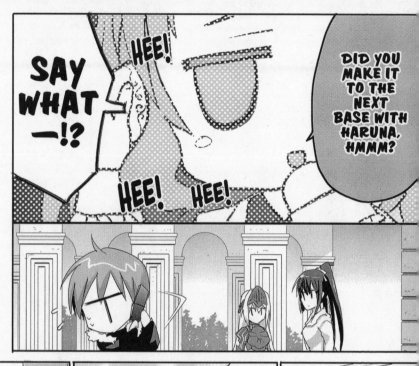

SAY WHAT —!?

HEE!

DID YOU MAKE IT TO THE NEXT BASE WITH HARUNA, HMMM?

HEE! HEE!

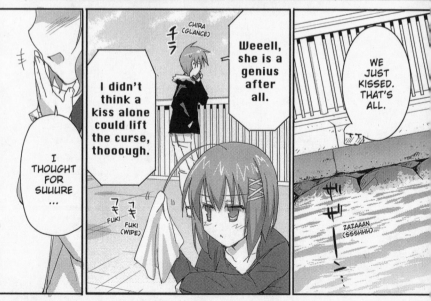

I THOUGHT FOR SUUURE ...

I didn't think a kiss alone could lift the curse, thooough.

CHIRA (GLANCE)

FUKI FUKI (WIPE)

Weeell, she is a genius after all.

WE JUST KISSED. THAT'S ALL.

ZAZAAAN (SSSHHH)

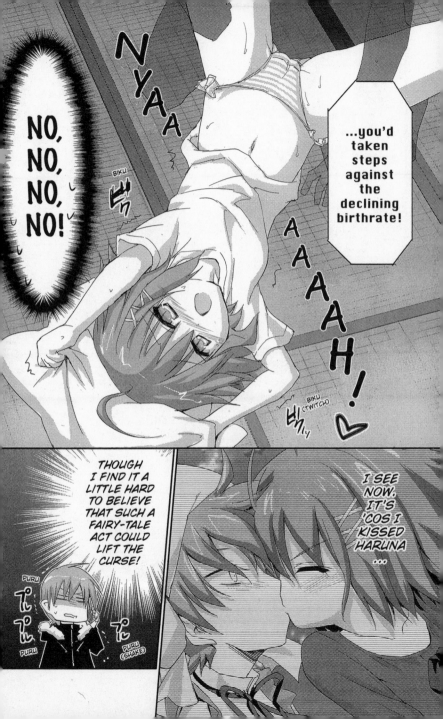

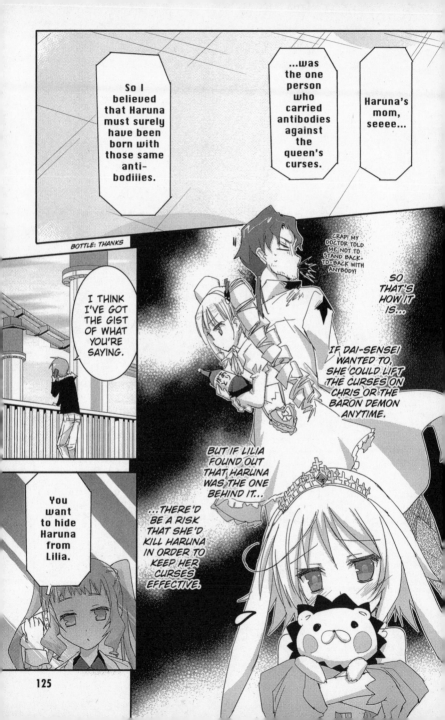

So I believed that Haruna must surely have been born with those same anti-bodiiies.

...was the one person who carried antibodies against the queen's curses.

Haruna's mom, seeee...

BOTTLE: THANKS

I THINK I'VE GOT THE GIST OF WHAT YOU'RE SAYING.

CRAP! MY DOCTOR TOLD ME NOT TO STAND BACK-TO-BACK WITH ANYBODY!

SO THAT'S HOW IT IS...

IF DAI-SENSEI WANTED TO, SHE COULD LIFT THE CURSES ON CHRIS OR THE BARON DEMON ANYTIME.

BUT IF LILIA FOUND OUT THAT HARUNA WAS THE ONE BEHIND IT...

You want to hide Haruna from Lilia.

...THERE'D BE A RISK THAT SHE'D KILL HARUNA IN ORDER TO KEEP HER CURSES EFFECTIVE.

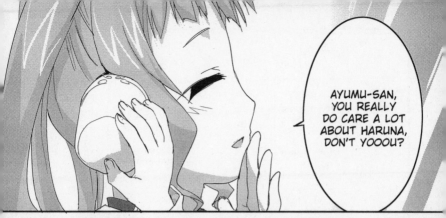

AYUMU-SAN, YOU REALLY DO CARE A LOT ABOUT HARUNA, DON'T YOOOU?

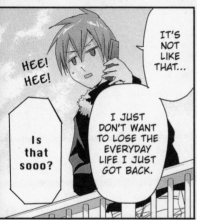

HEE! HEE!

IT'S NOT LIKE THAT...

I JUST DON'T WANT TO LOSE THE EVERYDAY LIFE I JUST GOT BACK.

Is that sooo?

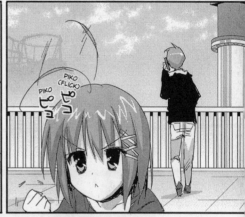

PIKO (FLICK)

PIKO

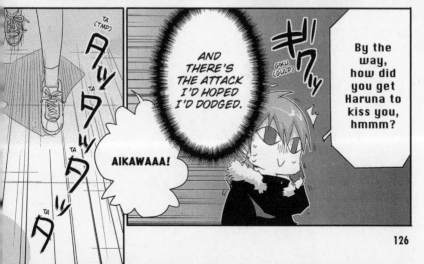

TA (TMP)

AND THERE'S THE ATTACK I'D HOPED I'D DODGED.

GIKU (GULP)

By the way, how did you get Haruna to kiss you, hmmm?

AIKAWAAA!

TA

TA

TA

126

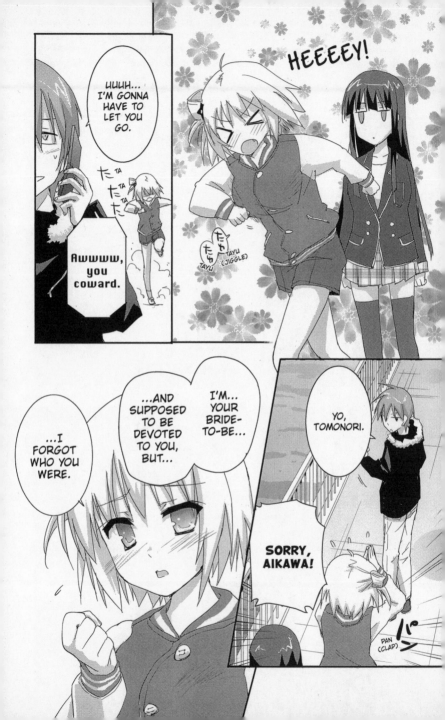

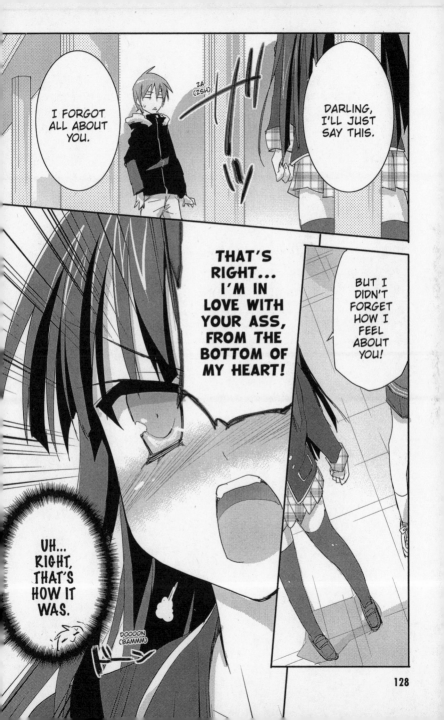

128

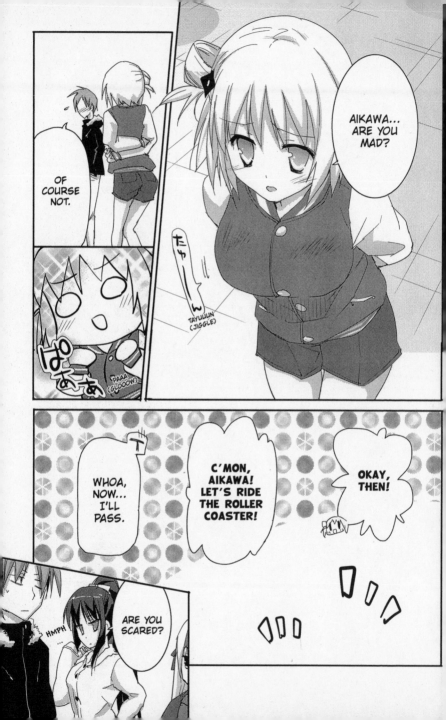

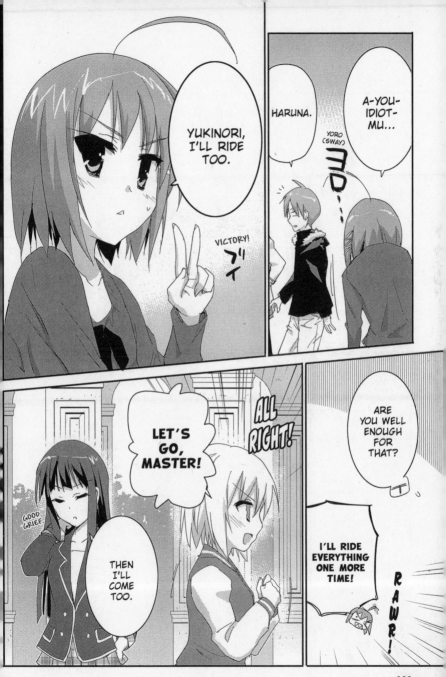

130

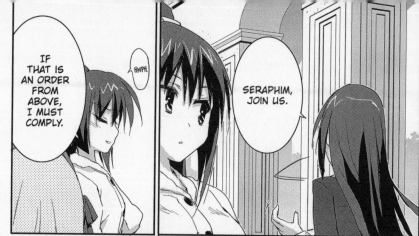

IF THAT IS AN ORDER FROM ABOVE, I MUST COMPLY.

HMPH.

SERAPHIM, JOIN US.

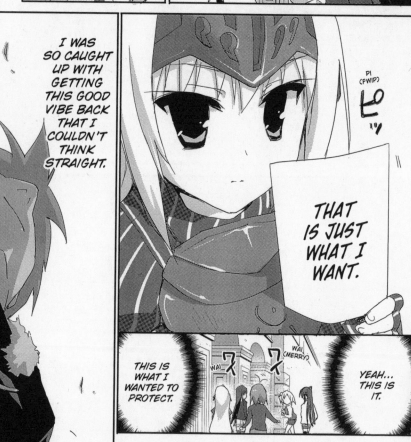

I WAS SO CAUGHT UP WITH GETTING THIS GOOD VIBE BACK THAT I COULDN'T THINK STRAIGHT.

PI (FWIP)

THAT IS JUST WHAT I WANT.

THIS IS WHAT I WANTED TO PROTECT.

WAI WAI (MERRY)

YEAH... THIS IS IT.

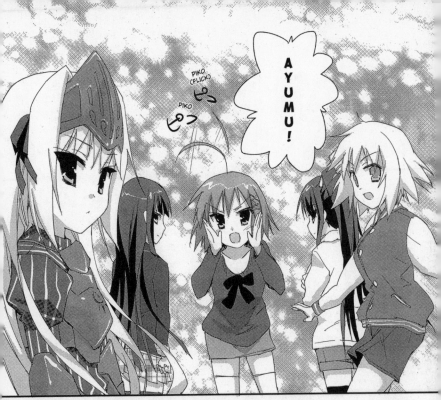

PIKO
(FLICK)

PIKO

A Y U M U !

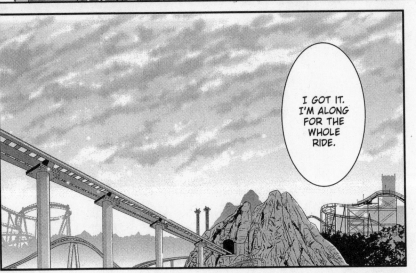

I GOT IT.
I'M ALONG
FOR THE
WHOLE
RIDE.

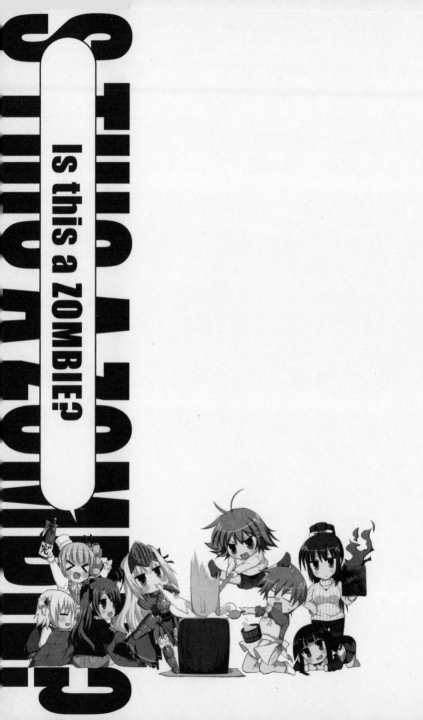

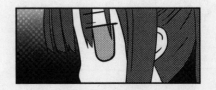

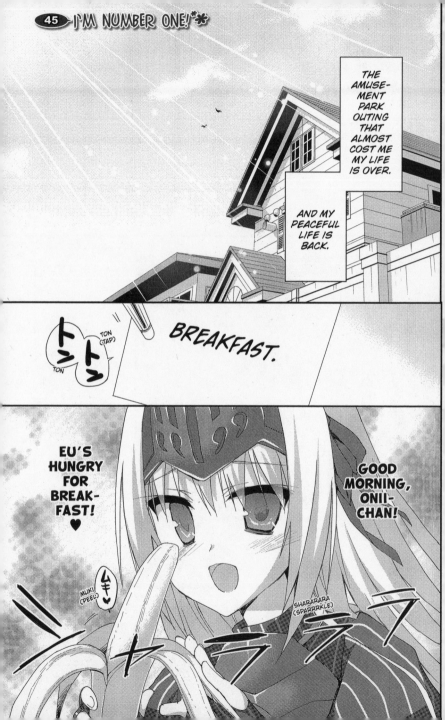

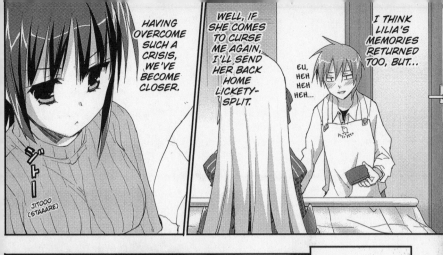

HAVING OVERCOME SUCH A CRISIS, WE'VE BECOME CLOSER.

JITOOO (STAAARE)

WELL, IF SHE COMES TO CURSE ME AGAIN, I'LL SEND HER BACK HOME LICKETY-SPLIT.

I THINK LILIA'S MEMORIES RETURNED TOO, BUT...

EU, HEH HEH HEH...

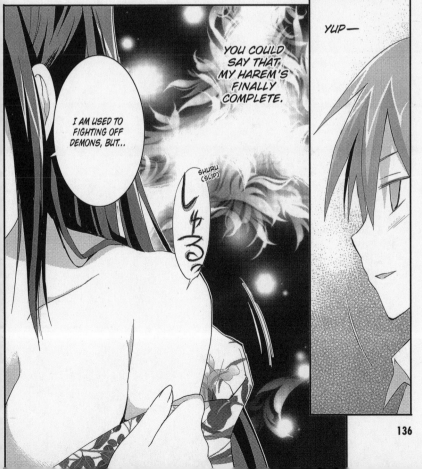

YUP—

YOU COULD SAY THAT, MY HAREM'S FINALLY COMPLETE.

I AM USED TO FIGHTING OFF DEMONS, BUT...

SHURU (SLIP)

136

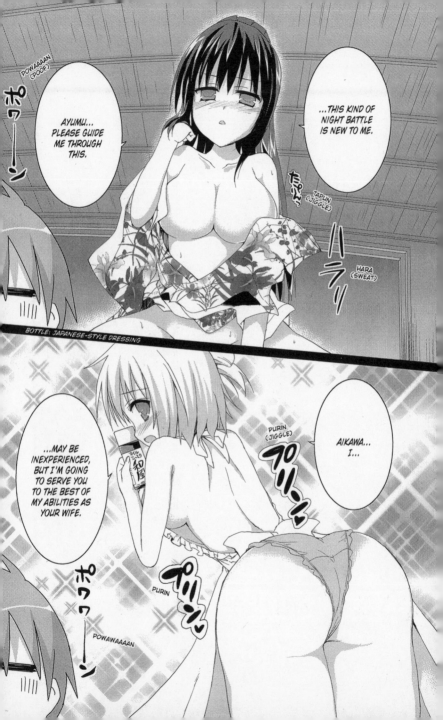

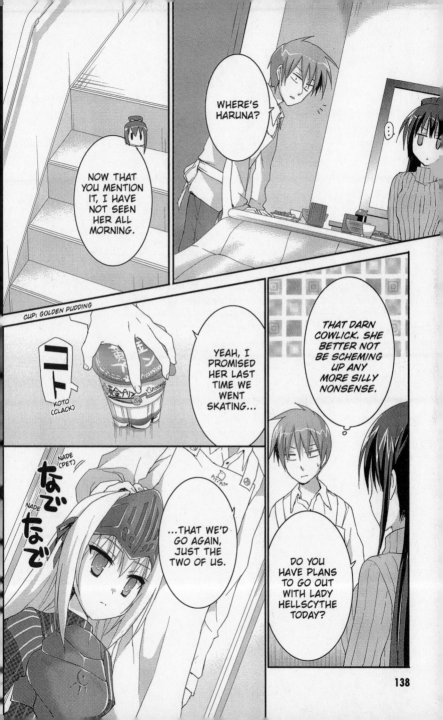

WHERE'S HARUNA?

NOW THAT YOU MENTION IT, I HAVE NOT SEEN HER ALL MORNING.

CUP: GOLDEN PUDDING

コト

KOTO (CLACK)

YEAH, I PROMISED HER LAST TIME WE WENT SKATING...

THAT DARN COWLICK. SHE BETTER NOT BE SCHEMING UP ANY MORE SILLY NONSENSE.

なで

NADE (PET)

なで

NADE

...THAT WE'D GO AGAIN, JUST THE TWO OF US.

DO YOU HAVE PLANS TO GO OUT WITH LADY HELLSCYTHE TODAY?

138

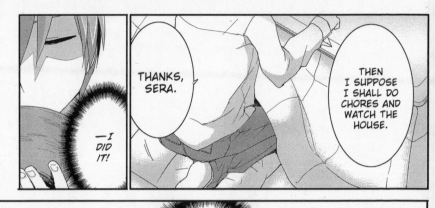

—I DID IT!

THANKS, SERA.

THEN I SUPPOSE I SHALL DO CHORES AND WATCH THE HOUSE.

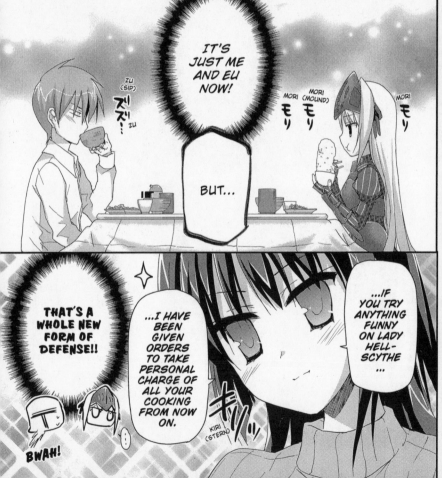

ZU (SIP)
ズズ・・
ZU

IT'S JUST ME AND EU NOW!

MORI   MORI (MOUND)   MORI
モリ   モリ   モリ

BUT...

THAT'S A WHOLE NEW FORM OF DEFENSE!!

...I HAVE BEEN GIVEN ORDERS TO TAKE PERSONAL CHARGE OF ALL YOUR COOKING FROM NOW ON.

KIRI (STERN)

...IF YOU TRY ANYTHING FUNNY ON LADY HELL-SCYTHE...

BWAH!

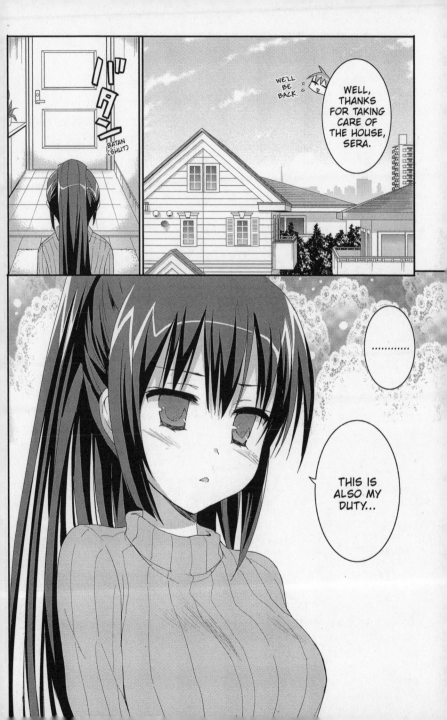

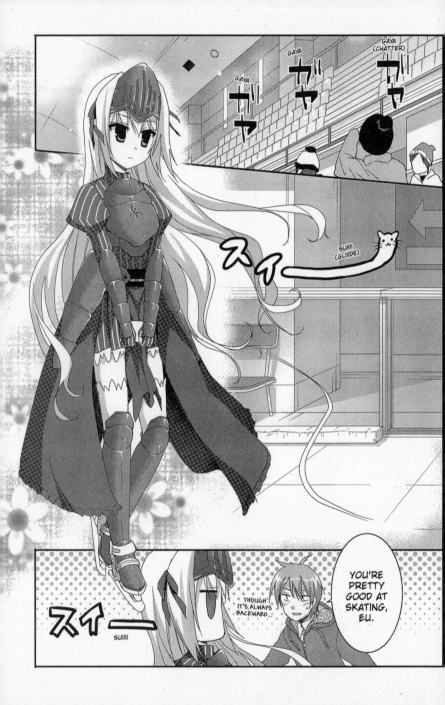

COMPARED TO WHEN WE FIRST MET, HER CURT HANDWRITING HAS GOTTEN A LITTLE SOFTER.

OKAYYY, HERE GOES!

YOUR TURN NEXT, AYUMU.

ELI DOESN'T EXPRESS HOW SHE FEELS, BUT I DISCOVERED SOMETHING THANKS TO THE QUEEN'S CURSE.

KUI (TUG)

ツ
ツ
ツ
ツ
KUI

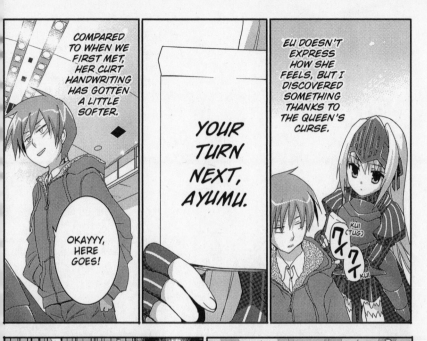

DA (DASH)

DA

DA

DA

IT SURPASSES THE DIFFICULTY LEVEL OF ULTRA TO ULTRA D...!

...AND THEN TWIRL ONE TIME—

YOU HOLD YOUR ARMS BEHIND YOU AND DO TWO SOMERSAULTS...

GUKI (TRIP)

WAI

WAI (MERRY)

SHAAA (SWIIISH)

I'LL SHOW YOU THE MOVES I'VE BEEN DEVELOPING JUST FOR THIS DAY.

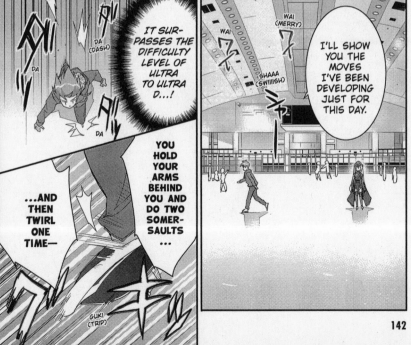

142

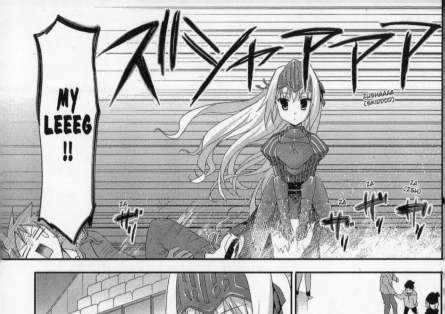

ズシャアアア
ZUSHAAAA
(SKIDDDD)

MY LEEEG !!

ZA (ZSH)
ZA
ZA (ZSH)

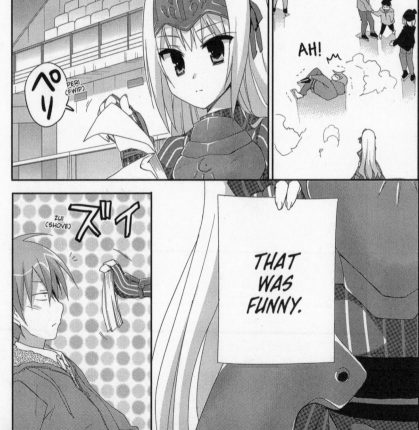

ペリ
PERI
(FWIP)

AH!

ズイ
ZUI
(SHOVE)

THAT WAS FUNNY.

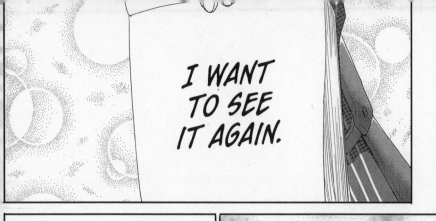

I WANT TO SEE IT AGAIN.

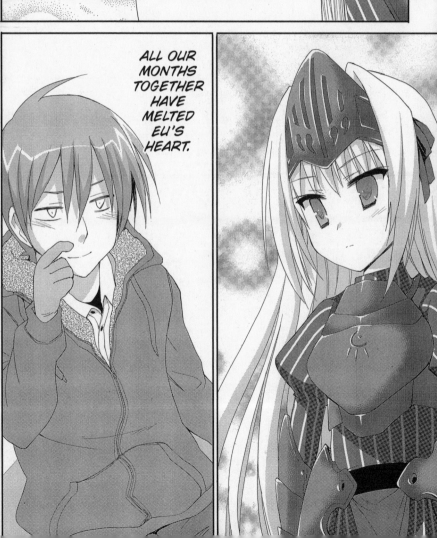

ALL OUR MONTHS TOGETHER HAVE MELTED ELI'S HEART.

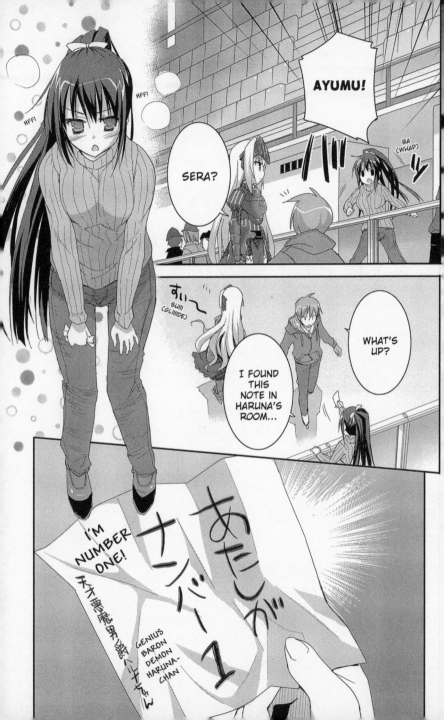

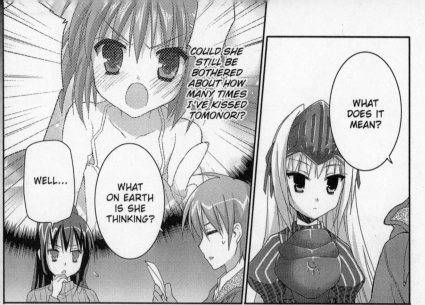

COULD SHE STILL BE BOTHERED ABOUT HOW MANY TIMES I'VE KISSED TOMONORI!?

WHAT DOES IT MEAN?

WELL...

WHAT ON EARTH IS SHE THINKING?

ART: YUKINORI YOSHIDA

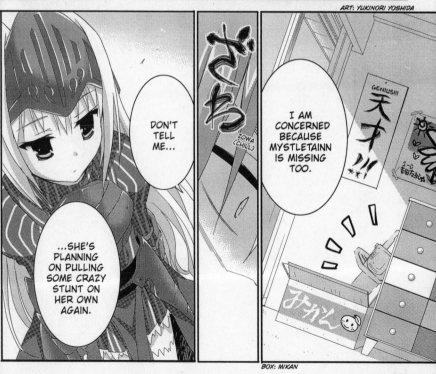

DON'T TELL ME...

...SHE'S PLANNING ON PULLING SOME CRAZY STUNT ON HER OWN AGAIN.

ZOWA (CHILL)

I AM CONCERNED BECAUSE MYSTLETAINN IS MISSING TOO.

GENIUS!!! 天才!!!

BOX: MIKAN

146

WENT BACK ......?

SU (SWF)

ス...

HARUNA WENT BACK.

EU.

DID YOU KNOW THAT HARUNA WAS LEAVING?

HOW...?

......!

I AM SORRY I KEPT IT FROM YOU.

AYUMU!

ばっ

BA (DASH)

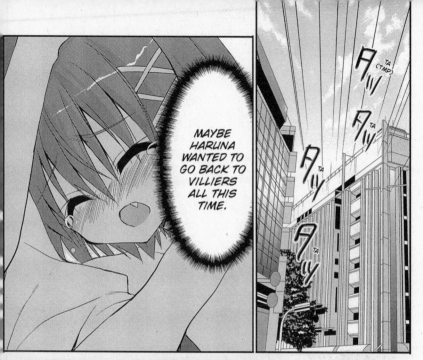

MAYBE HARUNA WANTED TO GO BACK TO VILLIERS ALL THIS TIME.

TA (CTMP)

TA
TA
TA

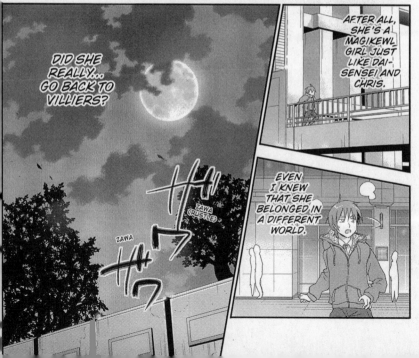

DID SHE REALLY... GO BACK TO VILLIERS?

HH!
ZAWA (CRUSTLE)

ZAWA

AFTER ALL, SHE'S A MAGIKEWL GIRL JUST LIKE DAI-SENSEI AND CHRIS.

EVEN I KNEW THAT SHE BELONGED IN A DIFFERENT WORLD.

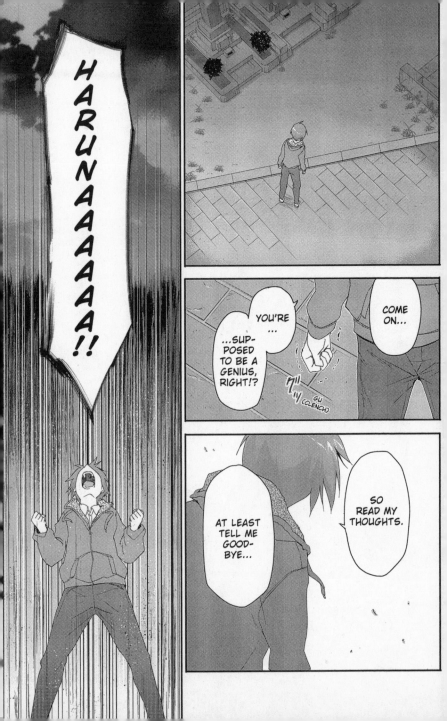

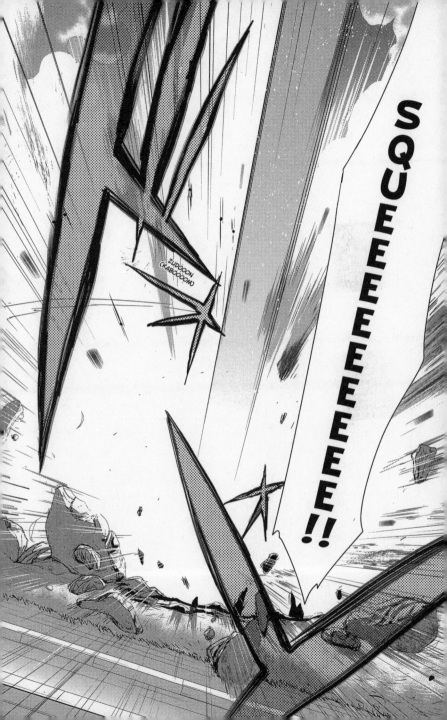

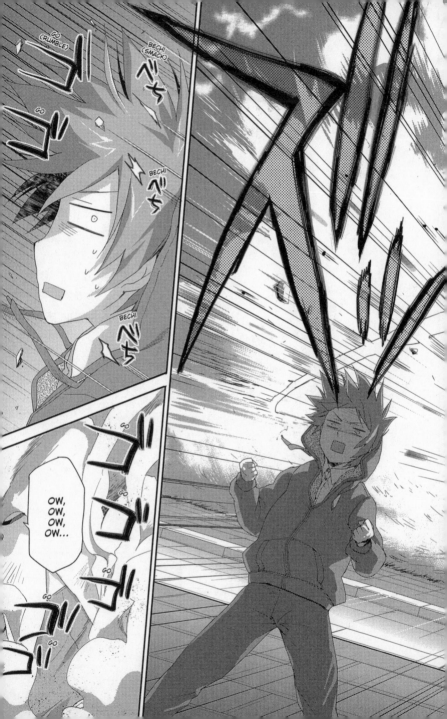

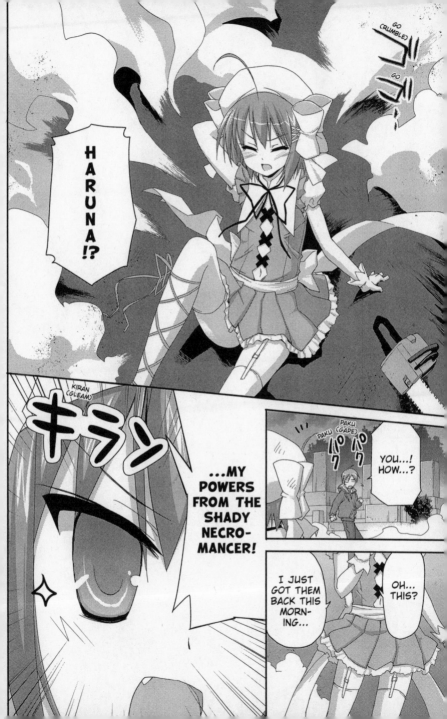

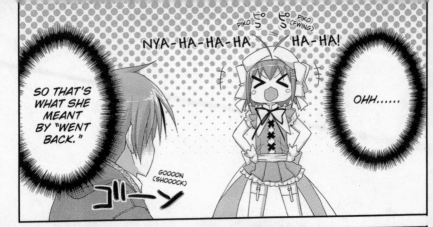

NYA-HA-HA-HA HA-HA!

PIKO ピ° PIKO (FWING)

SO THAT'S WHAT SHE MEANT BY "WENT BACK."

OHH......

GOOOON (SHOOOCK)

コ||ーン

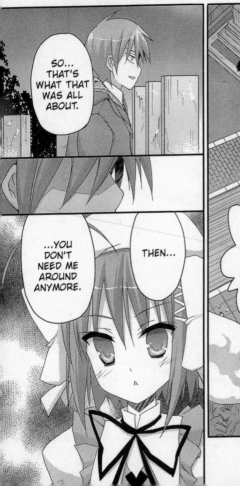

SO... THAT'S WHAT THAT WAS ALL ABOUT.

...YOU DON'T NEED ME AROUND ANYMORE.

THEN...

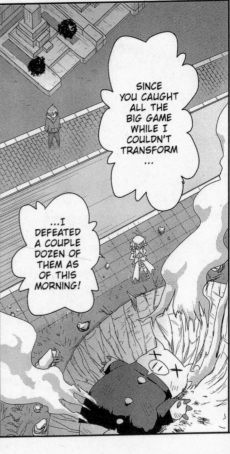

SINCE YOU CAUGHT ALL THE BIG GAME WHILE I COULDN'T TRANSFORM...

...I DEFEATED A COUPLE DOZEN OF THEM AS OF THIS MORNING!

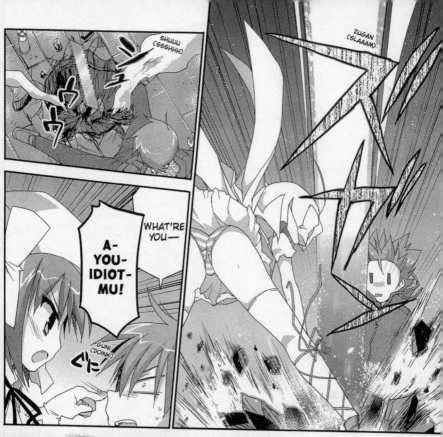

SHUUU
(SSSHHH)

ZUGAN
(SLAAAM)

WHAT'RE YOU—

A-YOU-IDIOT-MU!

GUNI
(DOINK)

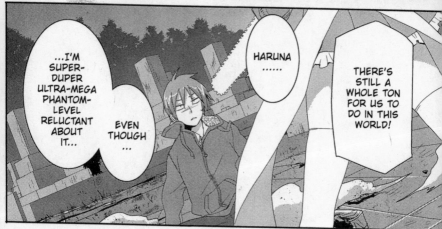

...I'M SUPER-DUPER ULTRA-MEGA PHANTOM-LEVEL RELUCTANT ABOUT IT...

EVEN THOUGH...

HARUNA......

THERE'S STILL A WHOLE TON FOR US TO DO IN THIS WORLD!

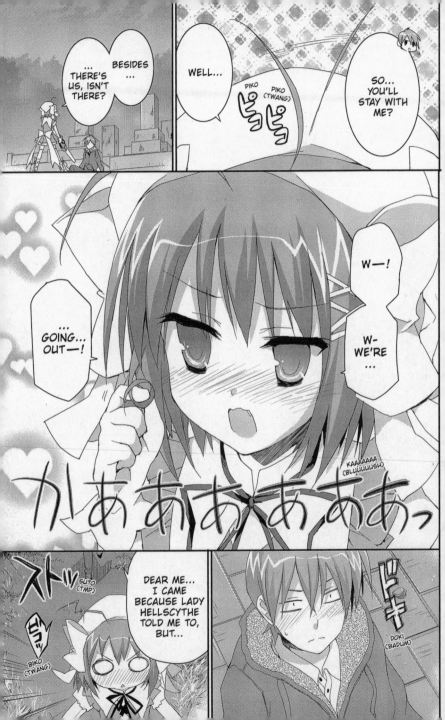

... BESIDES ... ... THERE'S US, ISN'T THERE?

WELL...

PIKO PIKO (TWANG)

SO... YOU'LL STAY WITH ME?

W—!

W-WE'RE ...

... GOING... OUT—!

KAAAAAAA (BLUUUUUUSH)

かあああああああっ

ストゥ SUTO (TMP)

ビコ BIKO (TWANG)

DEAR ME... I CAME BECAUSE LADY HELLSCYTHE TOLD ME TO, BUT...

ド╪ DOKI (BADUM)

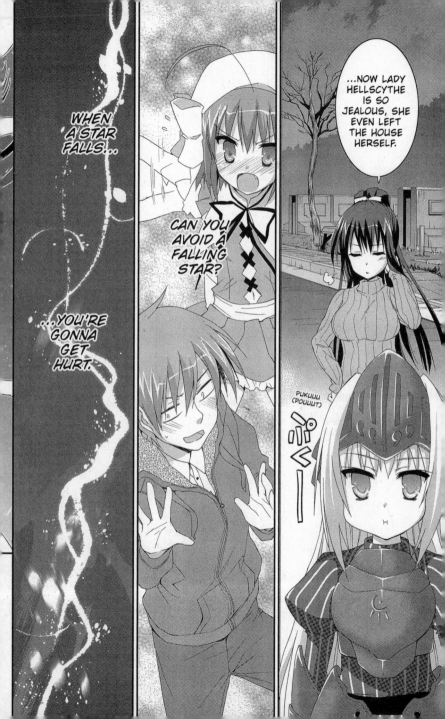

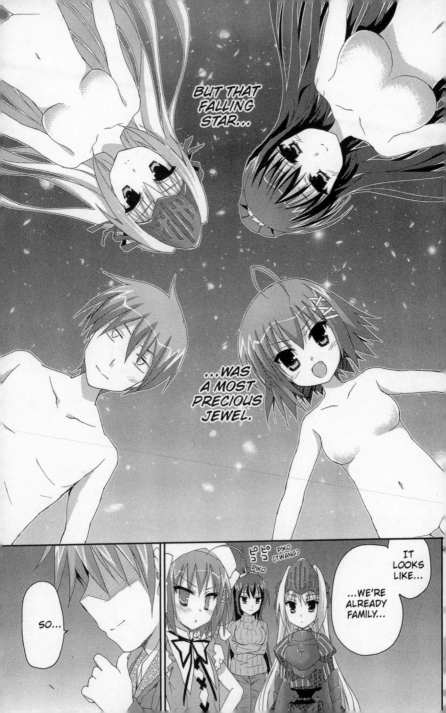

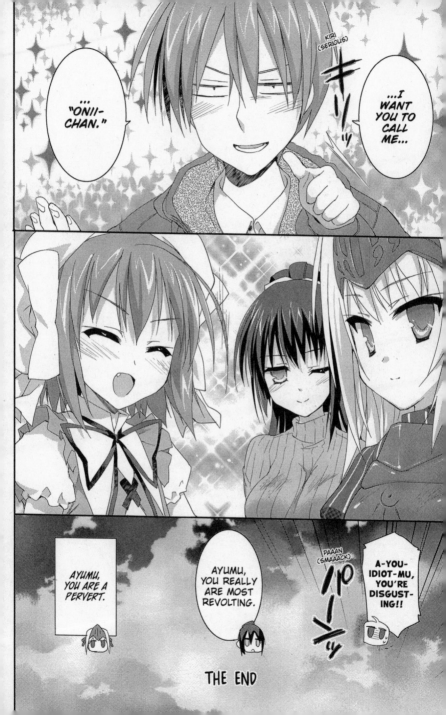

THE END

Is this a page of TRANSLATION NOTES?

PAGE 21 - Ero-Lawson: (*Erooson*) In the original, this is the nickname for a character from *Idol Master*, Ritsuko Akizuki. It is the combination of the words *ero* ("erotic") and *Lawson* (a popular convenience store). The nickname is supposed to refer to how she emits salaciousness at every turn.

PAGE 26 - Clara stood up: This is a reference to a famous scene in the anime *Heidi: Girl of the Alps* where the crippled Clara finally regains the function of her legs.

PAGE 29 - Stop it, J●ker!! I'll send you flying!: A line from the show *Kamen Norida*, a parody of the famous *Kamen Rider* series. The line is spoken by the main character, Takeshi, during the opening of the show where you see Takeshi bound to an operating table as another character, Dr. Joker Shinigami, appears to be operating on his upper body.

PAGE 35 - Natto: A traditional Japanese food made of fermented soybeans, typically eaten in the morning. It has a slimy texture that becomes even more webby and threaded as you mix it, which is a necessary step for its consumption.

PAGE 54 - Century Egg: A Chinese dish prepared by preserving quail, chicken, or duck eggs for several months.

PAGE 59 - 86: The number of the vehicle driven by the main character in the popular car manga/anime *Initial D*. The full name of the vehicle is a Toyota Sprinter Trueno AE86.

PAGE 66 - Through Skill: A play off the idea of things being "see-through," the words *through skill* in Japanese mean the skill to ignore or pretend not to hear words or questions that are unfavorable.

PAGE 68 - Excalibur Masamune: The two most famous swords of legend in the Western and Eastern traditions.

PAGE 116 - Ponyo: The main character of the 2008 Ghibli film, *Ponyo on the Cliff*.

PAGE 146 - Mikan: A Japanese citrus fruit very much like clementines.

PAGE 164 - Baby Star: a brand of crispy noodle snacks.

PAGE 164 - Sarasaty: a famous brand of disposable cotton/paper goods, like Kleenex in the United States.

PAGE 173 - Diablo Chaos Broker: A hammer-type weapon from the *Monster Hunter* game. Its original name is Chaos Render.

PAGE 173 - Master Shen: A character from the *Dragon Ball* universe.

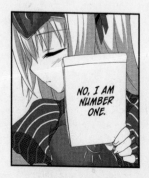

NO, I AM
NUMBER
ONE.

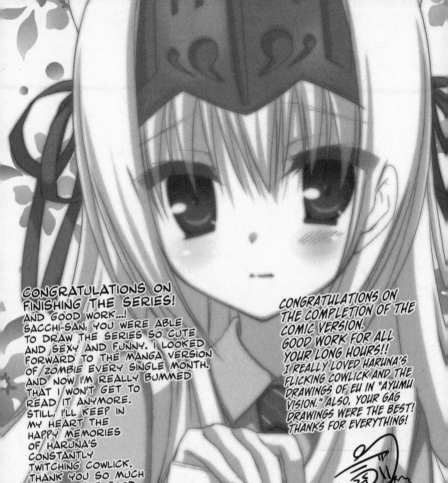

CONGRATULATIONS ON FINISHING THE SERIES! AND GOOD WORK....! SACCHI-SAN, YOU WERE ABLE TO DRAW THE SERIES SO CUTE AND SEXY AND FUNNY. I LOOKED FORWARD TO THE MANGA VERSION OF ZOMBIE EVERY SINGLE MONTH. AND NOW I'M REALLY BUMMED THAT I WON'T GET TO READ IT ANYMORE. STILL, I'LL KEEP IN MY HEART THE HAPPY MEMORIES OF HARUNA'S CONSTANTLY TWITCHING COWLICK. THANK YOU SO MUCH FOR ALL THE GOOD TIMES!

MURIRIN

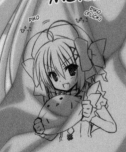

PIKO
PIKO GPIKO

CONGRATULATIONS ON THE COMPLETION OF THE COMIC VERSION. GOOD WORK FOR ALL YOUR LONG HOURS!! I REALLY LOVED HARUNA'S FLICKING COWLICK AND THE DRAWINGS OF EU IN "AYUMU VISION." ALSO, YOUR GAG DRAWINGS WERE THE BEST! THANKS FOR EVERYTHING!

KOBUICHI

GOOD MORNING. KIMURA HERE. SO WE'VE REACHED THE FINAL VOLUME, AT LAST. THIS IS A DEEPLY EMOTIONAL EVENT. IN THE FIGHT AGAINST TIME DURING ITS SERIALIZATION, QUITE A BIT OF MY LIFE GOT SHAVED OFF WITH ALL THAT I HAD TO DO. AND BECAUSE I HAD TO BE IN MY HOUSE TO WORK ON IT, I GAVE UP A LOT OF MY HOBBIES. I THINK IT CAUSED ITS OWN FAIR SHARE OF HARDSHIP.

GOOD WORK ON A JOB WELL DONE.
SHINICHI KIMURA

AFTERWORD

THANK YOU FOR READING ALL THE WAY TO THE END OF THE COMIC VERSION OF *IS THIS A ZOMBIE?* THIS IS THE PERSON IN CHARGE OF THE COMIC ADAPTATION, SACCHI. LOOKING BACK ON IT NOW, THE COMIC ONLY STARTED FOUR YEARS AGO BUT LASTED ALL THE WAY TO EIGHT VOLUMES. I THINK THIS IS REALLY ALL THANKS TO THE CONSTANT LOVE AND SUPPORT FROM THE READERS. THANK YOU SO VERY MUCH.

WELL, SINCE THIS IS MY LAST OPPORTUNITY TO LEAVE SOME PARTING WORDS, I THINK I'LL HOLD BACK BRINGING UP ALL THE PENT-UP BOOB STUFF I WANT TO TALK ABOUT AND WRITE ABOUT MY THOUGHTS ON THE WORK. UPON COMPLETING THIS COMIC VERSION, THE EIGHTH VOLUME HAD TIMES OF BOTH ENJOYMENT AND ALSO INTENSE SADNESS. HAVING A LITTLE MORE FREEDOM WITH THIS FORM OF THE STORY, I HAD ALWAYS IMAGINED THAT I'D WRITE A CHRIS ARC. BUT WHEN I TRIED TO WORK IT IN THAT DIRECTION, I INSTEAD FELT I HAD A DUTY TO EXPRESS, IN MY OWN WAY, THE EVERYDAY LIFE OF HARUNA AND THE GANG AS BASED IN THE ORIGINAL STORY.

SO WHEN IT FINALLY CAME TIME TO DO THE FINAL CHAPTER, THE DIRECTION I TOOK WAS "GOING BACK TO WHERE WE STARTED." THAT'S WHY I INCLUDED A SCENE REMINISCENT OF THEIR FIRST MEETING. AND YOU MAY RECALL HOW IN VOLUME 6, DURING THE SCENE WHERE AYUMU IS TALKING TO SERA ON THE WAY BACK HOME FROM HELPING NENE-SAN WITH HER ROUGH DRAFTS, HE ASKS HIMSELF WHAT HIS HAPPY ENDING WOULD BE. LOOKING BACK ON IT NOW, I THINK AYUMU ALREADY HAD THE ANSWER TO THAT EVEN BACK THEN.

HE REALIZED THE EVERYDAY LIFE WITH HIS NEW FRIENDS WHO INFLUENCED ONE ANOTHER AND HELPED EACH OTHER GROW WAS THE MOST PRECIOUS OF ALL.

EVEN THOUGH IT WAS SHROUDED IN A VEIL OF TITTIES, I HOPE ALL YOU READERS WERE ABLE TO FEEL HOW MUCH I LOVE THIS SERIES THROUGH ITS MANGA VERSION.

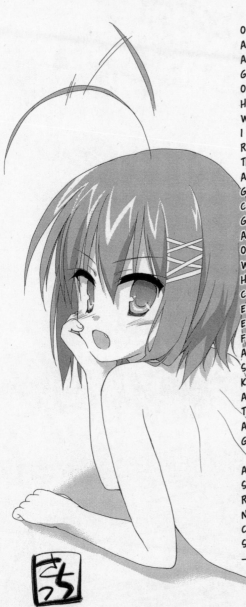

ON A FINAL NOTE, I REALLY
APPRECIATE THE ORIGINAL
AUTHOR, KIMURA-SENSEI, FOR
GIVING ME THIS INVALUABLE
OPPORTUNITY. I'M SORRY FOR
HOW INADEQUATE I SOMETIMES
WAS. YOUR KIND WORDS WHEN
I WAS FEELING MY LOWEST
REALLY SAVED ME. THANKS TO
THE ARTISTS KOBUICHI-SENSEI
AND MURIRIN-SENSEI FOR
GIVING ME SUCH ADORABLE
CHARACTERS THAT I REALLY
GREW TO ENJOY DRAWING. EU
AND CHRIS HAD SUCH DETAIL
ON THEM THAT MY HAND
WOULD START SHAKING, BUT
HARUNA'S TWITCHING COWLICK
CURED ALL OF THAT. TO THE
EDITORS AND EVERYONE IN THE
EDITORIAL DEPARTMENT, SORRY
FOR ALL THE TIMES I TOOK
ANY WIGGLE ROOM OUT OF THE
SCHEDULE, AND PLEASE LOOK
KINDLY ON ME IN THE FUTURE. I
AM FULL OF GRATITUDE FOR ALL
THE SUPPORT MY ASSISTANTS
AND A NUMBER OF OTHER FOLKS
GAVE ME.

AND I'M GOING TO WORK HARD
SO THAT I CAN SEE ALL OF YOU
READERS AGAIN IN SOME OTHER
NEW TITLE, SO PLEASE KEEP
CHEERING ME ON. THANK YOU
SO, SO MUCH.
—SACCHI

2013.12

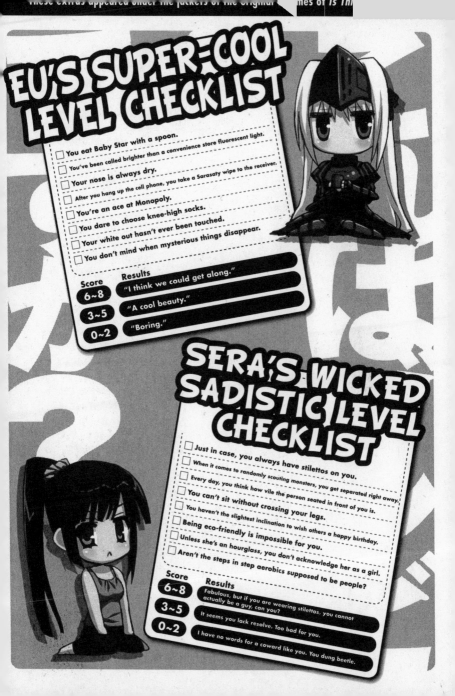

EU'S SUPER-COOL LEVEL CHECKLIST

- [ ] You eat Baby Star with a spoon.
- [ ] You've been called brighter than a convenience store fluorescent light.
- [ ] Your nose is always dry.
- [ ] After you hang up the cell phone, you take a Sarasaty wipe to the receiver.
- [ ] You're an ace at Monopoly.
- [ ] You dare to choose knee-high socks.
- [ ] Your white out hasn't ever been touched.
- [ ] You don't mind when mysterious things disappear.

Score	Results
6~8	"I think we could get along."
3~5	"A cool beauty."
0~2	"Boring."

SERA'S WICKED SADISTIC LEVEL CHECKLIST

- [ ] Just in case, you always have stilettos on you.
- [ ] When it comes to randomly scouting monsters, you get separated right away.
- [ ] Every day, you think how vile the person seated in front of you is.
- [ ] You can't sit without crossing your legs.
- [ ] You haven't the slightest inclination to wish others a happy birthday.
- [ ] Being eco-friendly is impossible for you.
- [ ] Unless she's an hourglass, you don't acknowledge her as a girl.
- [ ] Aren't the steps in step aerobics supposed to be people?

Score	Results
6~8	Fabulous, but if you are wearing stilettos, you cannot actually be a guy, can you?
3~5	It seems you lack resolve. Too bad for you.
0~2	I have no words for a coward like you. You dung beetle.

HARUNA'S MEGA-PERVERT LEVEL CHECKLIST

☐ Your commander calls you "incorrigible."

☐ You're proud of your happy trail.

☐ If anything ever happens to me...take me to the Women's Medical University.

☐ A wet napkin is for wiping away sweat.

☐ You dream of becoming a cosmetologist who waxes hair off of the shin.

☐ You express yourself in "Look out! Here I come!"

☐ Your heart races when you see huge at the beginning of anything.

☐ When you cross at a zebra crossing, you get off thinking about striped panties.

Score / Results

Score	Results
6~8	You oughta change your name to Maximum Sicko!
3~5	Every day's so easygoing, isn't it...? As if! I'll put you in a sleeper hold!
0~2	You have what it takes to uphold the future! Keep it up for at least another one hundred years!

CHECK IT OUT!

THINGS LIKE NEGATIVE IONS **CAN'T HEAL ME!**

FOR EVERYONE TO BECOME THE BRIDE THEY THINK I WANT, YOU HAVE TO MASTER THE **APPROPRIATE KUNG FU!**

ME, I'M A ZOMBIE... A "MAGIKEW..." AND I HAVE

When I go into a pool, I can't help but do the butterfly.

...IS SETTLING INTO

I THOUGHT UP A NEW TECHNIQUE! ...'S BUILDING WITH HIS NEW ROOMMATE... ...WHEN THE OPPORTUNITY ARISES TO FACE HIS

MUKI... ...UP TO THE TASK??

THE GERMAN SUPLEX BLINDING HOL...

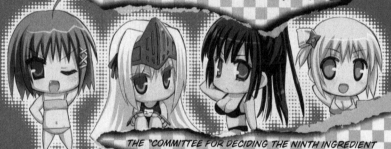

THE "COMMITTEE FOR DECIDING THE NINTH INGREDIENT IN THE EIGHT TREASURE DISH" DECIDED IT.

I THINK!

Is this a ZOMBIE?

P-PERVEEEERT!

GO TO SLEEP— ♪
GO TO SLEEP— ♪

SWEETENING UP MY COFFEE WITH SUGAR AND THEN DUNKING MY BREAD IN IT IS HOW I DO DESSE

SACCHI COMIC

SHINICHI KIMURA ORIGINAL

KOBUICHI • MURIRIN CHARACTER DESIGN

LET'S CUT THE VOLTAGE ONE STEP BEFORE IT REACHES ITS C

Is that so? I figured you're such a genius, Haruna-chan, that you wrote the code without even rea it!

Is this a ZOMBIE?

LEAF LADY! WERE YOU SWIFTLY STRUCK BACK?

Y-YOU IDIOT! I...I MUST BE HALLUCINATING. HARUNA-CHAN, YOU'RE SERIOUSLY AN E GIRL?

LD IT, YOU'RE SKIPPING OUT EAR

YOU'RE TOTALLY BRAVE!

NOW SAY IT WITH YOUR HEART IN IT! EH...F!

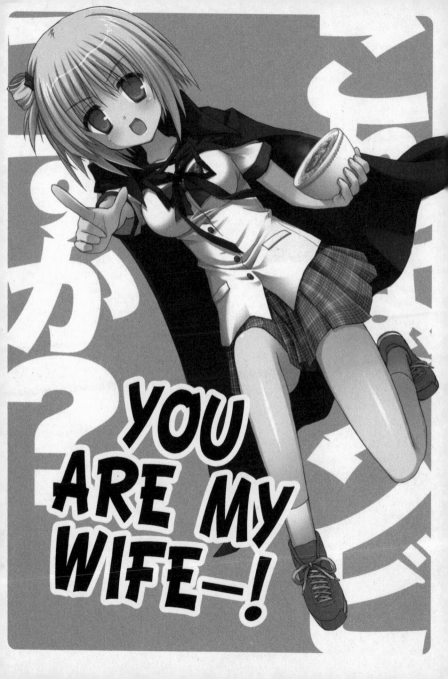

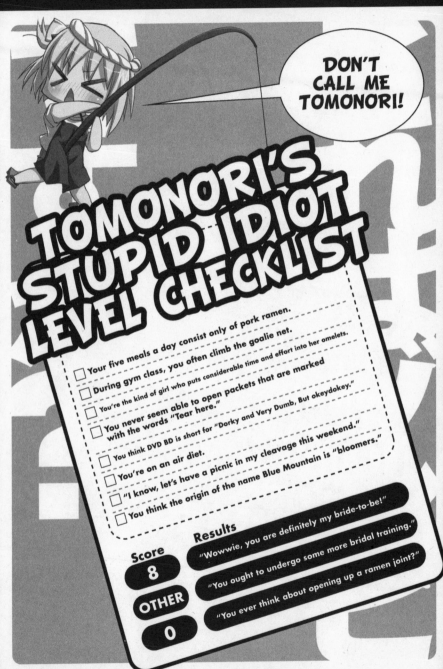

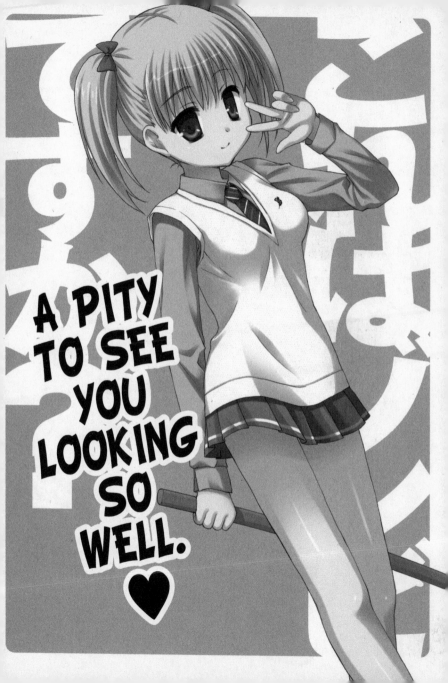

I DON'T THINK THAT. ♥

KYOUKO'S WICKEDNESS LEVEL CHECKLIST

☐ You befriend girls just a little less cute than you.

☐ You have an unhealthy fondness for toys like Gloomy Bear.

☐ You feel bad for the little chick that will never be...that's why you don't eat eggs.

☐ You make a little pouty mouth when in public.

☐ Your go-to pose is the upward glance.

☐ You trip. A lot.

☐ You hide your palms and just let your fingers peek out of your sleeves.

☐ Your cooking forte is meat and potatoes. ♥

☐ You face plant on your desk crying, "I'm screwed. I got a zero on that."

☐ Pon vinegar? Hmm? Is that like ponzu sauce?

☐ You eat like a squirrel.

☐ Only in front of the opposite sex will you point out cats on the roadside and say, "Aaw, a kitty cat!"

Score	Results
12	Aha! Well, would you look at that? You're wicked as can be! You take the "cute" out of "wicked cute"...
OTHER	You're wicked by nature, but only barely. ♥ Oozing dark gray flatters you so well it's positively obnoxious. ♪
0	You have to learn the ways of life or else you'll never get by in this world.

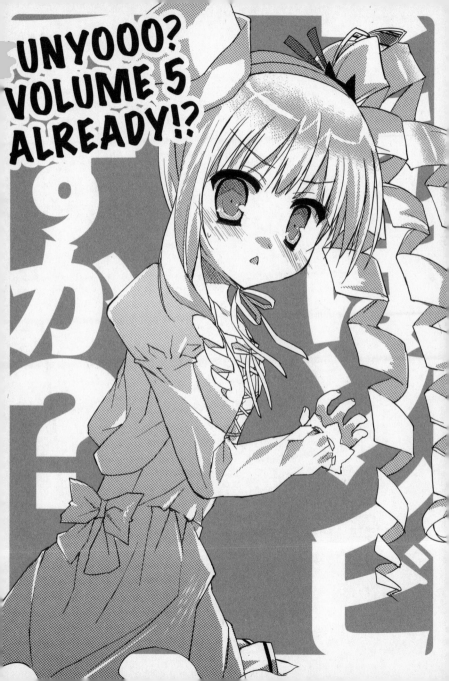

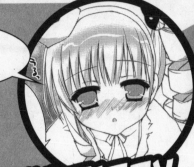

HMMM?

CHRIS'S TINY TITTY LEVEL CHECKLIST

☐ Those are decorations.

☐ I won't say they're beautiful, but their tiny size makes them pretty enough.

☐ It's always the places that hold nothing at all that hold the most potential.

☐ More than the cup, it's the *top* that matters.

☐ More than a roast, it's a fillet that people like.

☐ It's a fact that when you're too big you can't find a cute bra.

☐ Gravity is not a problem for you.

☐ Your weapon of choice is the Diablo Chaos Broker.

Score	Results
8	"Well done, brother! I just wanna give you a great big squeeze — just kidding!"
OTHER	"You're as lukewarm as Master Shen."
0	"You're an idiot for thinking that 'if only they were bigger, you could get featured in a pinup!'"

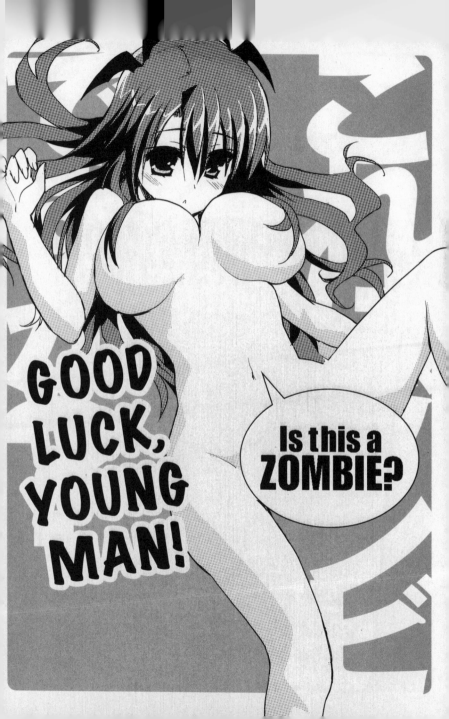

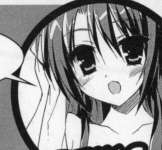

BOOBIES?

NENE-SAN'S BUSTING-OUT LEVEL CHECKLIST

- ☐ My car doesn't need air bags. It's already got air boobs.
- ☐ When singing the alphabet song, you get tense right around the middle of it.
- ☐ Your shirt forms a diamond between buttons, exposing a good 75 cm² of your bra.
- ☐ Some people have secretly nicknamed you "Ms. Rocket."
- ☐ If you don't mind, I'll wipe the sweat from below your underboob.
- ☐ Boob mouse pads don't do it for me. But I still own one.
- ☐ You fold your bills lengthwise so that you can sandwich them in your cleavage.
- ☐ When you see that you still have Mt. Everest on your chest even when lying on your back, you begin to doubt that they're even boobs.
- ☐ Even though you know that they'd never let you smoosh your face into their tits, you can't help calling to the Playboy Bunnies in bars.

Score	Results
9	My neck's so stiff. Maybe I could rest my head in your cleavage.
OTHER	Isn't there a saying that "anybody who likes boobs can't be all bad"?
0	Youth must be spent in innocence!

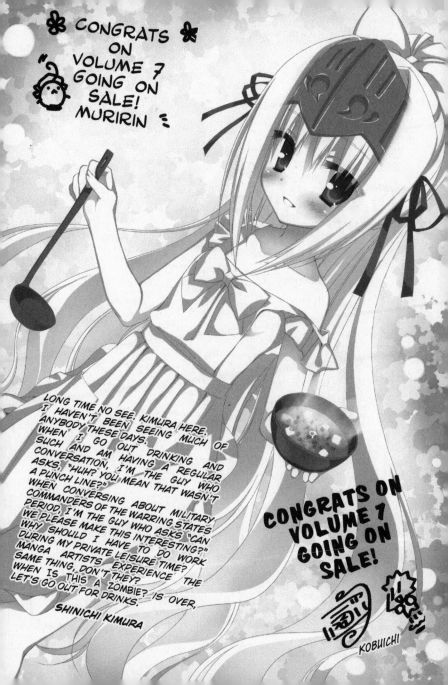

✿ CONGRATS ✿
ON
VOLUME 7
GOING ON
SALE!
MURIRIN

LONG TIME NO SEE. KIMURA HERE. I HAVEN'T BEEN SEEING MUCH OF ANYBODY THESE DAYS. WHEN I GO OUT DRINKING AND SUCH AND AM HAVING A REGULAR CONVERSATION, I'M THE GUY WHO ASKS, "HUH? YOU MEAN THAT WASN'T A PUNCH LINE?" WHEN CONVERSING ABOUT MILITARY COMMANDERS OF THE WARRING STATES PERIOD, I'M THE GUY WHO ASKS "CAN WE PLEASE MAKE THIS INTERESTING?" WHY SHOULD I HAVE TO DO WORK DURING MY PRIVATE LEISURE TIME? MANGA ARTISTS EXPERIENCE THE SAME THING, DON'T THEY? WHEN IS THIS A ZOMBIE? IS OVER, LET'S GO OUT FOR DRINKS.

SHINICHI KIMURA

CONGRATS ON
VOLUME 7
GOING ON
SALE!

KOBUICHI

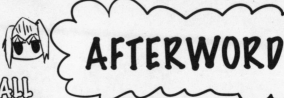

AFTERWORD

ALL RIGHTY THEN!!

IF YOU'RE READING THIS FIRST, PLEASE STOP AND COME BACK AFTER YOU'VE FINISHED THE VOLUME!

THANK YOU FOR BUYING VOLUME 7!!!

I KNOW I SAY THIS EVERY TIME, BUT IT'S REALLY ALL THANKS TO YOU READERS THAT THE SERIES HAS CONTINUED THIS LONG! THANKS!!

THE OTHER DAY, WHEN I E-MAILED KIMURA-SAN ABOUT WHAT WOULD BE IN STORE FOR THE STORY NEXT, HE SAID TO ME, "WHY DON'T YOU COME UP WITH SOMETHING ORIGINAL?" (I LIKE TO IMAGINE HIM SAYING THAT IN HIS BATHROBE, HOLDING A BRANDY IN ONE HAND.) AND SO I DID CHRIS'S STORY AT MY OWN DISCRETION AND STYLE OF PRESENTATION. (SORRY TO ALL THE FANS OF THE ORIGINAL STORY.) THE NEXT VOLUME IS GOING TO BE THE LAST ONE OF THIS COMIC VERSION, BUT I HOPE YOU WILL STILL STICK AROUND FOR THE ENTIRETY OF THE SERIES!

—SACCHI, MAY 9, 2013

KIMURA-SENSEI, KOBUICHI-SENSEI, AND MURIRIN-SENSEI— THANK YOU SO MUCH AS ALWAYS.

THE REASON I'M SO GROSS IS PROBABLY BECAUSE I NEVER GO OUT (IT'S AN OCCUPATIONAL DISEASE). SO PLEASE TAKE ME OUT DRINKING WITH YOU, KIMURA-SAN! HEH-HEH.

SPECIAL THANKS

THE COMICS EDITORIAL DEPARTMENT
OUR EDITOR, M-SAN
YAMAMOTO-SAN
MIMIZU-SAN
EKAKIBITO-SAN
HAKKII-SAN
RIN-SAN

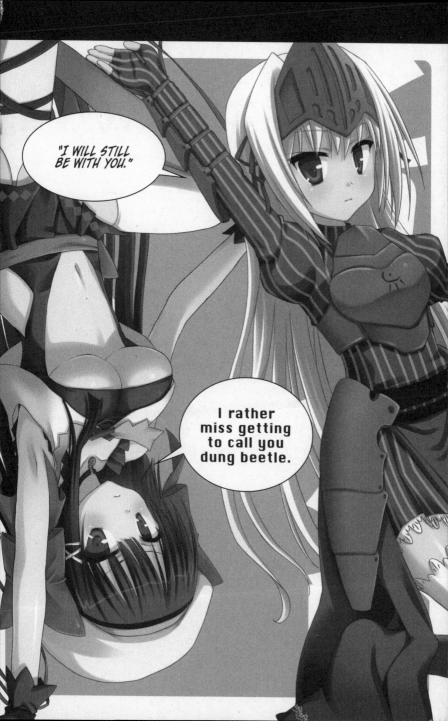

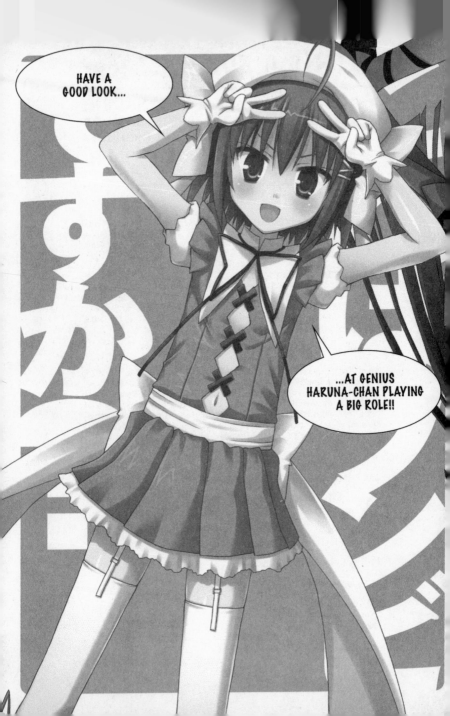

IS THIS A ZOMBIE? 8 ✽

SACCHI
SHINICHI KIMURA
KOBUICHI • MURIRIN

Translation: Christine Dashiell

Lettering: AndWorld Design

KOREHA ZOMBIE DESUKA? Volume 8
© 2013 SACCHI © 2013 SHINICHI KIMURA • KOBUICHI • MURIRIN.
Edited by FUJIMISHOBO. First published in Japan in 2013 by KADO-KAWA CORPORATION, Tokyo. English translation rights arranged with KADOKAWA CORPORATION, Tokyo, through TUTTLE-MORI AGENCY, INC., Tokyo.

Translation © 2014 Hachette Book Group, Inc.

Yen Press
Hachette Book Group
237 Park Avenue, New York, NY 10017

www.HachetteBookGroup.com
www.YenPress.com

Yen Press is an imprint of Hachette Book Group, Inc. The Yen Press name and logo are trademarks of Hachette Book Group, Inc.

First Yen Press Edition: July 2014

ISBN: 978-0-316-37677-8

10 9 8 7 6 5 4 3 2 1

BVG

Printed in the United States of America

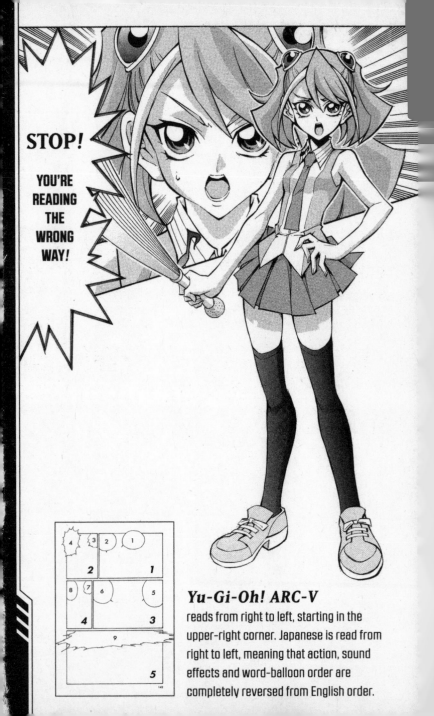

STOP!

YOU'RE READING THE WRONG WAY!

Yu-Gi-Oh! ARC-V

reads from right to left, starting in the upper-right corner. Japanese is read from right to left, meaning that action, sound effects and word-balloon order are completely reversed from English order.

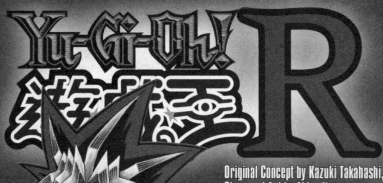

Yu-Gi-Oh! R

Original Concept by Kazuki Takahashi,
Story and Art by Akira Ito

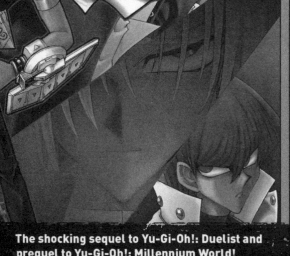

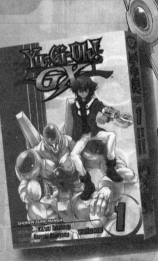

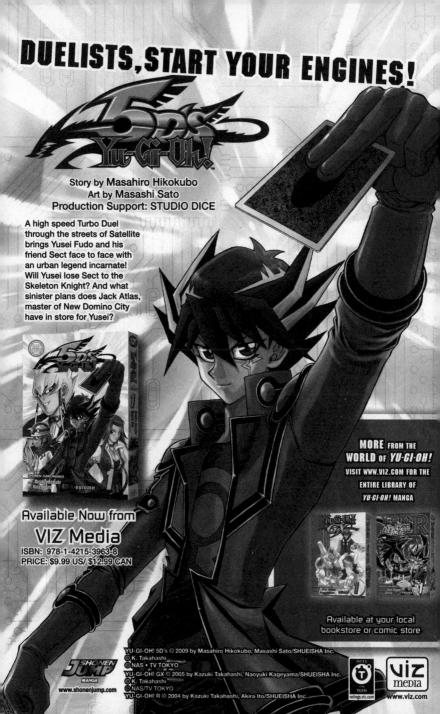

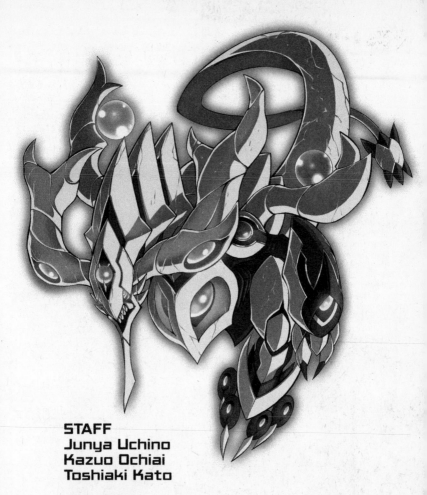

STAFF
Junya Uchino
Kazuo Ochiai
Toshiaki Kato

COLORING
Toru Shimizu

EDITING
Takahiko Aikawa

SUPPORT
Gallop
Wedge Holdings

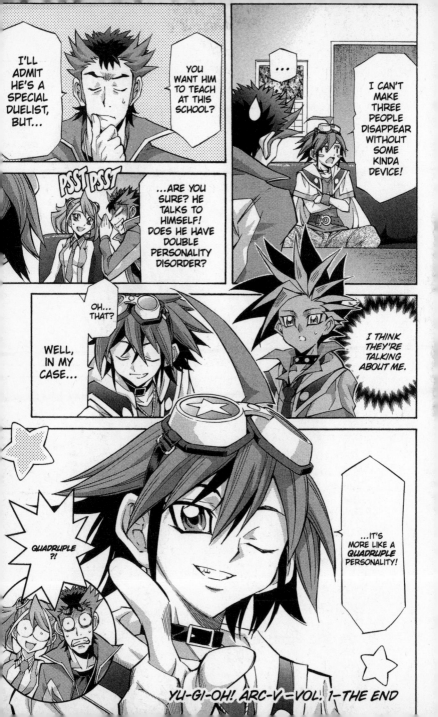

I'LL ADMIT HE'S A SPECIAL DUELIST, BUT...

YOU WANT HIM TO TEACH AT THIS SCHOOL?

...

I CAN'T MAKE THREE PEOPLE DISAPPEAR WITHOUT SOME KINDA DEVICE!

PSST PSST

...ARE YOU SURE? HE TALKS TO HIMSELF! DOES HE HAVE DOUBLE PERSONALITY DISORDER?

OH... THAT?

WELL, IN MY CASE...

I THINK THEY'RE TALKING ABOUT ME.

QUADRUPLE?!

...IT'S MORE LIKE A *QUADRUPLE* PERSONALITY!

YU-GI-OH! ARC-V —VOL. 1—THE END

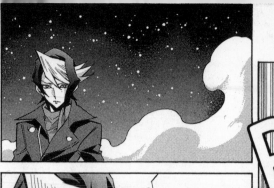

POM

THAT'S SO EMBAR-RASSING!!

YUYA...?!

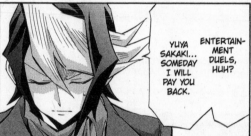

ENTERTAIN-MENT DUELS, HUH?

YUYA SAKAKI... SOMEDAY I WILL PAY YOU BACK.

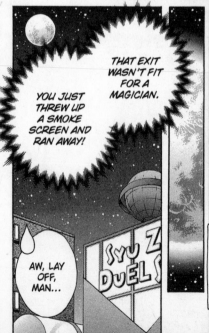

THAT EXIT WASN'T FIT FOR A MAGICIAN.

YOU JUST THREW UP A SMOKE SCREEN AND RAN AWAY!

AW, LAY OFF, MAN...

SYU Z DUELS

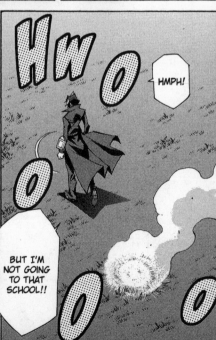

HWOO

HMPH!

BUT I'M NOT GOING TO THAT SCHOOL!!

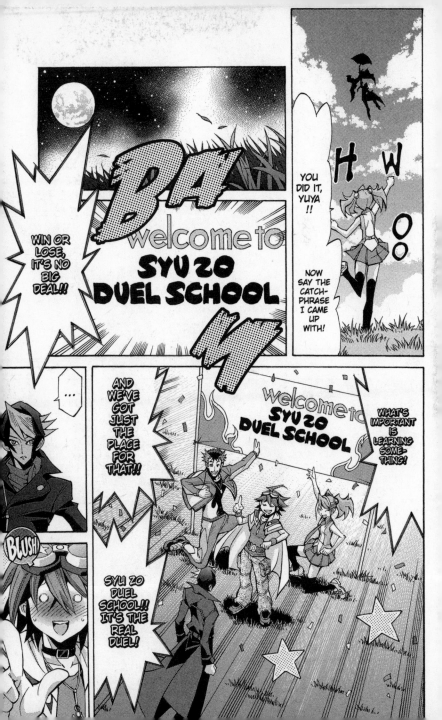

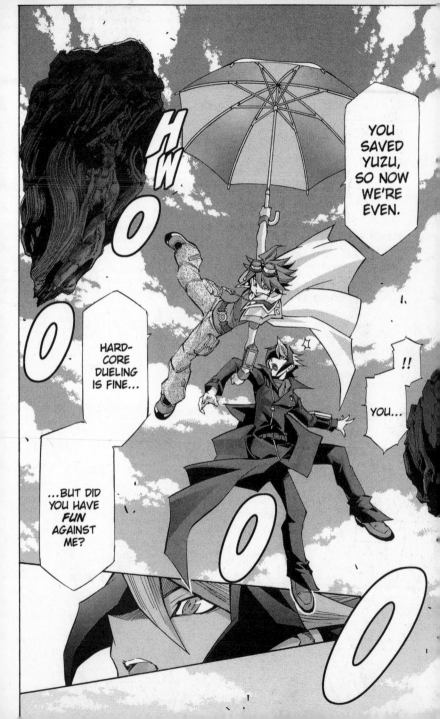

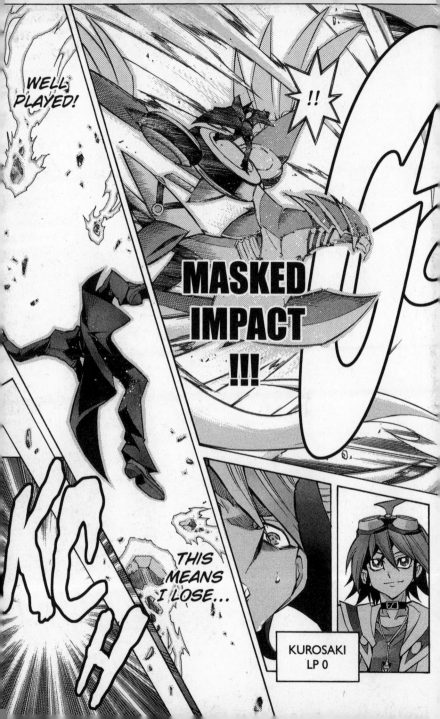

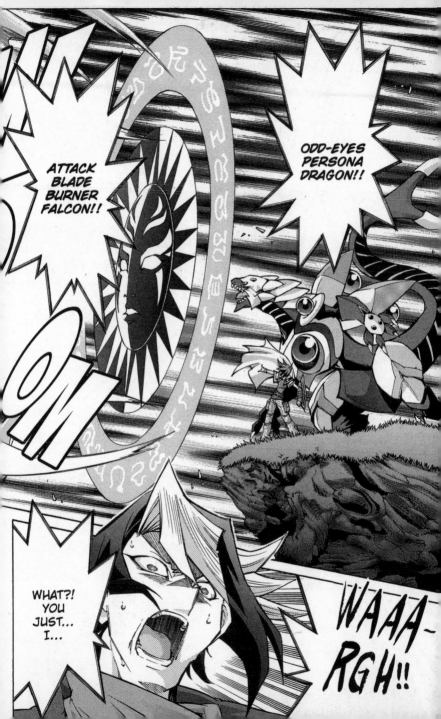

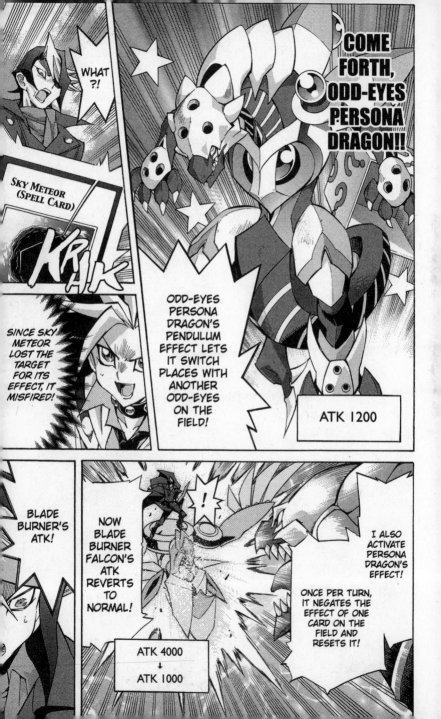

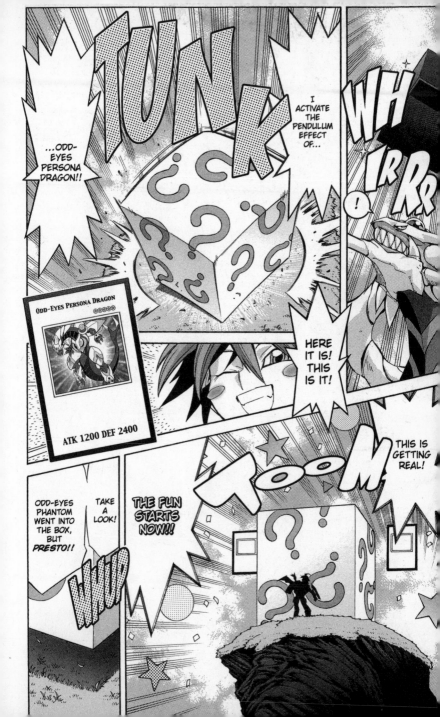

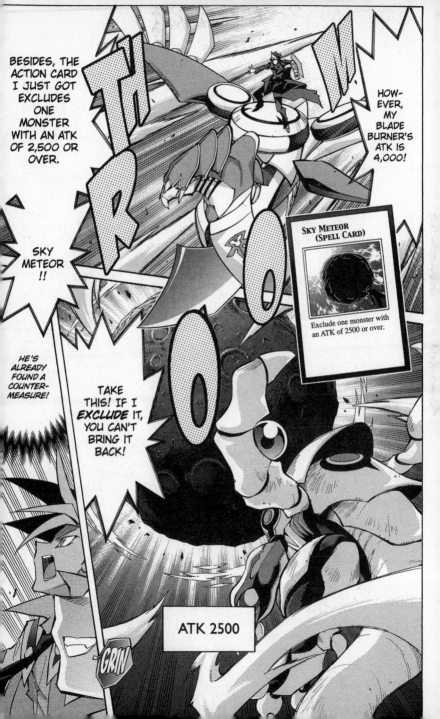

IF A PENDULUM MONSTER GETS DESTROYED AND GOES INTO THE EXTRA DECK...

OH... I GET IT!

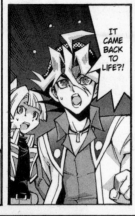

IT CAME BACK TO LIFE?!

WHAT A POWERFUL SUMMONING METHOD!!

...THEN IT CAN COME BACK AGAIN AS LONG AS THE PENDULLUM CARD IS STILL IN PLAY!!

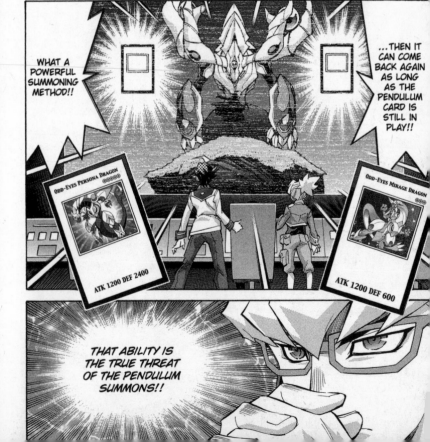

ODD-EYES PERSONA DRAGON

ATK 1200 DEF 2400

ODD-EYES MIRAGE DRAGON

ATK 1200 DEF 600

THAT ABILITY IS THE TRUE THREAT OF THE PENDULUM SUMMONS!!

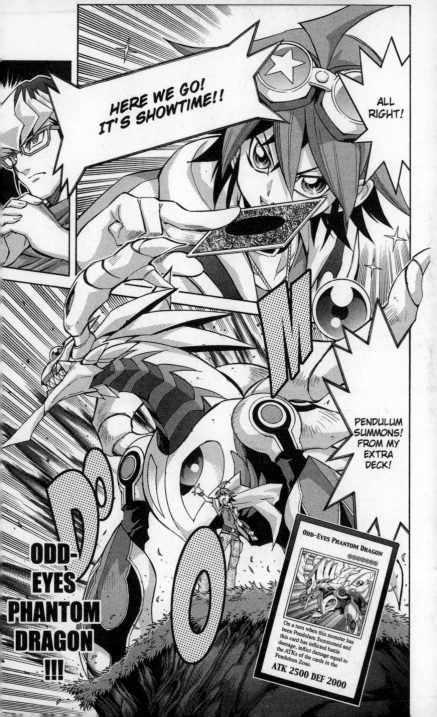

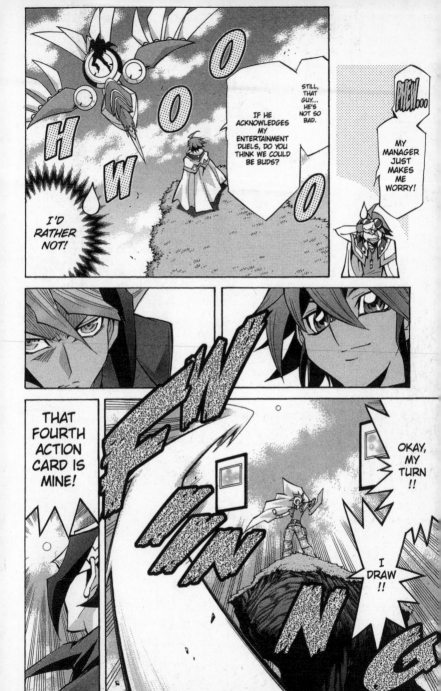

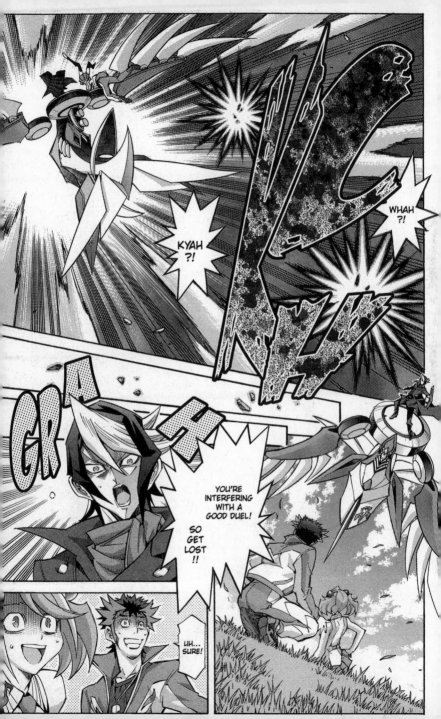

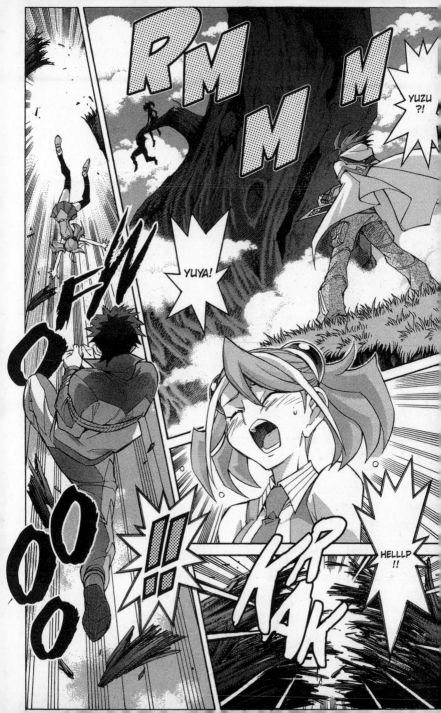

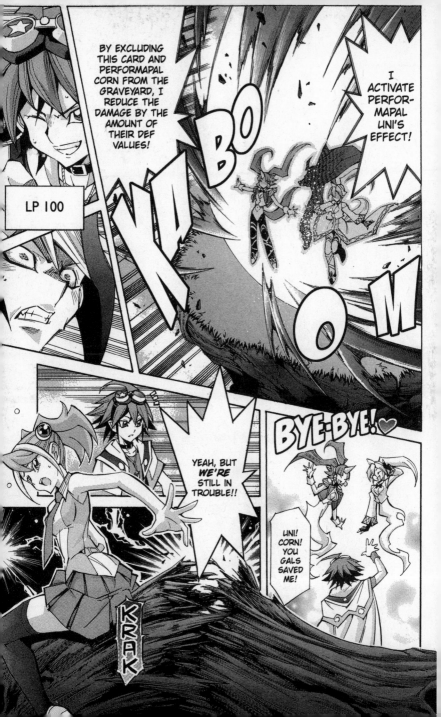

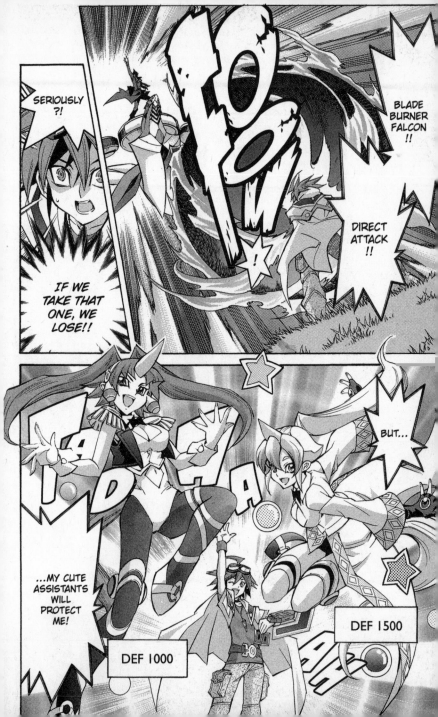

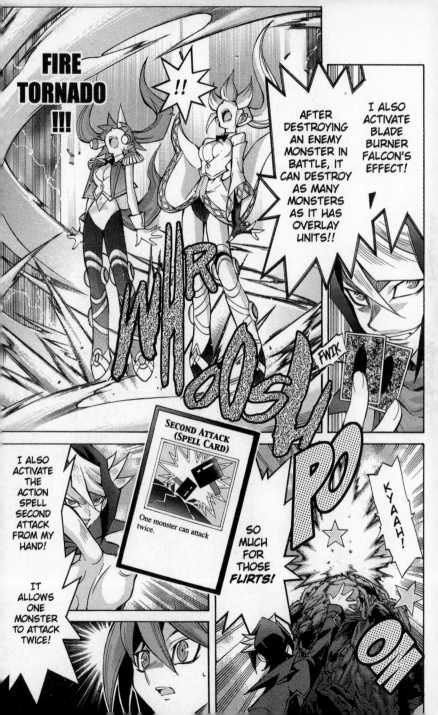

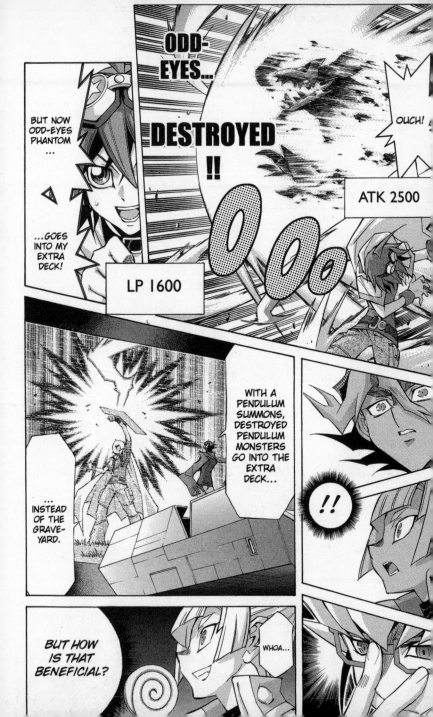

ODD-EYES...

DESTROYED!!

OUCH!

BUT NOW ODD-EYES PHANTOM...

ATK 2500

...GOES INTO MY EXTRA DECK!

LP 1600

WITH A PENDULUM SUMMONS, DESTROYED PENDULUM MONSTERS GO INTO THE EXTRA DECK...

...INSTEAD OF THE GRAVE-YARD.

!!

BUT HOW IS THAT BENEFICIAL?

WHOA...

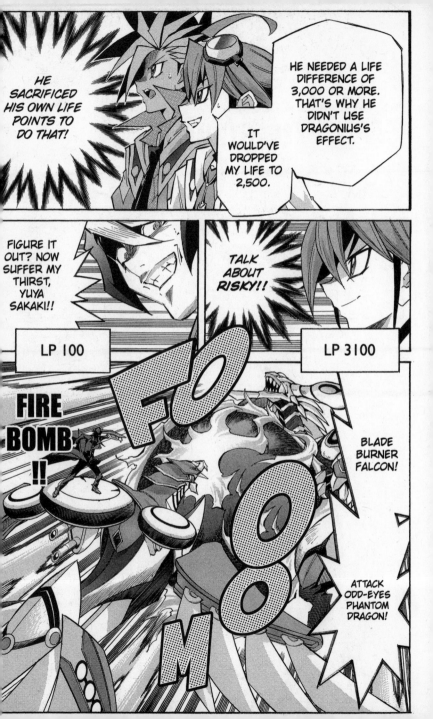

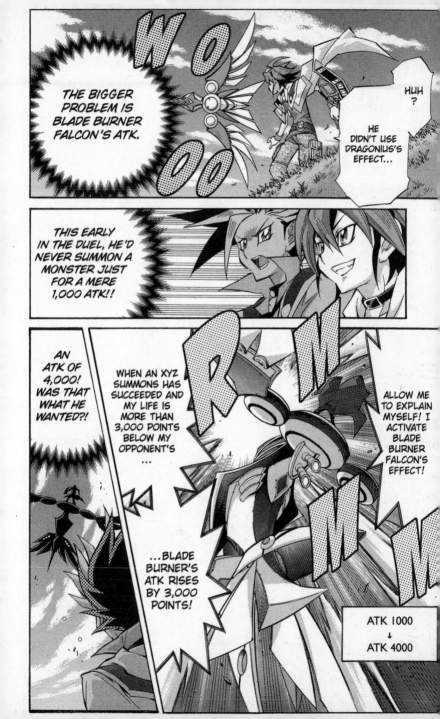

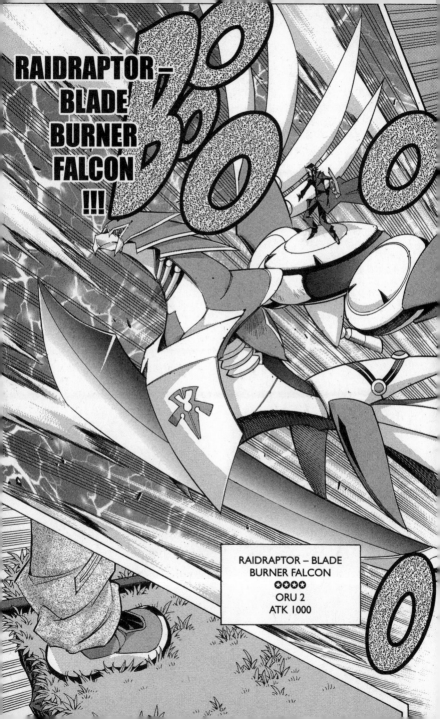

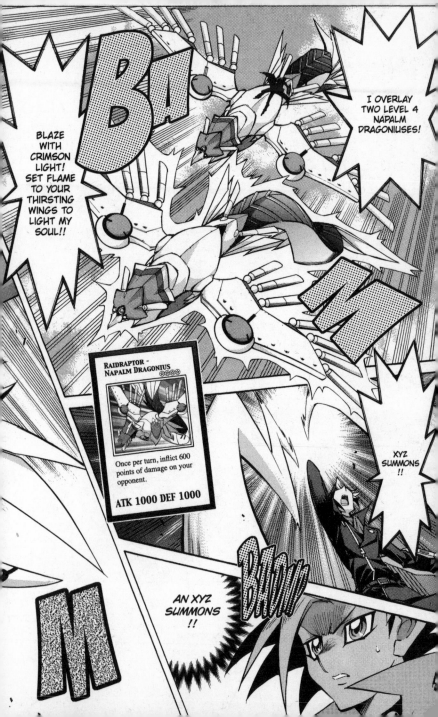

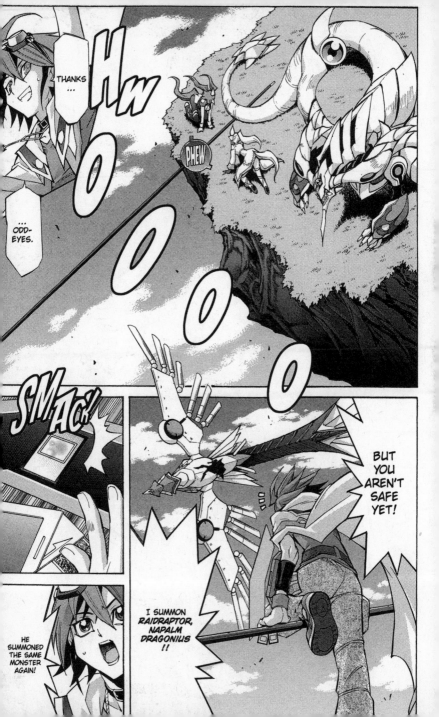

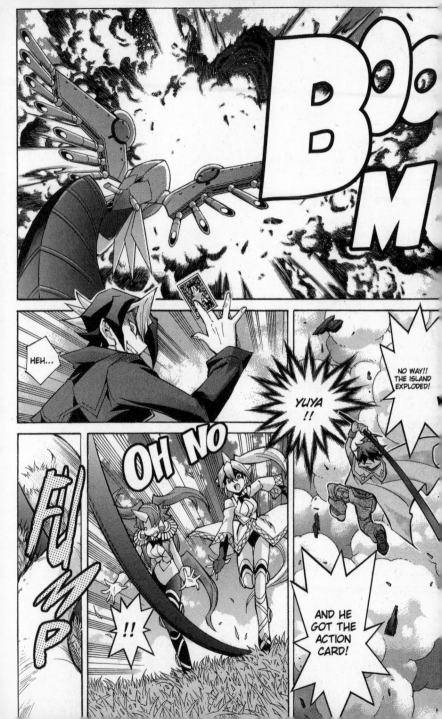

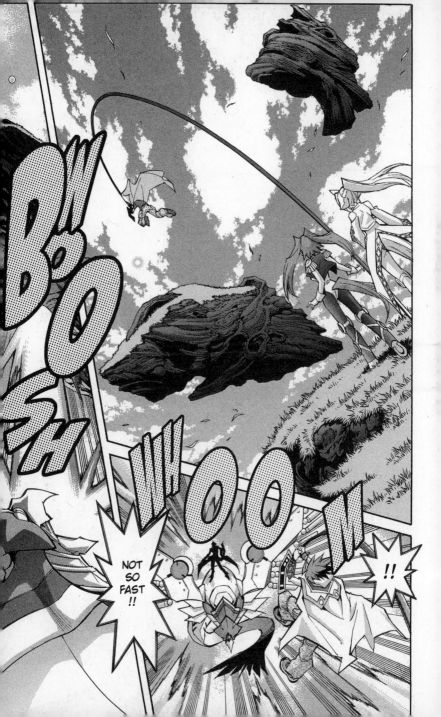

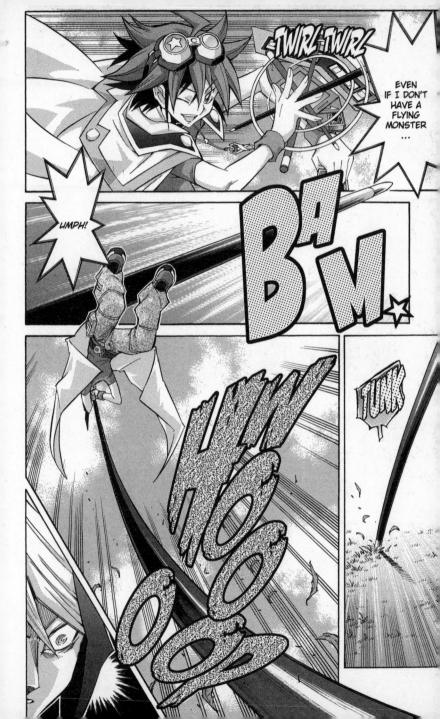

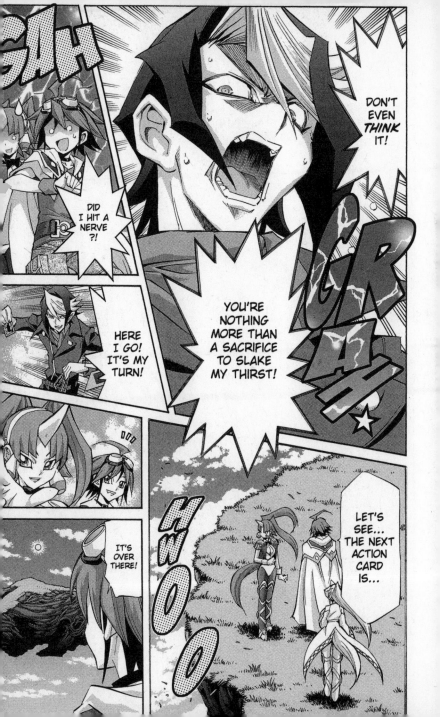

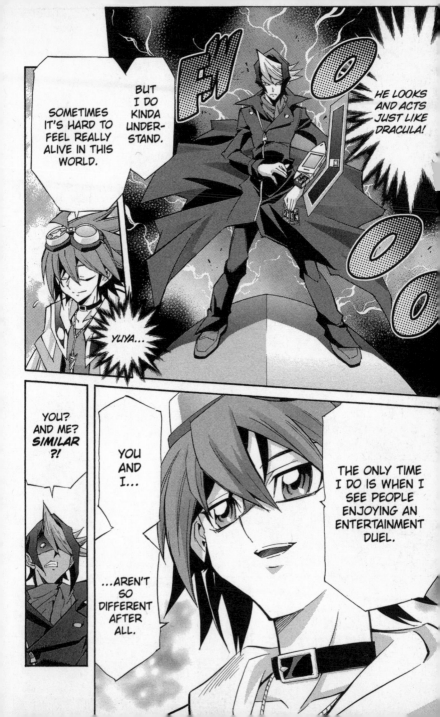

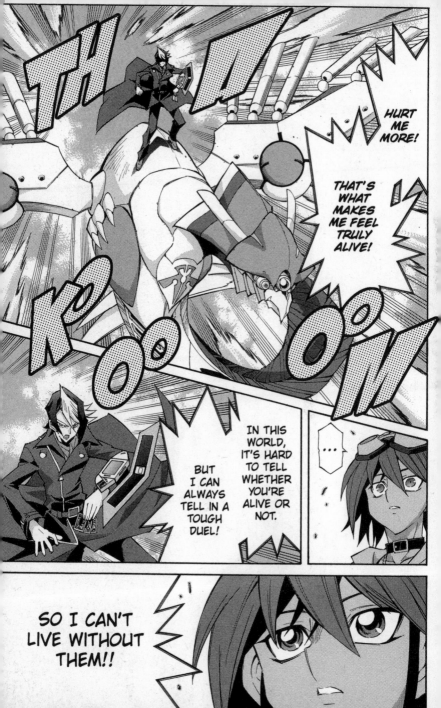

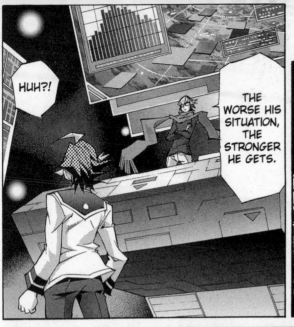

HUH?!

THE WORSE HIS SITUATION, THE STRONGER HE GETS.

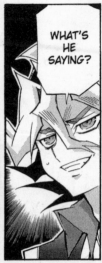

WHAT'S HE SAYING?

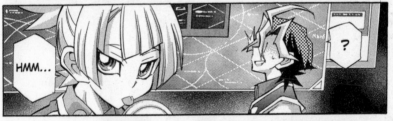

HMM...

?

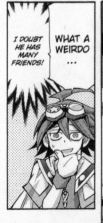

I DOUBT HE HAS MANY FRIENDS!

WHAT A WEIRDO...

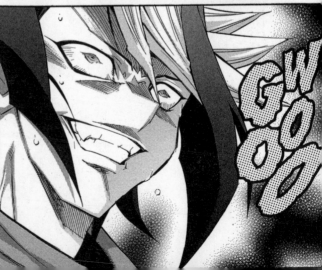

GWOOO

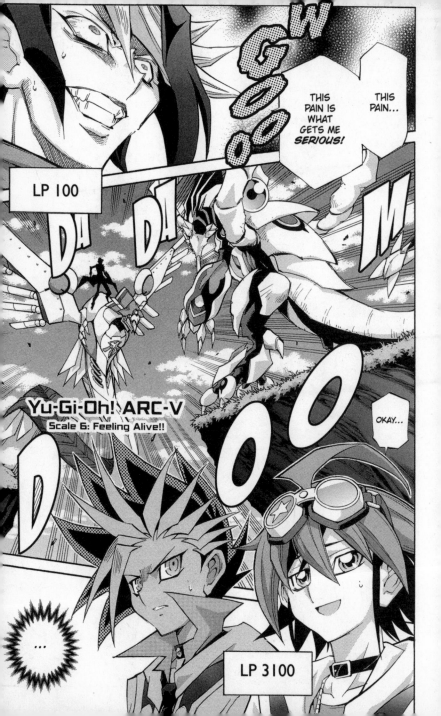

YUZU HIRAGI

Yuzu Hiragi

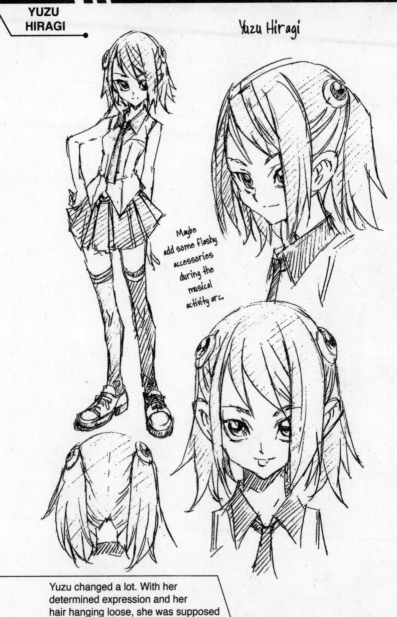

Maybe add some flashy accessories during the musical activity arc.

Yuzu changed a lot. With her determined expression and her hair hanging loose, she was supposed to be like a big sister to Yuya.

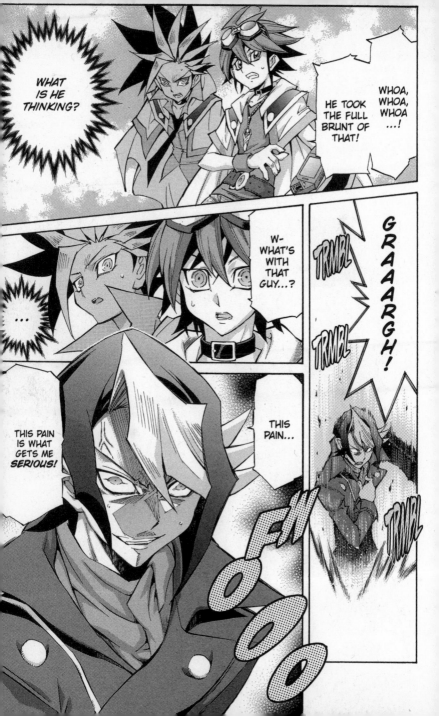

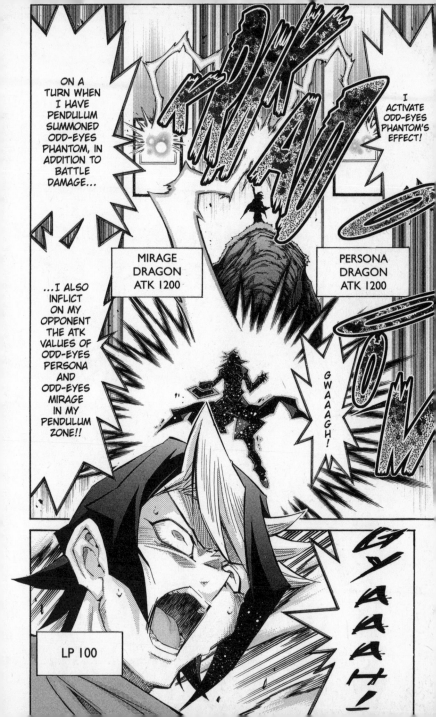

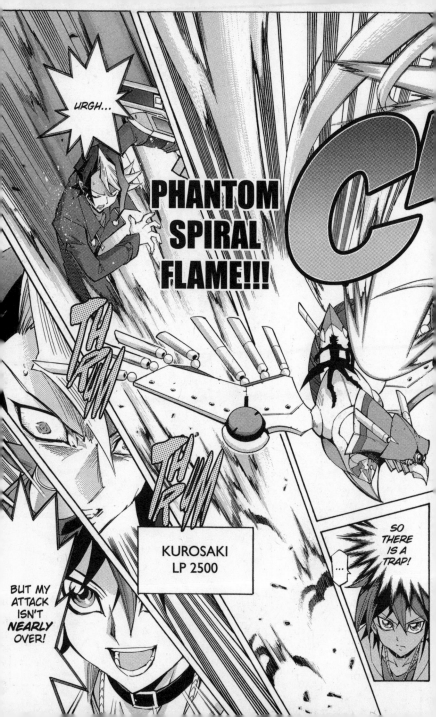

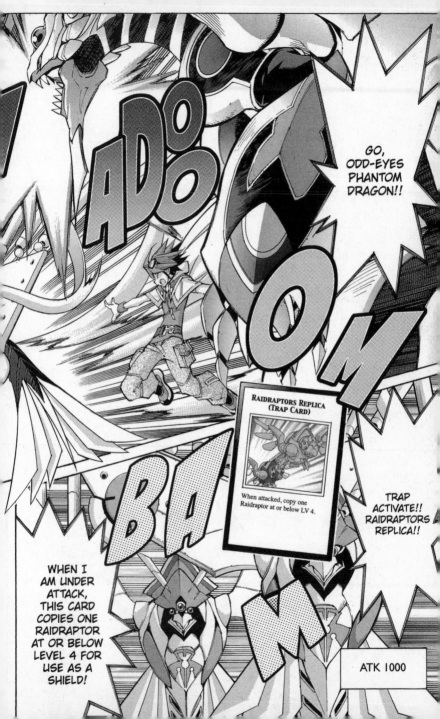

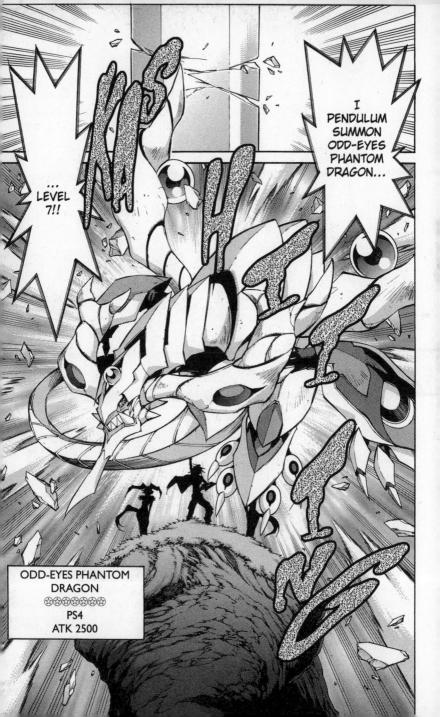

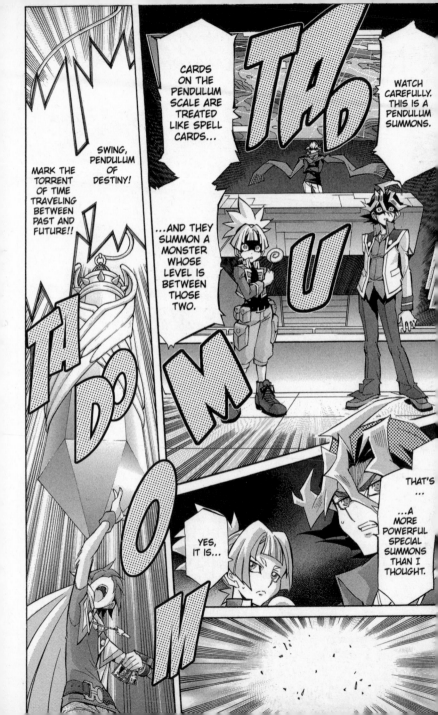

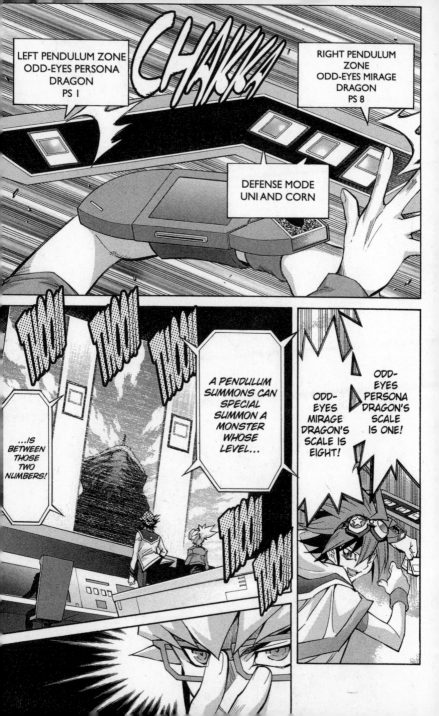

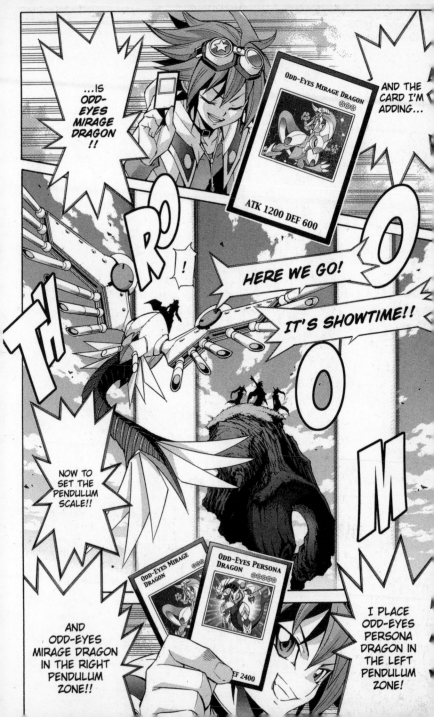

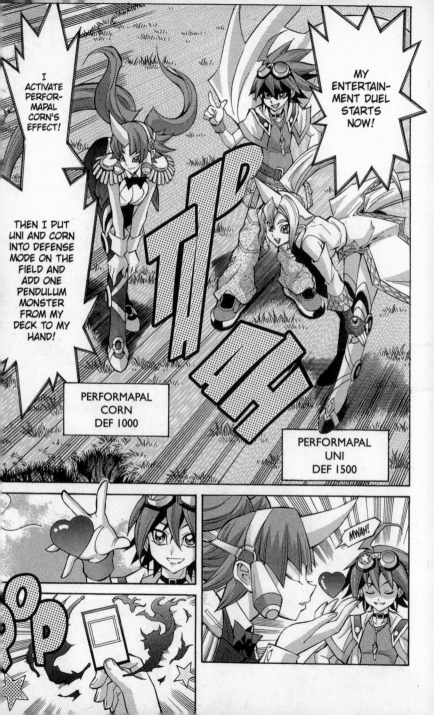

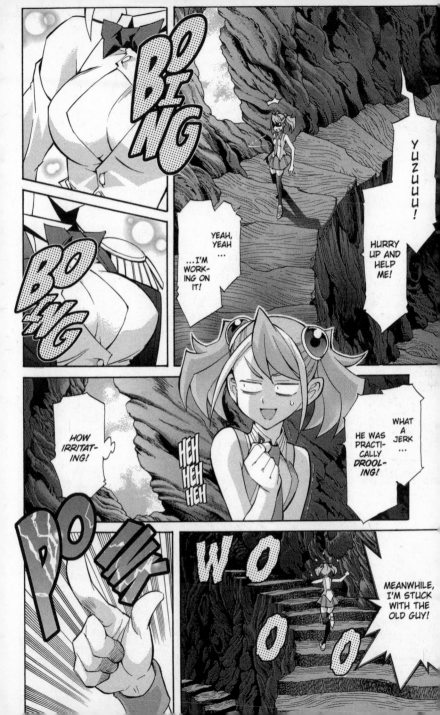

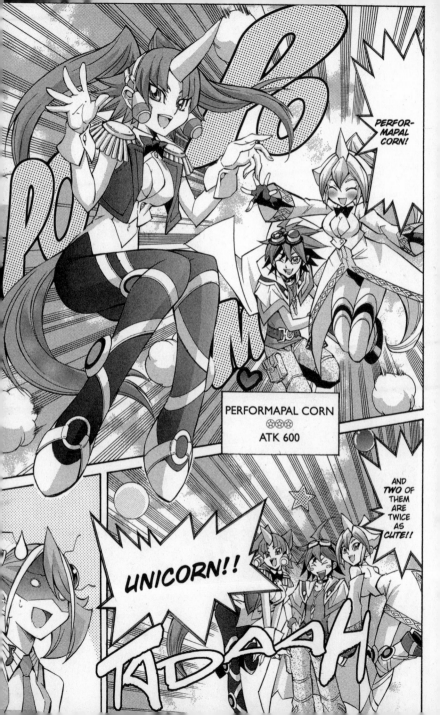

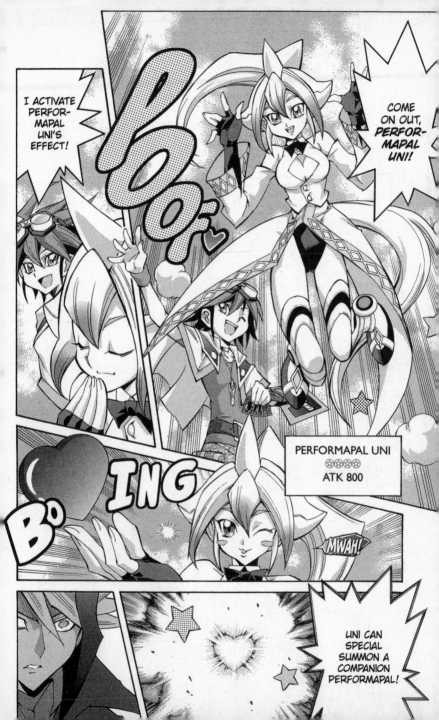

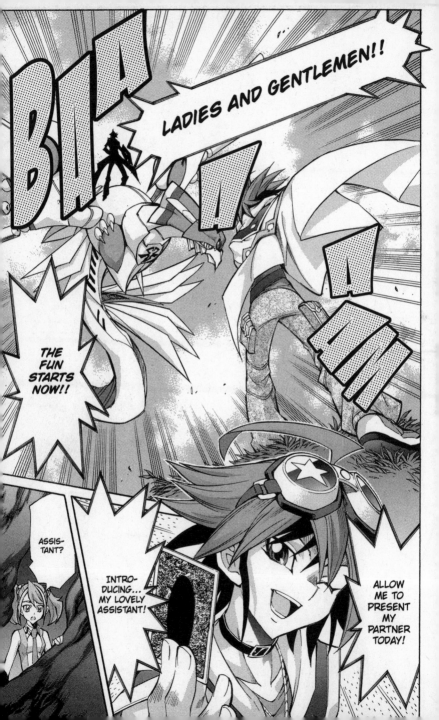

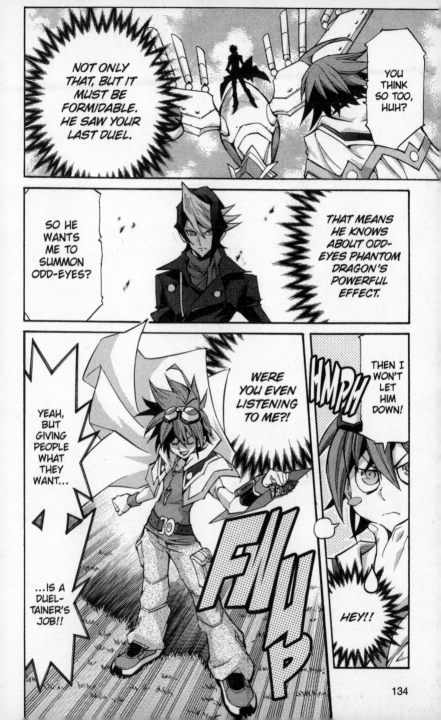

134

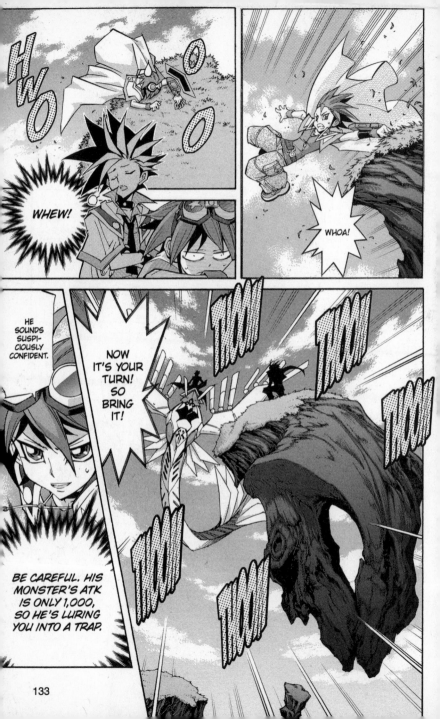

WHEW!

WHOA!

HE SOUNDS SUSPICIOUSLY CONFIDENT.

NOW IT'S YOUR TURN! SO BRING IT!

BE CAREFUL. HIS MONSTER'S ATK IS ONLY 1,000, SO HE'S LURING YOU INTO A TRAP.

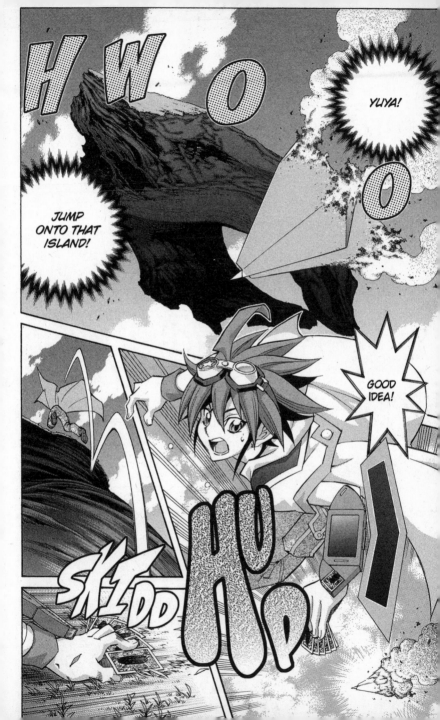

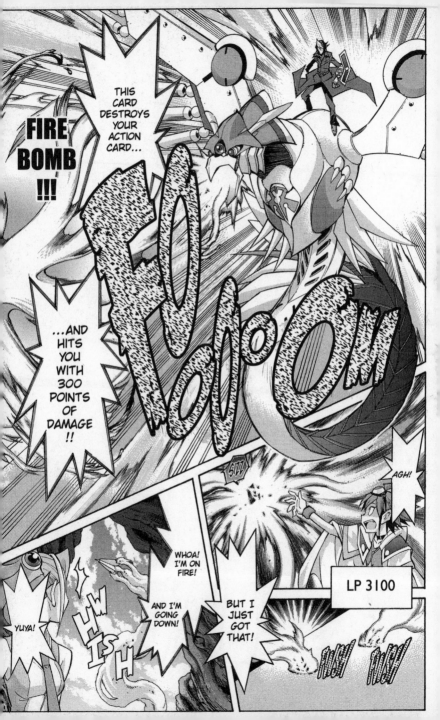

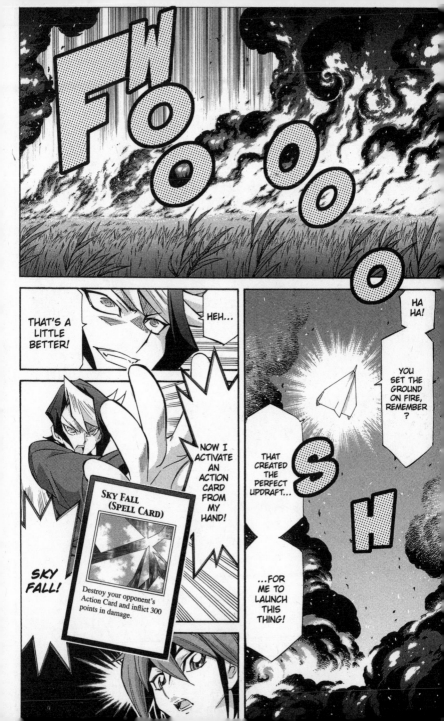

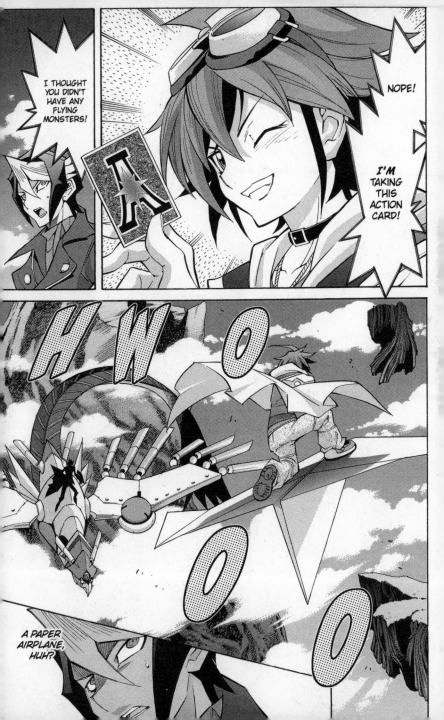

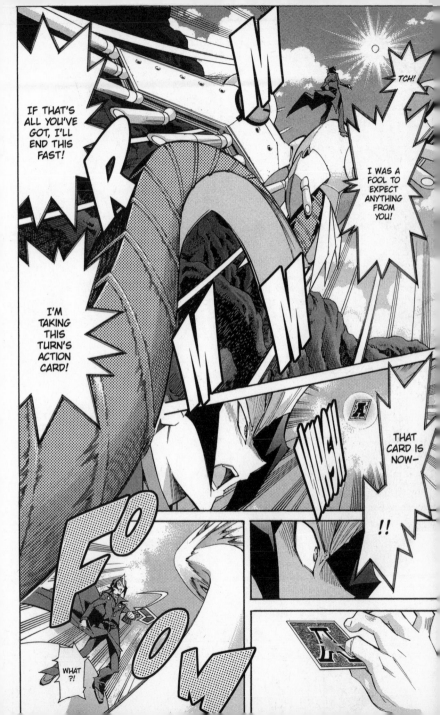

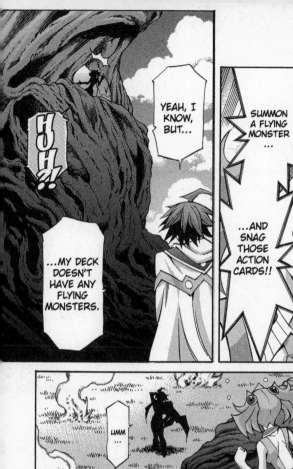

YEAH, I KNOW, BUT...

HUH?!!

...MY DECK DOESN'T HAVE ANY FLYING MONSTERS.

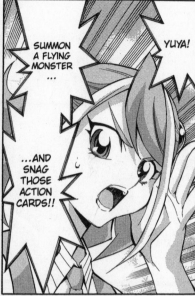

YUYA!

SUMMON A FLYING MONSTER...

...AND SNAG THOSE ACTION CARDS!!

UMM...

THEN WHAT'RE YOU GONNA DO?!

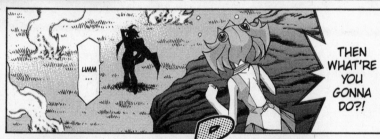

IF YOU CAN'T FLY, THEN RISK YOUR LIFE AND RUN UP THAT TOWER!

QUIT MESSING AROUND! A DUEL IS SERIOUS!

GRAAH

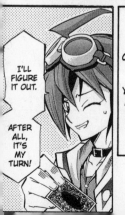

I'LL FIGURE IT OUT.

AFTER ALL, IT'S MY TURN!

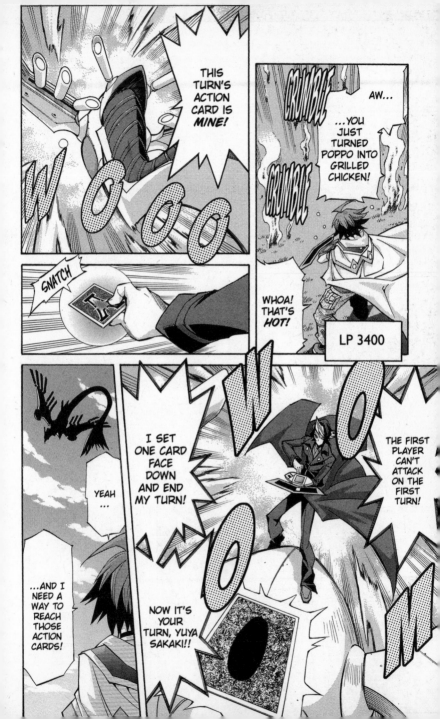

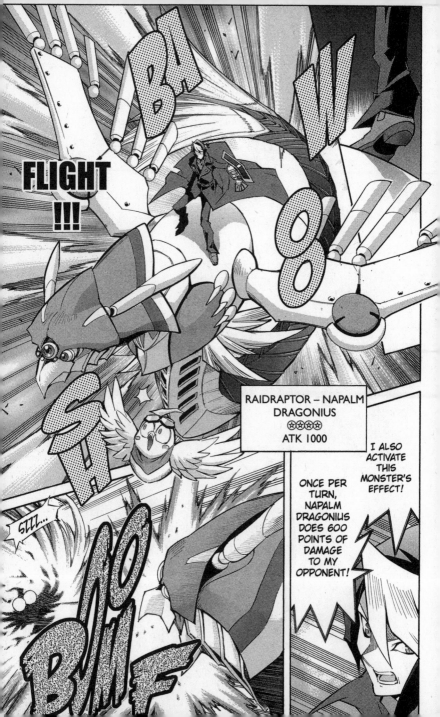

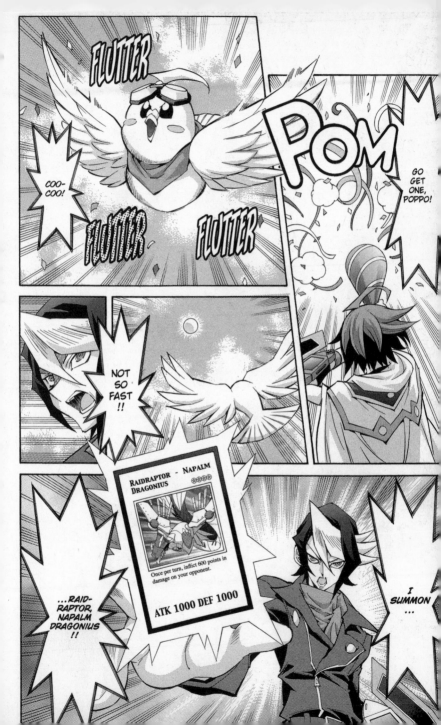

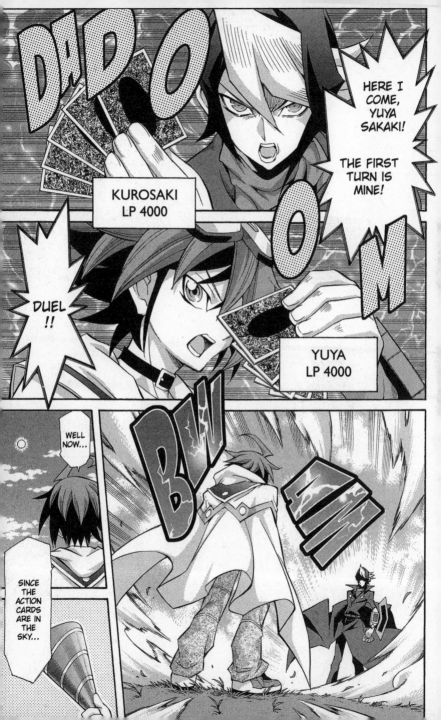

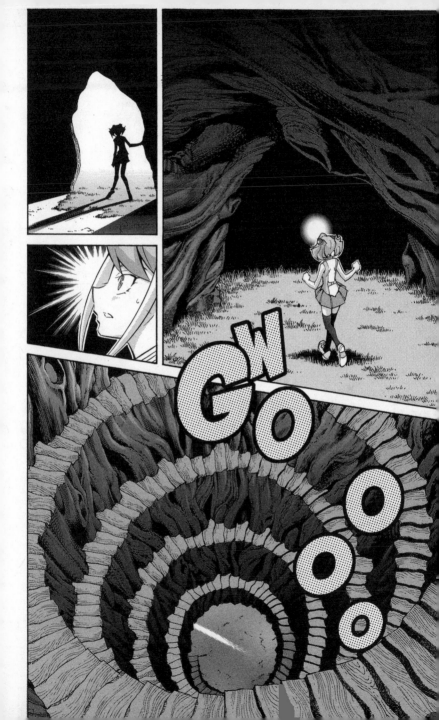

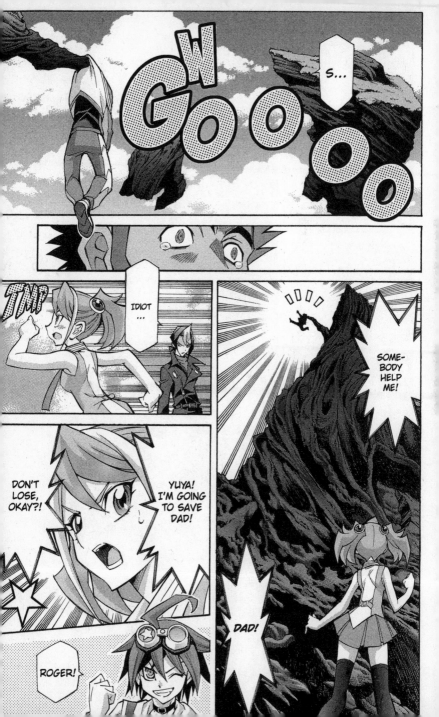

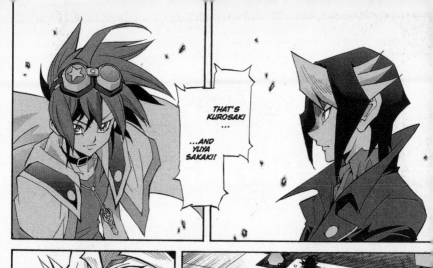

THAT'S KUROSAKI...

...AND YUYA SAKAKI!

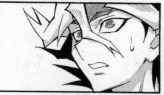

NO, DON'T.

HE'S NOT CLEARED TO DO THAT!

I'LL GO STOP HIM RIGHT AWAY, SIR!

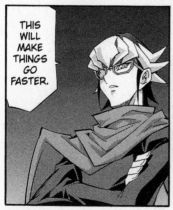

THIS WILL MAKE THINGS GO FASTER.

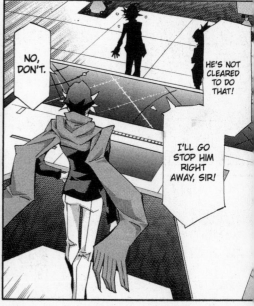

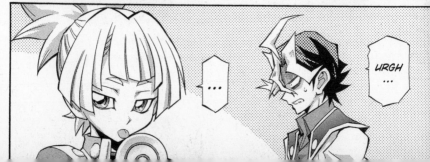

...

URGH...

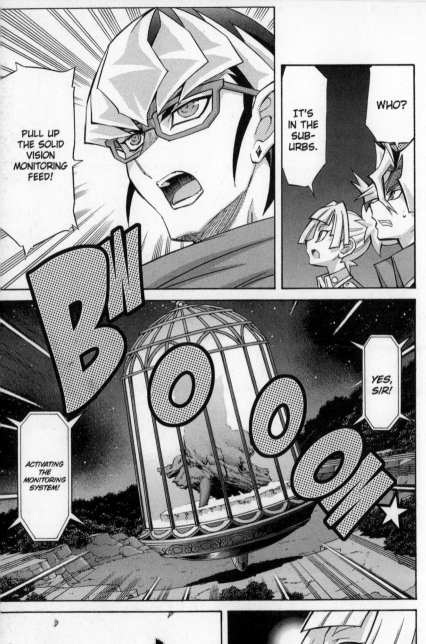

PULL UP THE SOLID VISION MONITORING FEED!

IT'S IN THE SUB-URBS.

WHO?

ACTIVATING THE MONITORING SYSTEM!

YES, SIR!

B" BOOOM!!★

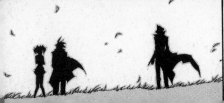

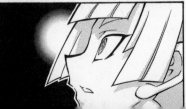

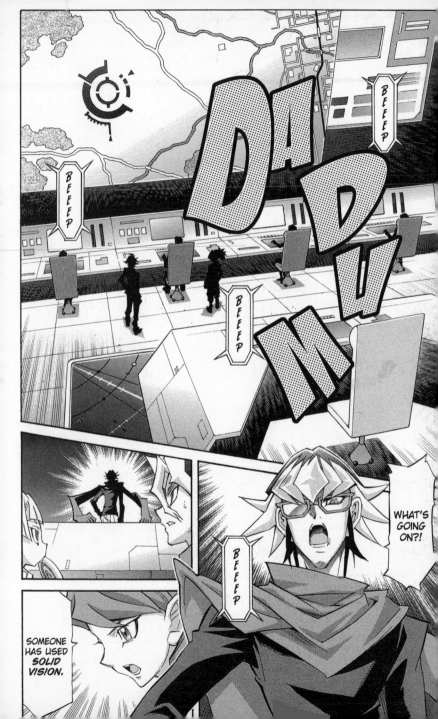

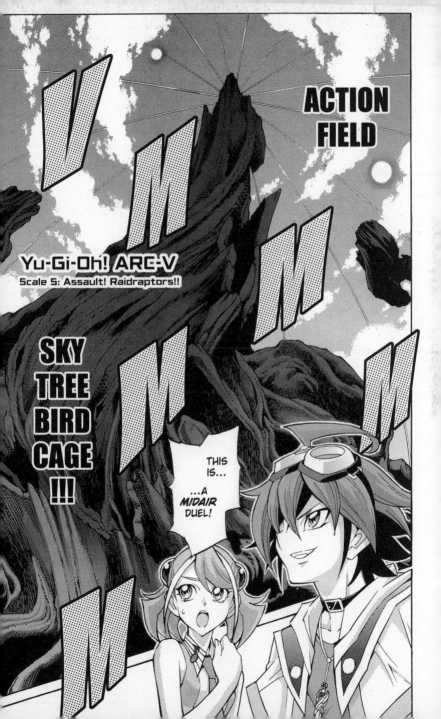

scale**4**

**REIJI
AKABA**

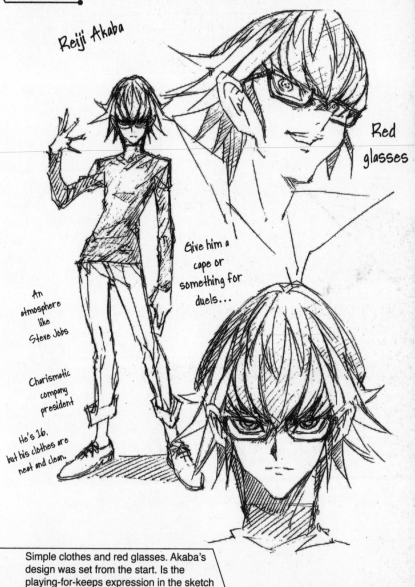

Reiji Akaba

Red
glasses

Give him a
cape or
something for
duels...

An
atmosphere
like
Steve Jobs

Charismatic
company
president

He's 16,
but his clothes are
neat and clean.

Simple clothes and red glasses. Akaba's
design was set from the start. Is the
playing-for-keeps expression in the sketch
going to show up in the story?

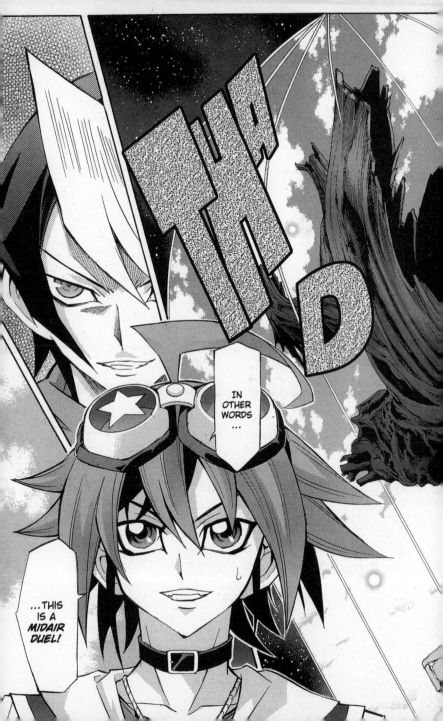

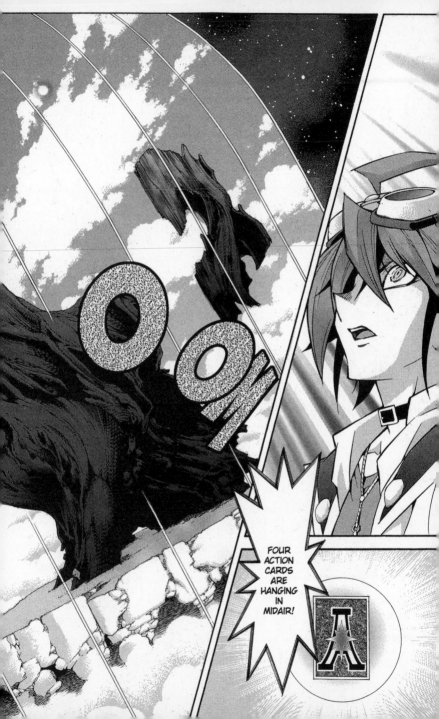

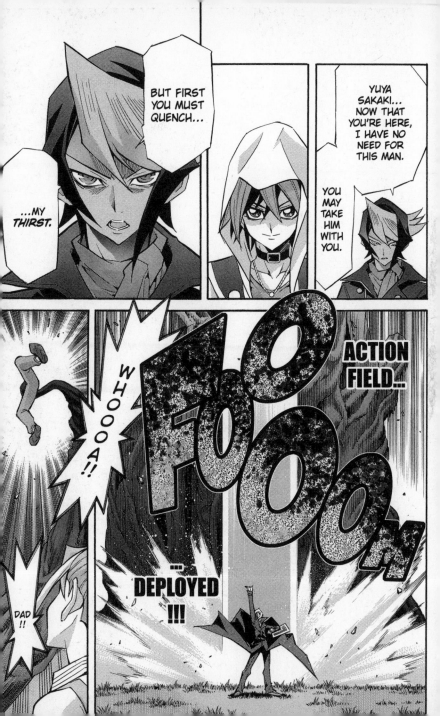

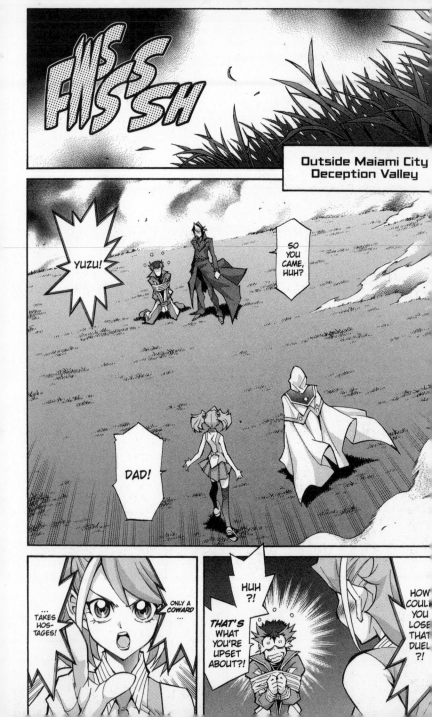

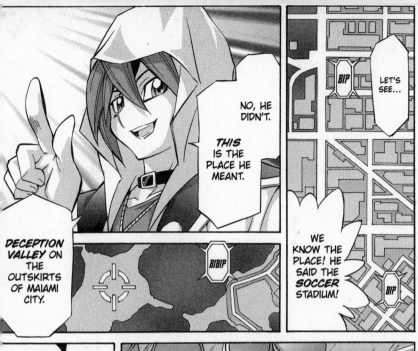

NO, HE DIDN'T.

THIS IS THE PLACE HE MEANT.

LET'S SEE...

BIP

WE KNOW THE PLACE! HE SAID THE *SOCCER* STADIUM!

BIP

DECEPTION VALLEY ON THE OUTSKIRTS OF MAIAMI CITY.

BIBIP

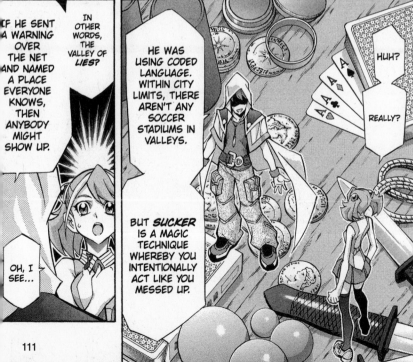

IF HE SENT A WARNING OVER THE NET AND NAMED A PLACE EVERYONE KNOWS, THEN ANYBODY MIGHT SHOW UP.

IN OTHER WORDS, THE VALLEY OF *LIES?*

HE WAS USING CODED LANGUAGE. WITHIN CITY LIMITS, THERE AREN'T ANY SOCCER STADIUMS IN VALLEYS.

HUH?

REALLY?

BUT *SUCKER* IS A MAGIC TECHNIQUE WHEREBY YOU INTENTIONALLY ACT LIKE YOU MESSED UP.

OH, I SEE...

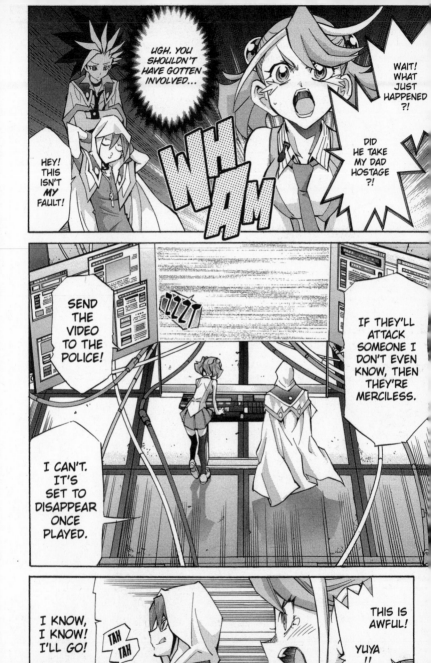

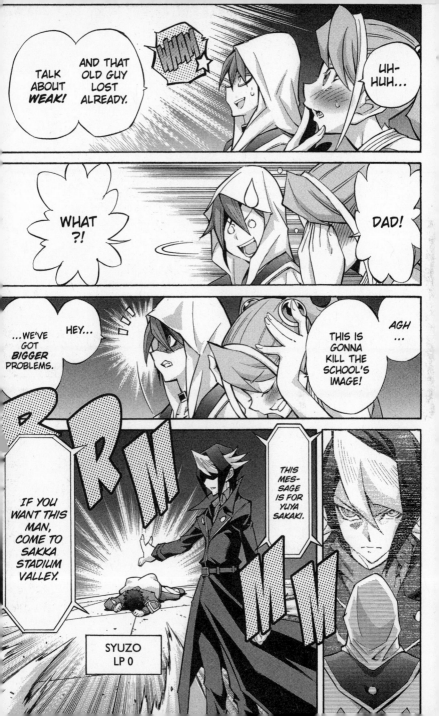

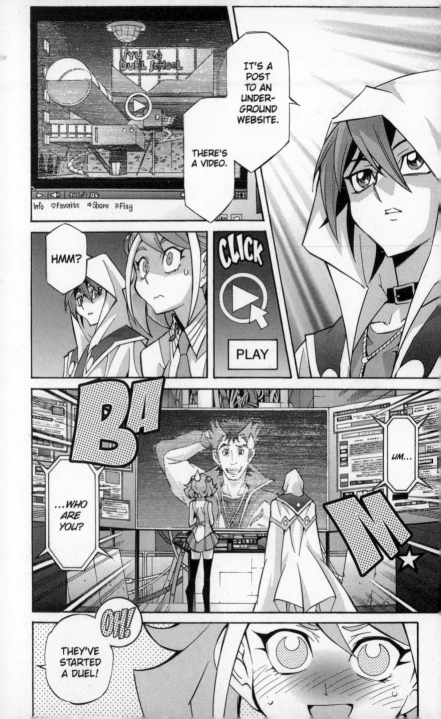

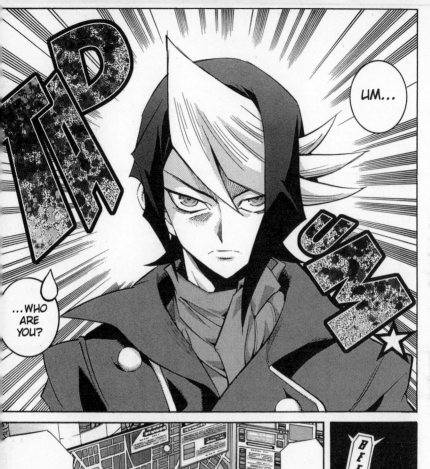

UM...

...WHO ARE YOU?

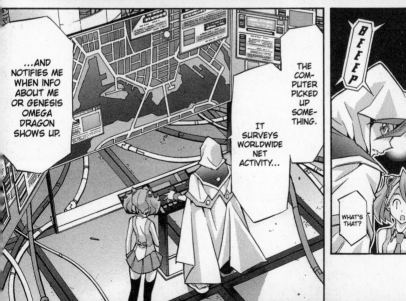

...AND NOTIFIES ME WHEN INFO ABOUT ME OR GENESIS OMEGA DRAGON SHOWS UP.

IT SURVEYS WORLDWIDE NET ACTIVITY...

THE COMPUTER PICKED UP SOMETHING.

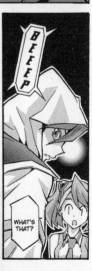

BEEP

WHAT'S THAT?

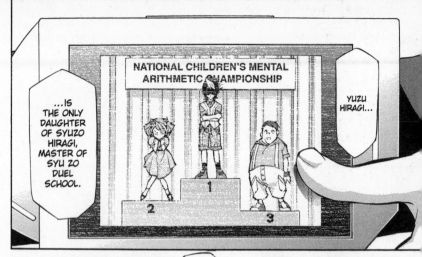

NATIONAL CHILDREN'S MENTAL ARITHMETIC CHAMPIONSHIP

YUZU HIRAGI...

...IS THE ONLY DAUGHTER OF SYUZO HIRAGI, MASTER OF SYU ZO DUEL SCHOOL.

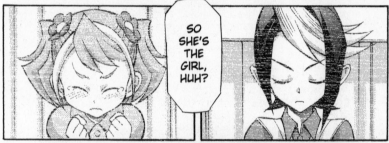

SO SHE'S THE GIRL, HUH?

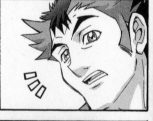

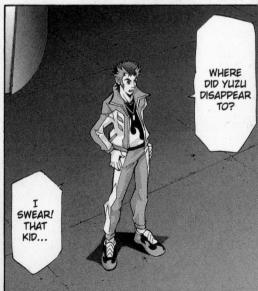

WHERE DID YUZU DISAPPEAR TO?

I SWEAR! THAT KID...

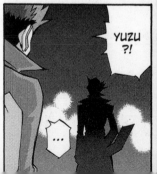

YUZU ?!

...

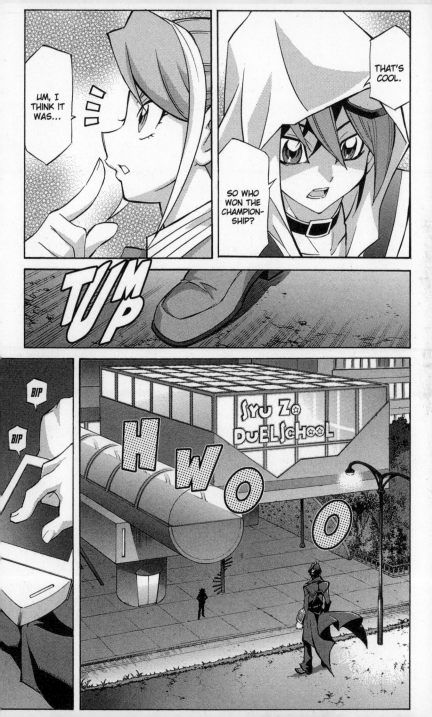

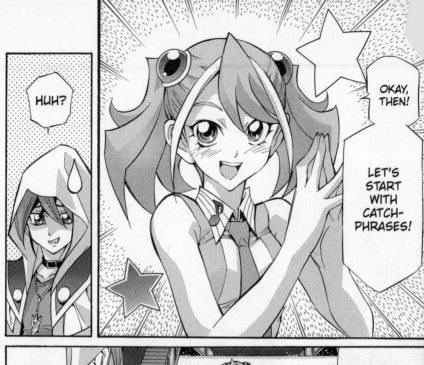

HUH?

OKAY, THEN!

LET'S START WITH CATCH-PHRASES!

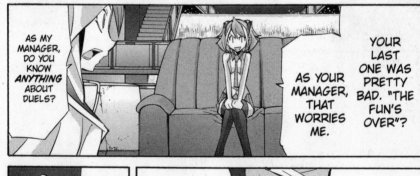

AS MY MANAGER, DO YOU KNOW *ANYTHING* ABOUT DUELS?

AS YOUR MANAGER, THAT WORRIES ME.

YOUR LAST ONE WAS PRETTY BAD. "THE FUN'S OVER"?

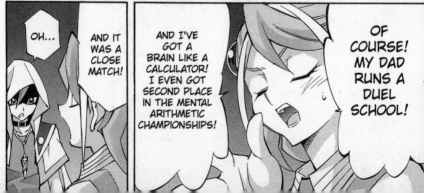

OH...

AND IT WAS A CLOSE MATCH!

AND I'VE GOT A BRAIN LIKE A CALCULATOR! I EVEN GOT SECOND PLACE IN THE MENTAL ARITHMETIC CHAMPIONSHIPS!

OF COURSE! MY DAD RUNS A DUEL SCHOOL!

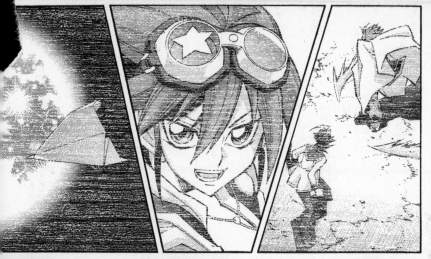

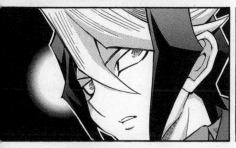

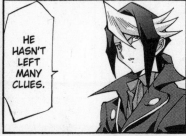

HE HASN'T LEFT MANY CLUES.

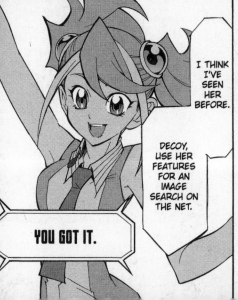

I THINK I'VE SEEN HER BEFORE.

DECOY, USE HER FEATURES FOR AN IMAGE SEARCH ON THE NET.

YOU GOT IT.

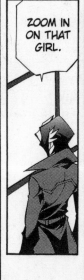

ZOOM IN ON THAT GIRL.

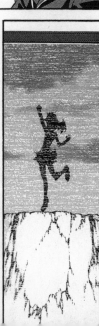

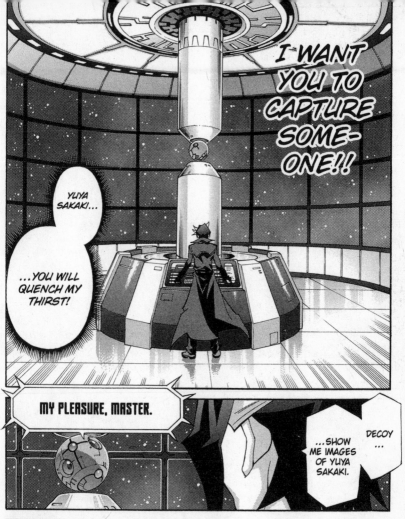

I WANT YOU TO CAPTURE SOME- ONE!!

YUYA SAKAKI...

...YOU WILL QUENCH MY THIRST!

MY PLEASURE, MASTER.

DECOY...

...SHOW ME IMAGES OF YUYA SAKAKI.

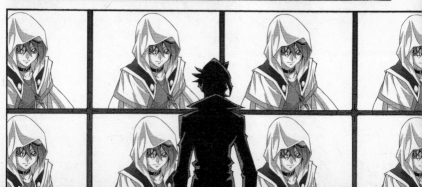

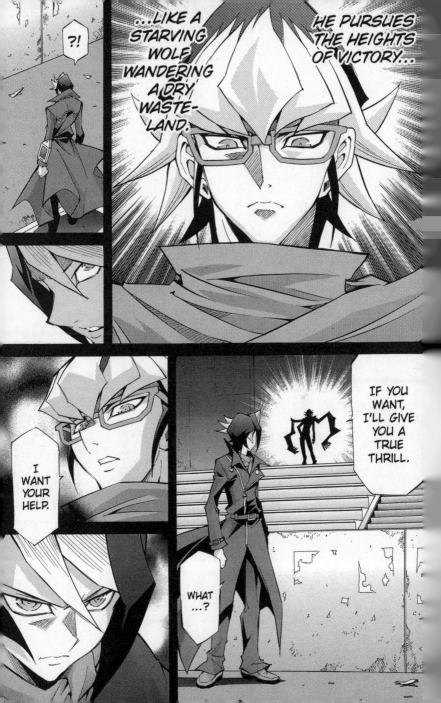

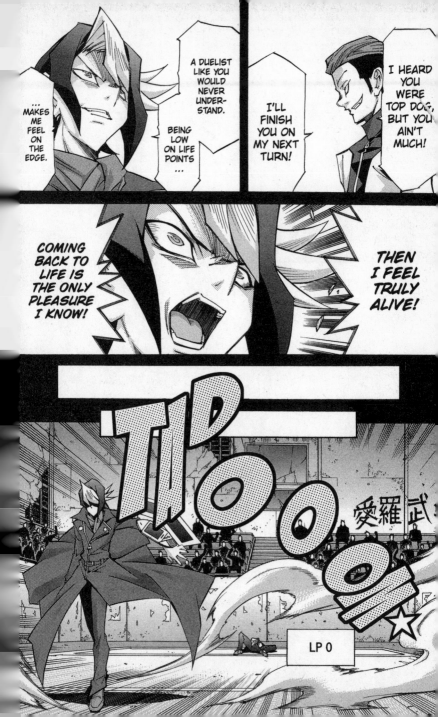

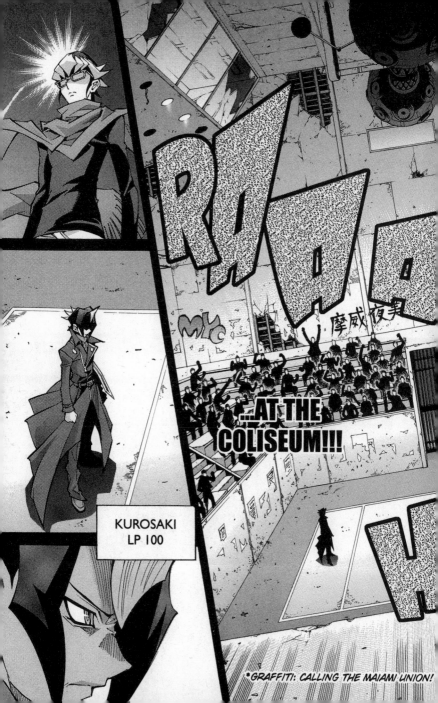

...AT THE COLISEUM!!!

KUROSAKI
LP 100

*GRAFFITI: CALLING THE MAIAMI UNION!

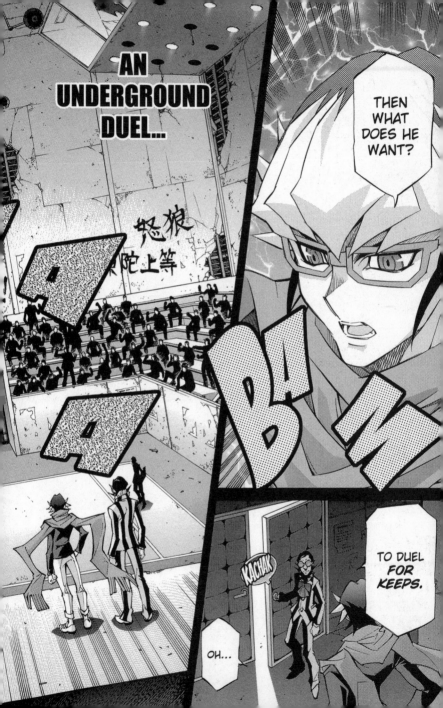

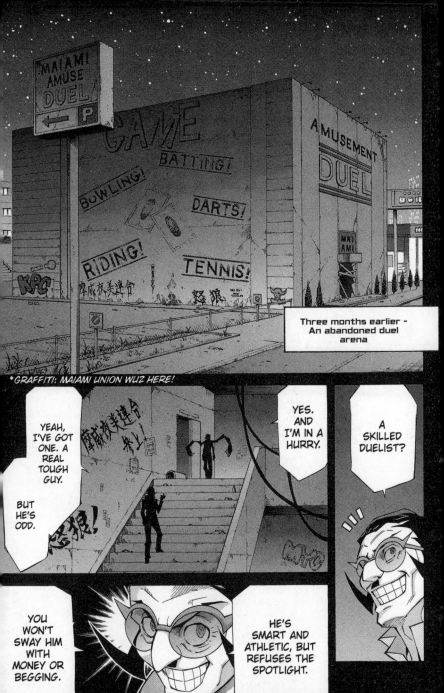

*GRAFFITI: MAIAMI UNION WUZ HERE!

Three months earlier -
An abandoned duel
arena

A
SKILLED
DUELIST?

YES.
AND
I'M IN A
HURRY.

YEAH,
I'VE GOT
ONE. A
REAL
TOUGH
GUY.

BUT
HE'S
ODD.

YOU
WON'T
SWAY HIM
WITH
MONEY OR
BEGGING.

HE'S
SMART AND
ATHLETIC, BUT
REFUSES THE
SPOTLIGHT.

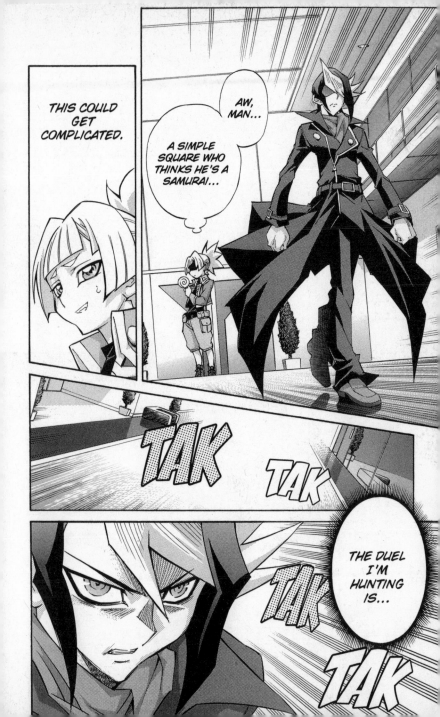

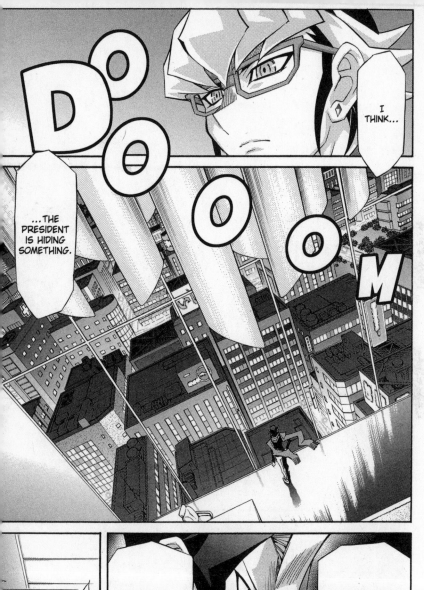

I THINK...

...THE PRESIDENT IS HIDING SOMETHING.

DOOOOM

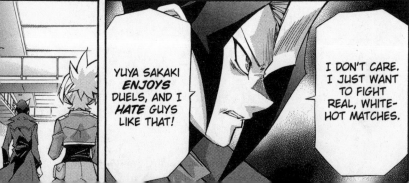

YUYA SAKAKI *ENJOYS* DUELS, AND I *HATE* GUYS LIKE THAT!

I DON'T CARE. I JUST WANT TO FIGHT REAL, WHITE-HOT MATCHES.

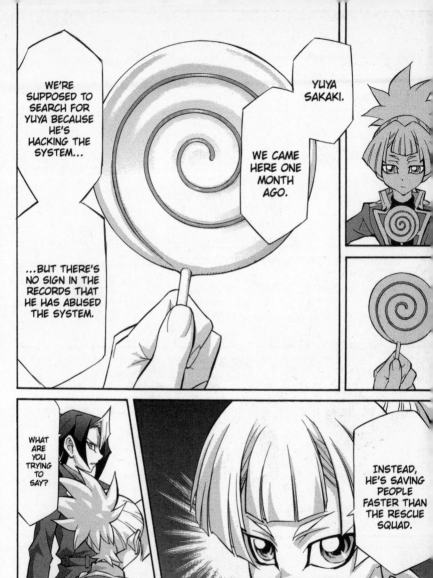
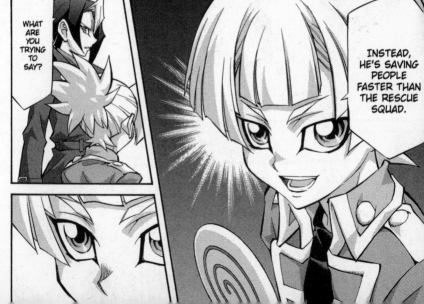

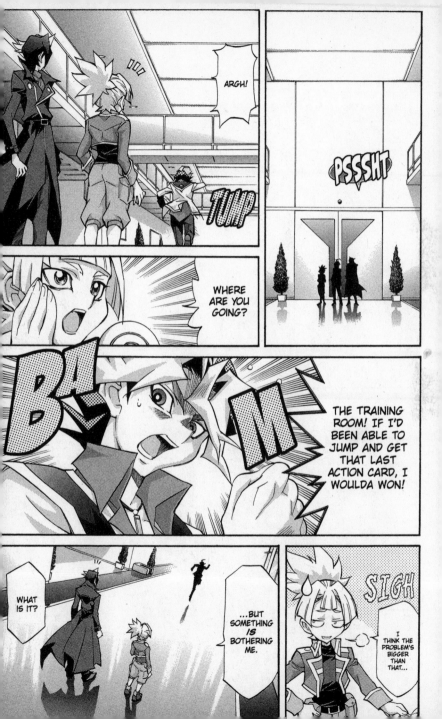

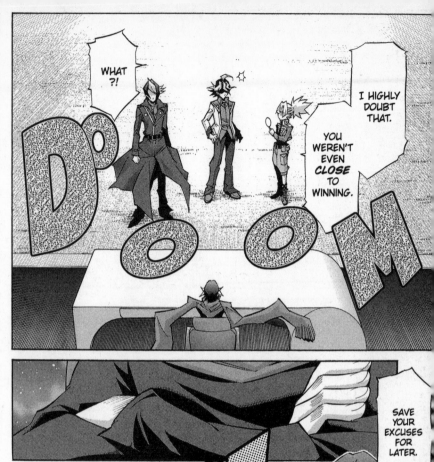

WHAT ?!

I HIGHLY DOUBT THAT.

YOU WEREN'T EVEN *CLOSE* TO WINNING.

D OO OO M

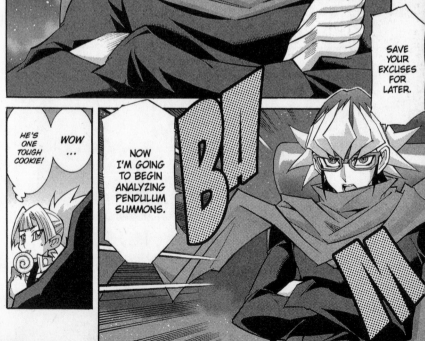

SAVE YOUR EXCUSES FOR LATER.

HE'S ONE TOUGH COOKIE!

WOW ...

NOW I'M GOING TO BEGIN ANALYZING PENDULUM SUMMONS.

BA!

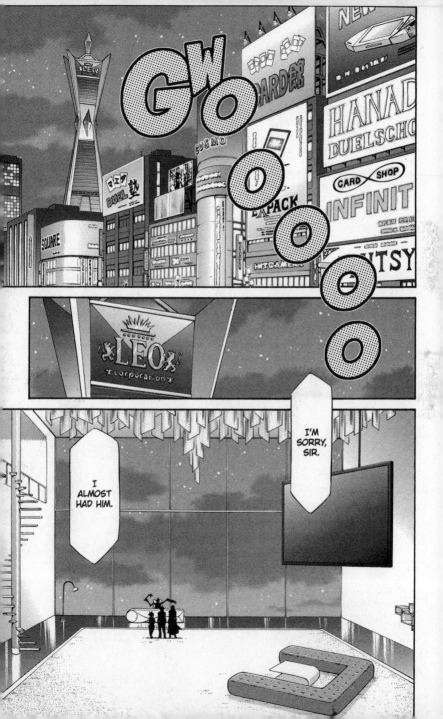

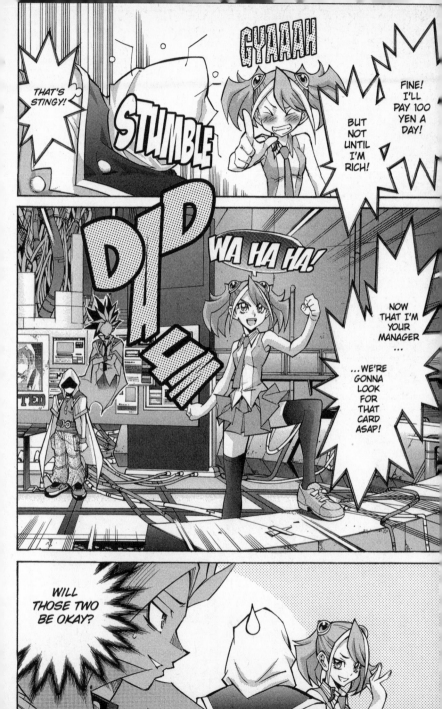

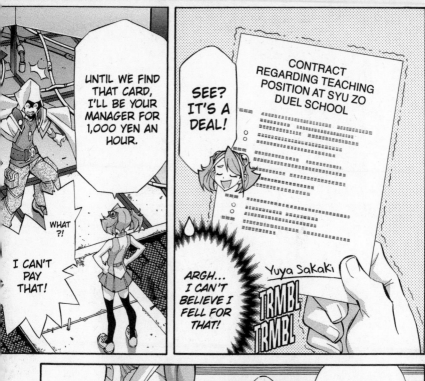

UNTIL WE FIND THAT CARD, I'LL BE YOUR MANAGER FOR 1,000 YEN AN HOUR.

WHAT?!

I CAN'T PAY THAT!

SEE? IT'S A DEAL!

CONTRACT REGARDING TEACHING POSITION AT SYU ZO DUEL SCHOOL

ARGH... I CAN'T BELIEVE I FELL FOR THAT!

Yuya Sakaki

TRMBL TRMBL

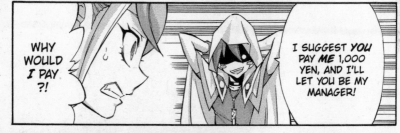

WHY WOULD I PAY?!

I SUGGEST *YOU* PAY *ME* 1,000 YEN, AND I'LL LET YOU BE MY MANAGER!

HMM...

I DON'T *NEED* A MANAGER.

I DON'T CARE EITHER WAY.

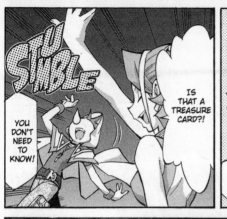

IS THAT A TREASURE CARD?!

YOU DON'T NEED TO KNOW!

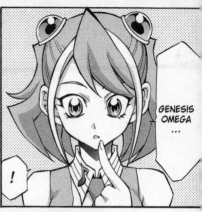

GENESIS OMEGA...

!

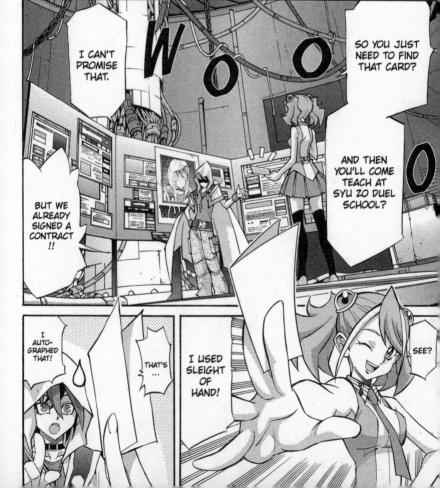

I CAN'T PROMISE THAT.

WOOO

SO YOU JUST NEED TO FIND THAT CARD?

AND THEN YOU'LL COME TEACH AT SYU ZO DUEL SCHOOL?

BUT WE ALREADY SIGNED A CONTRACT!!

I AUTO-GRAPHED THAT!

THAT'S...

I USED SLEIGHT OF HAND!

SEE?

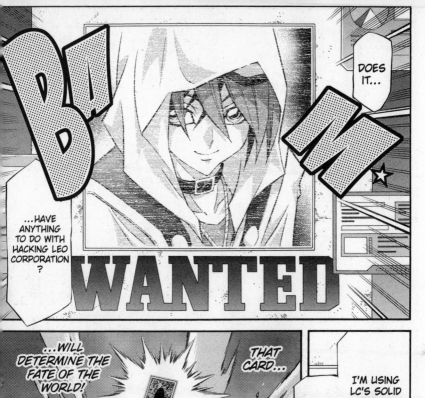

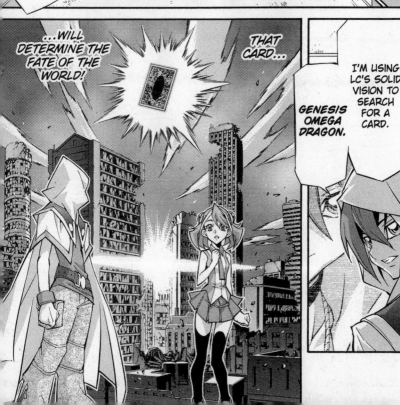

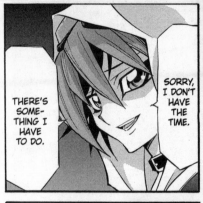

THERE'S SOME-THING I HAVE TO DO.

SORRY, I DON'T HAVE THE TIME.

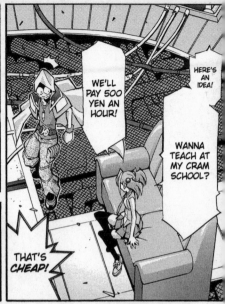

HERE'S AN IDEA!

WE'LL PAY 500 YEN AN HOUR!

WANNA TEACH AT MY CRAM SCHOOL?

THAT'S CHEAP!

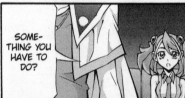

SOME-THING YOU HAVE TO DO?

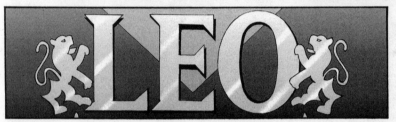

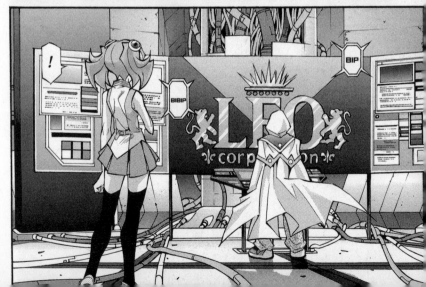

BIBIP

BIP